THE ART OF COEXISTENCE

THE ART OF COEXISTENCE

Pioneering Role of Fethullah Gülen
and the Hizmet Movement

Salih Yücel and İsmail Albayrak

TUGHRA
BOOKS
New Jersey

Published by Tughra Books
345 Clifton Ave., Clifton,
NJ, 07011, USA

www.tughrabooks.com

Library of Congress Cataloging-in-Publication Data
Yücel, Salih.
The art of coexistence : pioneering role of Fethullah Gülen and the Hizmet movement / Salih Yucel and Ismail Albayrak.
pages cm
Includes bibliographical references and index.
ISBN 978-1-59784-346-1 (alk. paper)
1. Gülen, Fethullah. 2. Gülen Hizmet Movement. 3. Dialogue--Religious aspects--Islam. 4. Toleration--Religious aspects--Islam. I. Albayrak, Ismail. II. Title.
BP80.G8Y83 2014
297.092--dc23
2014039404

ISBN: 978-1-59784-346-1

Printed by
Imak Ofset, Istanbul - Turkey

Contents

Introduction vii

PART ONE
EDUCATION, DIALOGUE, AND PEACE

The Hizmet Movement and Its Contribution to
the Global Peace and Tolerance / İsmail Albayrak 3

Muslim-Christian Dialogue: *Nostra Aetate* and Gülen's
Philosophy of Dialogue / Salih Yücel 21

Islamic Radicalism and Gülen's Response / Salih Yücel 35

Challenges in Inter-Religious Dialogue: Initiatives and Activities of
the Gülen (Hizmet) Movement in Turkey / İsmail Albayrak 57

The Concepts of Jihad and Terror from the Perspective
of Fethullah Gülen / İsmail Albayrak 91

PART TWO
SPIRITUALITY, ETHICS, AND KNOWLEDGE

Gülen as a Spiritual Leader in a Global Islamic Context / Salih Yücel 109

Istighna and *Ithar*: Two Forgotten Principles of *Da'wah* from
the Perspective of the Hizmet Movement / Salih Yücel 131

A Muslim Perspective on the Ethical Dimension of Life
in Relation to Its Beginnings and End: With Special References
to the Writings of Fethullah Gülen / İsmail Albayrak 147

Gülen's Approach to Qur'anic Exegesis / İsmail Albayrak 177

Bibliography 215

Index 231

Introduction

In this age of globalization, distance is no longer a problem. Mass communication technologies allow the local to become global. Thus, local areas are facing rapid change in various ways. While the cry for democratic values, human rights and intercultural dialogue is frequently heard, the global threat of war, terrorism, the increased gap between poor and rich, famine, malnutrition, global warming and pollution, and many other social and cultural problems, pose a real challenge for present citizens of the globe. Intellectuals and politicians take these challenges as their primary concerns. Despite the existence of some pessimists, there are a number of initiatives working for the common good and expending great effort to solve these problems.

The Hizmet (Gülen) Movement is one of the most influential initiatives that should be taken into consideration in this context. Fethullah Gülen is a Turkish Muslim scholar whose ideas have inspired and influenced many Turkish intellectuals, educators, students, businessmen, politicians and journalists inside and outside Turkey to establish schools, educational and intercultural centers, and humanitarian aids organization in more than one hundred fifty countries. Furthermore, it cannot be denied that the Hizmet Movement is of greatest interest to contemporary journalists and academics. It is currently the topic of numerous academic conferences, daily articles in major newspapers and conversations in social circles. Gülen is loved and praised by many Turkish people and others, but is also severely criticized by some people inside and outside Turkey.

In this book, authors will cover the Hizmet Movement under the leadership of Fethullah Gülen from various perspectives in order to shed lights on current discussions. This book consists of nine essays in two parts. In the first essay, İsmail Albayrak, after summarizing some important features of globalization briefly, provides short biographical information about the life of Gülen, and then focuses on a general description of the Movement and its main characteristic in the formation of an ideal person who is capable of internalizing the qualities of self-discipline, dialogue and the notion of *hizmet/khidmah* (service for humanity). The question of how the formal and informal educational activities of the Movement contribute to the solution of local and global problems is the second concern of this article. Finally, as an extension of the Movement's global educational activities, Gülen's approach to cultural and religious diversity and their relationship in modern societies will be analyzed.

The second essay by Salih Yücel extensively covers how Gülen and his followers have engaged in dialogue in Turkey and outside Turkey and looks at the distinguishing principles of Gülen and his followers in their dialogue activities with non-Muslim individuals and communities. According to Yücel, Gülen views dialogue as a forgotten Islamic principle which has long been neglected. He does not only state this in his books, but has also personally applied this principle since the 1990s and urges other Muslims to do the same. Yücel makes it very clear that Gülen played important role in breaking the taboo or the unwritten rule of not engaging with other non-Muslim leaders or religious adherents in Turkey by meeting with Pope John Paul II, as well as the Orthodox Patriarch in İstanbul and other senior religious leaders. Responses from within Turkey were for and against Gülen's acts of dialogue. Some critics went as far as to call Gülen a heretic and even a secret cardinal aiming to proselytize Muslims for this act. In spite of such responses, which often originated from radical groups, Gülen not only continued to engage in and encourage dialogue, but also proposed the institutionalization of interfaith relations to Pope John Paul II, by establishing a joint divinity school in Harran (Old Edessa), Turkey. Gülen's goal is not to set up a new religion, as some of Gülen's critics claimed at the time, but rather to bring Muslim and Christian theologians, scholars and students together under one roof for more inclusive dialogue and scholarship. Yücel briefly looks at Gülen's vision and practice of dialogue, and considers *Nostra Aetate* as a basis for Muslim-Christian dialogue.

In the third essay, Yücel begins his discussion quoting from major scholars who argue that one major problem affecting the contemporary Muslim world is the lack of good role models and representation (*tamthil/temsil* in Turkish) in all fields, from science to sports and religion. As a result, Muslims are not sure how to respond to acts that are perceived to be either for or against Islam and the Muslim world. In a time when sensationalist media receives the majority of airtime, negative role models who make the most noise are consequently taken as representatives. According to Yücel, the last two centuries have often seen Muslims perceived as reactive characters, instead of proactive citizens and leaders. Basing his analysis on the interpretations of several prominent scholars, Yücel examines the method and manner of reactionary and radical Muslims in the light of the Qur'an and Sunnah. He focuses on Gülen's views of reactionaries, which runs parallel to the major views of the Qur'anic exegetes and Sunnah scholars. While the manner of reactionary Muslims generally contradicts the methods for dealing with aggression prescribed in Islam's primary texts, the article also acknowledges the difficulties involved in applying the Islamically preferred methods today, because the leading political and economic systems that shape the world affect which responses are heard and which are buried. Yücel concludes that the universal principles in the Qur'an and Sunnah need to be absorbed, reflected on, interpreted and experienced based on contemporary needs and issues without straying from the essence of Islam.

In the fourth essay, Albayrak takes Yücel's arguments further and places it in a broader Turkish context. He discusses the uncertainty and suspicion non-Muslims may feel regarding the sincerity of dialogue activities in the Muslim world, despite the increasing participation of Muslims, which takes various forms. Albayrak analyzes the argument that some non-Muslims hold that Muslims engage in dialogue in Western or non-Muslim societies only and neglect such initiatives in nations where Muslims are in the majority. In this article, he first examines the relationship between majority and minority groups and then move to religious and cultural dialogue activities conducted in the Republic of Turkey, by the Gülen (Hizmet) Movement. Furthermore, he evaluates the activities of the supporters of the Gülen Movement and the theological and cultural criticisms expressed by other Muslims about its activities. Finally, he gives some examples to show how inter-faith activities are sincerely practised not only overseas, but in a Muslim majority nation whose constitution is considered secular. Thus, in this article, Albayrak presents the Movement's influences and effects on global dialogue activities in a broader framework.

In the final article of this part Albayrak begins with how in modern media, Islam and terror are frequently debated together. He says that because it is extremely common to identify terrorism with Islam, as if the two were natural allies, thus we feel that we are an under obligation to bring these two different terms together in our presentation. The author aim in this article is to show that this association is not very relevant to the discussion. To achieve this aim, Albayrak focuses mainly on these questions: What is the meaning of terror? What do Islamic teachings say about terror? What is the relationship between the notion of *jihad* and Islam? What status does Islam confer on suicide attacks? He points out the focus on the false justification of war in the modern world, which can only pave the way for more terrorist actions. The author endeavors to address these issues from the Gülen's perspective. Finally, he concludes with a summary of the positive effects of the interfaith and intercultural dialogue meetings that Gülen initiated both inside and outside of Turkey in order to promote national and international tolerance, peace and mutual understanding.

In Part Two, there are four articles which discuss directly Fethullah Gülen's approaches to various issues. In the first article of this Part Yücel argues, in the fifth essay, that while Gülen is not directly engaged with mass media, he nevertheless receives significant global media attention. *The Economist* described him as the most influential leader in the Muslim world. *Foreign Policy* also placed him in first position, even though the method of online voting was not academic. However, Yücel continues, it cannot be denied that Gülen is the religious leader of greatest interest to contemporary journalists and academics. He and the faith-based movement, the Hizmet Movement, is the topic of numerous academic conferences, daily articles in major newspapers and conversations in social circles. He is loved and praised by many Turkish people, but is also criticized heavily by some Turks and non-Turks. His critics include former communists, atheists, ultranationalists, fanatic secularists, radical Islamists as well as people who are influenced by these groups. Yücel looks at such criticisms and Gülen's responses to them, through an academic lens and discusses the accusations filed against him. Despite these criticisms, the Movement has grown gradually and continues to grow. Although Gülen does not accept the role of the head person, leader or inspiration of the global movement, the millions of people either directly involved or supportive of the Movement take him as an inspiration and view him as a great spiritual leader.

In the second essay of this Part, Yücel demonstrates how the Movement applies two major principles of Islam which lead to great output using fewer resources. These principles are *istighna* and *ithar*, applied religiously by Gülen and his close friends and followers in different degrees. This creates a positive image for the Movement and attracts greater local support in terms of volunteers and donors. Yücel researched the local Gülen-inspired school to find that 65–70% of the work is done through volunteer work by employees and affiliated individuals. This is a unique financing methodology that gives the Movement credibility and the chance to produce more with less input. Otherwise, the Movement would need three times the finance to produce the current level of success. Yücel points to the fact that the principles of *istighna* and *ithar* are characteristics of Prophets. Contemporary thinker Said Nursi (1883–1960) expounded on these principles in their relevance to the modern age and Gülen applied these strictly in his life. Gülen's self-sacrificing nature means that he does not accept any return, reward or financial help for himself. Though he is officially retired, he does not take his pension, but donates it instead to a family in need. He lives on a small percentage of his book sales, of which 90% goes to funding scholarships. This role-modelling affected his close friends and followers, who strive to take on these principles in their lives. Yücel concludes that applying these principles leads to altruism on part of the followers and builds trust in the communities and countries served by the Movement's followers.

In the third essay of this Part, Albayrak discusses certain topics relating to the sacred nature of life as viewed from a Muslim's perspective with special references to the relevant works of Gülen. Among these, abortion and euthanasia, which have been made subjects of lively and intense debate by religious and secular groups, is given priority in this article. Albayrak draws attention to some of the differences found within Muslim approaches: while in the West these topics are considered in the framework of bioethics, in Islamic traditions, in the light of Gülen's own discourse, their context is that of modern medicine, jurisprudence and morality together. Although some theological differences separate the two traditions, Albayrak hopes that this article can help Muslim scholars actively engage with other religious communities in the area of biomedical ethics, and work collectively and coherently for a common goal, helping to create awareness within the wider community of their care and sensitivity with respect to issues of life and death.

The final article focuses on Gülen's exegetical works. Although Gülen has not written a complete exegesis on the Qur'an, Albayrak will refer to Gülen's important exegetical works to show where he stands in relation to the diverse modern Muslim scholarship on the Qur'an. This article examines Gülen's re-reading of the Qur'anic text, his approach to the nature and status of the Qur'an as Divine revelation, the notions of abrogation, clear (*muhkam*) and allegorical (*mutashabih*) verses, thematic unity among the chapters and verses of the Qur'an, Qur'anic narratives and the occasion of revelation. The main questions that Albayrak tackles in this context are: what is the difference between Gülen's reading of the Qur'an and that of his counterparts adhering to both classical and modern approaches? Does Gülen offer a new reading differing from others, or does he follow very well established exegetical traditions? How does he deal with modern sciences and ongoing scientific developments in relation to Qur'anic verses? Do Muslims need a new type of hermeneutics in their interpretation of the Qur'an? Finally, Albayrak places Gülen in wider exegetical activities in Turkish context.

It is the authors' primary duty to express our sincere thanks to the friends and colleagues who read the manuscripts and offered generous and constructive criticism. We also thank Fikret Yaşar, Erkan Kurt and Yusuf Alan who edited the manuscript and made insightful suggestions. The Grace and Mercy of God has been an ever present help in our times of need. We cannot thank the Lord enough.

Part One

Education, Dialogue,
and Peace

The Hizmet Movement and Its Contribution to the Global Peace and Tolerance[1]

İsmail Albayrak

Australian Catholic University/Sakarya University

T his article will summarize some important features of globalization briefly, and then will provide the general description of the
Movement, its main characteristics in the formation of an ideal
person who is capable of internalizing the qualities of self-discipline, dialogue and the notion of *khidmah* (service for humanity/*hizmet*). The question of how the formal and informal educational activities of the Movement contribute to the solution of local and global problems is the second
concern of this article. Finally, as an extension of the Movement's global
educational activities, the article will deal with Gülen's approach to cultural and religious diversity and their relationship in modern communities.

Globalization

Globalization has multidimensional aspects therefore it is not easy to define.
This undefined character of globalization is strongly related to economic, political, social, cultural and ethical values of the globe. For some, the
process of globalization is a real nightmare which causes various types
of problems. They consider it a great threat to local traditions and cultures
by weakening the conventional borders or internal cohesion of communities to create super economic and social structures.[2] This homogeniza-

---

[1]   This article *was* published in *International Handbook of Inter-religious Education*,
(eds. Kath Engebretson, Marian de Souza, Gloria Durka). I would like to thank Prof.
Engebretson for her cordial permission to republish it *with some modifications*.
[2]   M.B. Steger, *Globalisation: A Very Short History*, 64.

tion is seen by many critics of globalization with great anxiety that the local is losing its meaning, values and is melted into the global. They strongly believe that if it continues uncontrolled, the powerful effect of globalization will eliminate various rivals. Shutting down many big firms or factories, undefined business and marketing laws and daily loss of jobs in great numbers are part of the usage of this unavoidable instrument, namely globalization.

The main reason for this mistrust lies in the economic imbalance among the nations of the world. For rich and developed countries, globalization is a revolution, a great success of Western civilization to be spread all over the world but for others, it is an ideology to be prevented. According to second group, this ideology accelerates the speed of change in societies and increases violence and war to seize power, control or impose authority over others. The underdeveloped countries seem to have no role to play in this one way project of globalization.

For others, globalization is a unique way to go forward. It is enough to look only at the development in information and mass media technologies to realize how people are involved in this inevitable process. Today, people are now communicating in a global language.[3] Via the internet, they daily transact large amount of money from one country to another. The impact of intergovernmental relations grows rapidly. This great potential of globalization makes people aware of their common problems. People who are very optimistic about globalization believe that this process, with its great technological progress, will bring wealth, freedom, good political arrangements and democracy for all beyond the local concern of nation states. It should also be remembered that people who are longing for globalization argue that contemporary common problems can only be solved by global initiative and enterprise.

Between these two radical understandings of globalization, there are various discourses which pronounce more cautious approaches. Glocalization[4], I think, is one of the important representatives of this middle way. While the society preserves its own local values, it also supports, active-

---

[3] It is important to note that today 80% of internet content is in English. This is good for understanding each other but this is alarmingly dangerous for the preservation of local cultures and languages.

[4] Erik Swyngedouw, 'Globalisation or glocalisation,' *Cambridge Review International Affairs*, 33.

ly participates in and contributes greatly to global values. When we take a Muslim's discourse of globalization into account, it will be seen that it is not very different from the modern discussion of globalization. There are extreme sceptics who consider it as a major threat to Islam and a conspiracy against Muslims all over the world. Especially after the collapse of the Soviet Union and the vast tragedy of 9/11, criticism and attacks on Islam everywhere lead many Muslims to mistrust global discourse of globalization. In addition, because the Muslim world in general is weak, powerless and quite passive in front of the globalization process, they display no significant contribution to either contemporary problems or the globalization process. Consequently, they prefer to stay away from the process where they have no influence. They also express their dissatisfaction with a globalization which lacks spiritual and ethical dimensions. This understanding makes many Muslims focus on only their own localities or societies in the globe. I think, because of its inability to embrace all the world in this global age, many activities and policies of this insufficient approach would not be able to continue for long.

There are also other Muslim intellectuals who welcome globalization without any hesitation. In contrast to above mentioned group, these intellectuals express their complete trust and appreciation of Western cultures and values. Because they believe that their present situation is not compatible with modernity, they zealously prefer a form of globalization from above to modernize their own communities. This confidence allows them to accept what they can get from the leading countries in globalization. However, it seems that their unquestioned acceptance of globalization marginalizes them among their own community.

Living in a world which is in constant and rapid change, it is easy to guess that there will be many other approaches too. Now we are not in a position to say which of these approaches will dominate on the basis of this changeable nature of our globe. However, when we talk about the Muslim world it is important to note that there are different versions of these approaches to globalization. Unfortunately, the disgrace brought about by occupation and the fragile nature of the war against terrorism creates many reactionaries to globalization among Muslims. The situation also forces many Muslim movements to establish political or military powers which do not seem to last long. The Gülen Movement,[5] in this respect, is unique in their approach to globalization. They are open to change but also respect their own traditional values and identities. In other words, the Gülen Movement does not display an antiglobalist reflection (not reactionary) but it has produced a counterglobalization (proactivist) view which bears its own seal. Before moving to the analysis of the Movement it is important to give brief information about Fethullah Gülen and the Movement.

Fethullah Gülen and His Movement

Fethullah Gülen is a Muslim intellectual, thinker and religious scholar. He was born in Turkey in 1941. He grew up in a very religious environment. His first teachers were his parents. He mastered the Qur'an and its lan-

---

[5] I come across different naming of the Movement in recently written books and articles. Some describe the Movement as a civil-society, social conservative or Anatolian Islam of faith based movement (Greg Barton, 'Progressive Islamic Thought, civil society and the Gülen Movement in the national context: parallels with Indonesia,' Proceedings from *Islam in the contemporary world: The Fethullah Gülen Movement in thought and practice,* Rice University/Houston, 2005, 2, 9), pietistic activism (Elisabeth Özdalga, 'Worldly Asceticism in Islamic Casting: Fethullah Gülen's Inspired Piety and Activism,' *Critique,* 17 (2000) 83–104), civil cosmopolitan movement (Joshua D. Hendrick, 'The Regulated Potential of Kinetic Islam: Antithesis in Global Activism,' *Muslim Citizens of the Globalized World: Contributions of the Hizmet Movement,* (eds.), Robert A. Hunt and Yüksel A. Aslandoğan, New Jersey: The Light Pub. 2006), while others name them as an ethic oriented or text based movement (M. Hakan Yavuz, 'Islam in the Public Sphere: The Case of the Nur Movement,' in *Turkish Islam and the Secular State: The Hizmet Movement,* (eds.) M. Hakan Yavuz and John L. Esposito, New York: Syracuse University Press, 2003, 2–3). There are others who describe the Movement as educational Islamism (Bekim Agai, 'The Hizmet Movement's Islamic Ethic of Education,' in *Turkish Islam and the Secular State: The Hizmet Movement,* (eds.) M. Hakan Yavuz and John L. Esposito, New York: Syracuse University Press 2003, 50), or a desecularisation and glocalisation or recularisation movement (John O. Voll, Fethullah Gülen: Transcending Modernity in the New Islamic Discourse,' in *Turkish Islam and the Secular State: The Hizmet Movement,* (eds.) M. Hakan Yavuz and John L. Esposito, New York: Syracuse University Press 2003, 242). I think none of these descriptions do justice to the broad definition of the Movement. Gülen's own definition 'A movement originating its own model' (Gülen, *Toward Global Civilization of Love and Tolerance,* New Jersey: The Light Pub. 2004, 210) seems better than others' description.

guage at a very early age and then continued his traditional *madrasa* (school) education in different villages of his home town. While in school, he met students of Bediüzzaman Said Nursi and was introduced to the *Risale-i Nur* collections, in one respect a 'complete' and 'contemporary' Islamic school that contributed a great deal to his intellectual and spiritual formation. Meanwhile, he privately continued his 'modern' education in science and philosophy, literature and history.

In 1959 Gülen moved to Edirne to work as an *imam*. Following his years in Edirne he was appointed as a Qur'anic teacher to İzmir, the third biggest city in Turkey, in 1966. These years were very fruitful for him. Besides teaching the Qur'an and Arabic he also travelled a lot in the Aegean part of Turkey to deliver speeches concerning religious, social and ethical issues. In the 1970s he became very well known as a preacher and respected scholar in Turkey. He was sent to different cities and finally to Bornova, İzmir, where he worked until September 12, 1980. After his retirement in 1980, he re-started his regular sermons unofficially in 1986 and continued up until the beginning of the 1990s. In 1994 he initiated the 'Foundation of the Journalists and Writers' Organization,' a group that promotes dialogue and tolerance among all social strata and has received a warm welcome from almost all walks of life. He visited the Vatican and had a meeting with the Late Pope John Paul II in 1998. In 1999 he went to the United States for medical treatment. Since then he continues to live in the USA.

A small group that started to form around his opinions served people in the light of his advice. Now, many people from all walks of life participate in this service. They continue to serve without thought of material reward. They preach, teach and establish private educational institutions and intercultural dialogue centers all over the world. They also publish books and magazines, as well as daily and weekly newspapers, participate in television and radio broadcasts, and fund scholarships for poor students. The companies and foundations set up by people of different world views who agree about serving people, especially in the field of education, have founded and are operating about 2,000 secondary and high schools and over 20 universities from England to Australia, the United States and Russia, and South Africa. Gülen's understanding of service permits no expectation of material or political gain. Sincerity and purity of intention should never be harmed or contaminated by these expectations.[6] This picture indicates clearly that, with thousands of followers inside and outside Turkey, the Gülen Movement has already become a part of globalization.

Main Characteristics of the Movement and the Importance of Education

As we have mentioned, many movements among Muslim countries in the modern period did not last long due to their short sighted dominant political engagement. Bearing in mind the colonized and oppressed position of many countries during the 19th and 20th centuries, Muslims generally produced various types of anti-Western and anti-modernity discourses in reaction to Western powers. Thus, liberation from the West was the primary requirement and many have tried to be sealed off from Western influence.[7] The case in the Gülen Movement is quite different. As many researchers have pointed out, the Movement originated in Turkey where the cultural and religious (together with mystical) richness of the uncolonized Ottoman state have still been preserved.[8] Although religion and culture play significant roles in the Gülen Movement, it is neither a fundamentalist reaction to the West and modernity nor a complete acceptance of it. As will be discussed further, the Gülen Movement represents middle and more balanced way in many respects. They are open to recognize the contribution of others. In fact, they are extremely positive about the use of mass communication technology in human service and very conscious of how globalization removes the borders among nations and brings people frequently together. The question of how Muslims can be involved and contribute to this process lies in their understanding of humanity and in their understanding of serving humanity in a global way. In order to summarize their overall approach to humanity we have to first look at Fethullah Gülen's philosophy and its perception.

---

[6]   en.fgulen.com/content/category/148/160/10/.

[7]   Even many Muslims who live in Western countries try to resolve their own problems on the basis of ethnic identity. American Muslims, who are mainly composed of Arabs, South Asians and Africans, are good illustration of this. Each group has political and social agendas which are quite different from others. (Oliver Roy, *Globalized Islam*) The fear of assimilation makes people live in a globalized world extremely locally.

[8]   Barton, 2005:5.

For Gülen, the value of our ancient earth originates from its noble inhabitants, namely humankind. To serve this honorable resident is our most honorable earthly duty.[9] The question of why the human being is very important, according to Gülen, lies in his full trust in and dependence on God. Because we love God, we should love and respect His best creation. If a person loves God, they feel a deep inclination towards His every creature.[10] This love is not a static proclamation or an abstract notion; it is in fact a transcendental immersion which come directly from Gülen's understanding of Islam. He believes that love is the strongest and most powerful weapon in the universe.[11] The dream of this universal love can only be realized by the 'person of ideals.' The 'person of ideals' constitutes the ideal society, this is a virtuous circle. Gülen says that their common feature is to love God fervently and to ask themselves questions about the meaning of life, existence, death, servanthood, their relationship with God and other creatures, the nature of sin, reward, why humanity is suffering, where humankind is going? Ultimately these are the ones who will serve humanity truly by their distinctive morals, spirit and reason.[12]

Gülen sees the realization of the person of ideals as the ultimate aim of human existence. Actually he calls them a 'Golden Generation' and sees their activities on a global level as a sign of hope for the salvation of all humanity. Because they equip themselves with values such as faith, love, a balanced view of science, freethinking, freedom, consultation etc.[13] Gülen believes that they will do their best, until finally the world becomes paradise.

The key term in the realization of the Golden Generation as a whole is education. Gülen has spent more than forty years encouraging and inspiring the people around him to invest materially and spiritually in education. For Gülen, education is a sublime duty that manifests the Divine name *Rabb* (Pedagogue, Upbringer, Sustainer).[14] This is a very important piece

---

[9]   Gülen, *Toward Global Civilization of Love and Tolerance*, 225.

[10] Gülen, *İrşad Ekseni*, 168–169.

[11] Camcı and Kudret Ünal, *Hoşgörü ve Diyalog İklimi*, 132.

[12] Gülen, *Zamanın Altın Dilimi*, 10–13.

[13] Ahmet Kuru, 'Fethullah Gülen's Search for the Middle Way Between Modernity and Muslim Tradition,' in *Turkish Islam and Secular State: The Hizmet Movement* (eds. M. Hakan Yavuz and John L. Esposito), 2003, 119.

[14] Gülen, *Essays, Perspectives, Opinions*, 71–72.

of notion which connects human beings with God. Real life, says Gülen, is only possible by knowledge. Whoever neglects teaching and learning could be considered dead. For Gülen, the reason we are created is to learn, communicate and teach.[15] Gülen, in his many writings, draws attention to the differences between humans and animals by underlying the importance of education. He says that animals are created with potential talent but a human being's journey in the world starts with impotence and a miserable position and they must wait for everything from others.[16]

Gülen is so insistent on education for several reasons. Not only does it train individuals but it is also the most vital factor for positive social change. In addition, he sees education as the most effective tongue for relations with others. Education is the aim of the aims. In his own words, the people who are educating their young today are actually investing in the next 25 years.[17] Nonetheless, despite the existence of a wide range of schools everywhere, Gülen, like his predecessor Said Nursi, expresses many times his dissatisfaction with the existing system of schooling. There are numerous state and private schools but they fail to take the whole need of children into consideration. Gülen frequently repeats that people who are responsible for the education of youth in the modern period have not developed a holistic approach to education. This failure results in the creation of a young generation with no ideals, as if they were animated corpses.[18] The pressure of globalization in this process cannot be denied. Educational institutions have come under pressure to focus more on meeting the demands of the economy rather than more sublime aims; the education for employment blinds many people to raising spiritually and bodily healthy children.

This is the gist of Gülen's educational philosophy. For Gülen, training the body of children is easy but very few train the minds and hearts of the pupils at the same time.[19] For him the distinction made between the mind and heart of students in modern school system is a calamity for all. Today, according to Gülen, this mistake is still being repeated. Despite

---

[15] Gülen, 2004:217.

[16] Gülen, 2002:67–68.

[17] Gülen, 2004:205.

[18] Thomas Michel, 'Fethullah Gülen as Educator,' in *Turkish Islam and the Secular State: The Hizmet Movement* (eds. M. Hakan Yavuz and John L. Esposito), 74.

[19] Gülen, 2004:202.

the production of many great scientists from contemporary schooling systems, modern men and women fail to establish real happiness in the globe. In fact, this one sided education increases the crises in societies and produces only youth with no ideals. Thus, there is a great need for new and fresh approaches to current education systems.[20] It is also urgent to redefine the frame of knowledge. Gülen thinks that in the modern period, knowledge is limited to empty theories and unabsorbed pieces of learning, which arouse suspicion in minds and darkness in hearts, is a heap of garbage around which desperate and confused souls flounder.[21] Nonetheless, he sees Nursi's approach as a sole prescription for this dilemma. The purpose of education is to make knowledge a guide in oneself and in others. To achieve such an aim is to see education as the illumination of the mind in science and knowledge and the light of the heart in faith and virtue.[22]

This is the middle way that Gülen wants to promote everywhere. He takes this heritage directly from the teachings of his predecessors and he also finds Qur'anic references to this concept.[23] He wisely interprets the Qur'anic term *al-sirat al-mustaqim* (straight path)[24] as a middle way to use in a wide variety of social and ethical issues. This middle way can be described as an extreme emphasis on avoidance of excesses and deficiencies while finding a balance between materialism and spiritualism, rationalism and mysticism, worldliness and asceticism, heart and mind, tradition and modernity.[25] This is the sole way to prevent young people from fanaticism and atheism. However, for Gülen, the acceptance of the middle way on the above mentioned issues is not a blind action. This understanding has been based on both religious and scientific knowledge. There are two laws (law of nature/religious law) which come from the Eternal which do not conflict between them. Actually, one aspect of the notion of *taqwa* (performing what God has commanded) is to learn how God's true religion and natural law (sciences) can be combined. In brief, both advise moderation and balance.[26] This middle way opens the doors of education

---

20   Ibid., 255.
21   Ibid,, 205.
22   Ibid., 197.
23   Gülen, *Prophet Muhammad: The Infinite Light*, 200–201.
24   Qu'ran 1:5.
25   Kuru, 2003:116–119.
26   Hendrick, 2006:19.

for many hesitant, conservative parents who face great difficulties in allowing their children to receive a modern education at the risk of losing their faith or keeping their faith but suffering from losing their chance to achieve a high standard of education in modern secular schools. Moreover, Gülen's philosophy of education also prevents Muslim students and others who live as a minority outside Turkey from experiencing cultural shock or complete assimilation, and also from alienation or ghettoization from the dominant cultures.

To fulfil such an important goal, Gülen, in contrast to many Muslims, has chosen education with a special emphasis on ethics at the center of his own Movement. Education is the most significant tool to compete with others on a global scale. His educational model does not exclude anyone from participation. In fact, its universally accessible nature empowers many marginalized groups to continue their education in this model. This is one way to bring an equal and just educational system to everyone in the growing inequality and unjust nature of global education for improvement of the conditions of the poor. Bearing in mind the existence of schools in nearly every part of the world and in various environments and different social conditions, as stated above, their main focus is on the development of ethical understanding of the global issues rather than teaching religion.

This stress on the universal dimension of humanity's common virtues allows the Movement's educational model to be more globalized and embrace a diverse number of nations. For this reason the Gülen Movement has prioritized schools rather than the mosque, which is chosen by many Islamically oriented movements. This shift from mosque to school also enables the Movement to see the world as a whole place of service (*dar al-khidmah—in Turkish: hizmet*), where one can serve for the common good of humanity. In other words, serving the community is a kind of worship and the school in modern period is the best place to serve the community, so the content of the mosque as a place of worship is transferred to the school where the lost soul is being saved. In this context, teachers replace the imams of the mosque and they (teachers) are understood by Gülen to be subjectively the equivalent of saintly men or women.[27] Furthermore, in order to elevate the job of the teacher to a very noble status, Gülen associates the profession of teaching with the task of

---

[27] Gülen, 2002:72.

the Prophets and many other Muslim saints.[28] Like the Prophets, the teachers of the Movement focus on communal salvation rather than individual happiness. So teachers, according to Gülen, become major figures in building the happiness of our globe.

It is also important to note that he makes a clear distinction between the educator and the teacher, stating that educators are very limited number in our modern world.[29] Despite their openness to new development and the contribution of others, educators in the Gülen Movement also share a common pedagogic vision, similar curriculum[30] and human and material resources[31] based on networks of advanced information and communication infrastructure. This collective consciousness is the unique attempt to respond and confront the challenging nature of globalization. The adoption of self-mission is of prime importance in this educational project, therefore teachers consider every individual as a different world and try to find a way to their heart.[32] In this process, the notion of *tamthil* (representation; temsil in Turkish) comes to the fore. *Tamthil* means to teach values through examples. Gülen believes this is the most effective way to prepare students for the future. The need for proper action is influential more than the words. In this way, he believes, both the teacher and student internalize the core values of education. Put another way, they not only teach but also show how to use knowledge.

Once again, in Gülen's project this interaction is not one or two sided (teacher-student) but is multidimensional and includes family, school environment and mass media etc. Gülen argues that the desired result can only be achieved by the cooperation of these different sides. Otherwise, the existence of opposing tendencies among these vital institutions will subject the students to contradictory influences that will distract them and dissipate their energy. In particular, mass media should contribute to the education of the young generation by following the education pol-

---

[28] Yüksel Doğan and Muhammed Çetin, 'The Educational Philosophy of Gülen in Thought and Practice,' in *Muslim Citizens of the Globalized World: Contribution of the Hizmet Movement* (eds. Robert A. Hunt and Yüksel Aslandoğan), 37.

[29] Gülen, *Criteria or the Lights of the Way*, 36.

[30] Every year many meetings are being held by teachers to develop and bring new material to their teaching. It is observed that the curriculum they use has never been static.

[31] Michel, 'Fethullah Gülen as Educator,' 70.

[32] Gülen, 2004:209.

icy approved by the community.[33] This is the dream of Gülen therefore, as a inspirer of a giant movement; he guides his followers to establish various institutions to satisfy this global need. This is an ongoing process and the institutions never stop. Within this process, teachers as well as parents and other people need to be educated constantly. Every stratum of the community should be taken into consideration and real energy should be expended for the salvation of the community. Interestingly enough, Gülen interprets being a good (*taqwa*) person not only on the basis of avoidance of sin but also as active participation in the improvement of society.[34] Thus in this global educational project not only men but also women have a great role to play.

Towards Global Peace and Tolerance

Besides education, another important activity initiated by Gülen in the cause of global peace is his emphasis on the notion of tolerance, dialogue and intercultural and interfaith relations. Dialogue activities are an extension of Gülen's global educational struggle; they also serve the education of humanity. Although he has been severely criticized by some people, he bravely argues that dialogue is primarily concerned with religion and is thus a religious duty.[35] Gülen constantly insists on the religious nature of the meetings because the basic Islamic sources advise Muslims to engage in dialogue with representatives of other faiths. Thus, Gülen says that dialogue is not his invention or innovation, but a revival of the most neglected aspect of Islam. His constancy in this regard is very sincere: he has said that even if the sensitive political balance of the world changes a thousand times he will never stop the dialogue meetings; the Islamic sources do allow him only to do so.[36]

First of all, he believes that the pluralism in our modern society is a fact not a problem. Religiously speaking it is the duty of believers to preserve this tension between the sameness and difference in the emergence of global homogeneities. A Qur'anic verse[37] clearly rejects cultural

---

[33] Gülen, 2004:206.
[34] Yavuz, 2003:25.
[35] Enes Ergene, *Geleneğin Modern Çağa Tanıklığı*, İstanbul: Yeni Akademi, 2005, 47.
[36] www.herkul.org.
[37] Qu'ran 49:13.

homogeneity propagated by dominant globalization: 'O mankind! We have created you male and female, and have made you nations and tribes that you may know one another. Lo! The noblest of you, in the sight of Allah, is the best in conduct (*taqwa*)...' It is safe to assume that one of the essential words of the Qur'an concerning plurality lies in this verse. In fact, the Qur'an sees diversity as one of the most important human strengths. *Taaruf* (knowing each other) should be reconsidered in the context of the need to find common grounds for the coexistence of diverse religious and cultural varieties. It is a key that could open the door to interfaith dialogue. Here the Qur'an draws attention to equality in regard to biology and to a dignity common to all. Thus no one can be justified in boasting of an inherent superiority over others.

Thus for Gülen, one of the prime functions of education is to foster intercultural understanding. Failure to take into account the diverse nature of society in education feeds the homogeneous and monocultural dominance in many host cultures. Denial or disregard of the diversity which already exists in society leads to misrepresentation of the others. This partisanship is the root of every turmoil and social conflict. In a world becoming more and more globalized, one has to know who will be his future next door neighbor. Furthermore, like neighbors, nations also need each other in global scale. One of the most important factors here is to eliminate causes that separate people, such as discrimination based on color, race, belief and ethnicity. Education, Gülen says, can uproot these evils.[38] Having held firmly to this belief, the Gülen Movement works very hard to promote tolerance both inside and outside Turkey. For Gülen, dialogue and tolerance mean accepting every person, irrespective of their status and learning to live together.[39] In this regard, education is considered as an island of unity. Tolerance and dialogue need to be taught in school. Teaching differences and giving the accurate picture of the unfamiliar other give opportunities to move on. Gülen thinks that this is a key for the improvement of relationships among the world's nations. Religiously speaking, in the understanding of Gülen, what is good for all is also good in Islam (and other religions). Education is the way to transmit these universal values. Education about tolerance also contributes to the solidarity of nations and their willingness to live together.

---

[38] Ali Ünal and Alphonse Williams, *Fethullah Gülen: Advocate of Dialogue*, 330.

[39] www.herkul.org.

In Gülen Movement schools, education of tolerance is being practiced vividly and it is fair to say that diversity is part of their existent schooling system. In many countries students from different ethnic, cultural and religious backgrounds study in the same peaceful atmosphere of these schools. For example, in Bosnia, Croatian and Serbian students—even though their numbers are small- study peacefully alongside Bosnian students, in spite of the brutal war. This is a powerful indication that the Gülen Movement's schools have succeeded in establishing a non-sectarian atmosphere in their educational system without neglecting to respect cultural and religious differences.

Today's global discourse teaches us that one's happiness depends on the other's happiness and many crises in the globe can be overcome only by the promotion of tolerance and dialogue. For Gülen, dialogue is a must. But it does not mean that it is a compromise or negotiation. Dialogue and tolerance are also not passive acceptance of others. For Gülen, tolerance is religious duty and a virtue to be gained. It is an indication of sincerity in the engagement of cultural relation. Gülen repeats several times the importance of forgetting revenge for the past, disregarding the polemics, elimination of hatred from the vocabulary. Gülen asks his followers to see their own mistakes and be blind the mistakes of others.[40] It is not wise to dictate what you believe, but it is meritorious to listen to others to understand them or learn from them. So respecting cultural, religious and social differences is crucial in the education of tolerance. Gülen sincerely believes that the existent cultures and religions have this potential to contribute to world peace provided that modern men take education of tolerance seriously.

Today, in every school of the Movement, the education of tolerance is being taught in a comprehensive way, including the interaction of both students-teachers and their families. Similarly, it is being taught through good examples which pave the way to mutual and respectful relations. Having internalized the value of tolerance education, teachers transmit this understanding to their students. In addition to schools, the last ten years have seen a great explosion in the establishment of cultural and interfaith centers to promote dialogue and tolerance. Bridge-builders of Gülen Movement have felt the need for general training in intercultural

---

[40] Gülen, *Key Concepts in the Practice of Sufism-1*, 98.

activities and have gone beyond schools to meet this need. These centers play a complimentary role to school education and have had a great impact on the internal cohesion of societies. In addition, these centers also contribute to the integration of minorities in different countries without losing their own identities and cultures.

Gülen is optimistic for the future of these activities and their contribution to global peace. However, he is also very cautious not to name the dialogue activities of his followers. He argues that this is an unceasing process and the future will show how beneficial it is. He is also confident that people will be very hopeful to see the future, common work of the three Abrahamic religions which come from the same root.[41] So, for Gülen this is a global responsibility and the followers of these great traditions should come together and try to build common ground among diverse societies. This common ground, tolerance, dialogue and peace, will heal most of our present wounds as a global nation. Like his predecessor, Gülen sees three great illnesses in front of humanity: ignorance, poverty and internal schism. Knowledge, capital work and unification can struggle against these. However, among them ignorance is the most serious sickness; it must be opposed with education, which has always been the important way of serving one's country. Now that we live in a global village, education is the best way to serve humanity and to establish a dialogue with other civilizations.[42]

Today, despite many good works of self-sacrificing people all over the world, there are still many who control by force, intolerance among different intra and international groups. After 9/11, I think, Islam and Muslims have been greatly affected by this global disinformation. The war against terror is being transformed into a war against Muslims and most Muslims are being seen as terrorists or most terrorists are being seen as Muslims. Similarly, Islam becomes a subtitle of terrorism and associated with violence. The efforts of some mass media and the mistakes of some individuals further diminish the image of Muslims and Islam around the globe. What we are facing today is a really clash of ignorance rather than the clash of civilization. Gülen sincerely believes that if one wants to win the hearts of suppressed people, wants to solve the conflict, the most secure shelter is education and dialogue. Unfortunately, vio-

---

[41] Gülen, 2004:231.
[42] Ibid., 198.

lence nourishes violence. This is an experimentally proven fact. It is easy to destroy but it is very difficult to rebuild. Today our multicultural societies' cohesion depends on this mutual understanding, engaging proactively in cooperation between communities and respecting each other. According to Gülen, this is a religious duty and we are responsible for the preparation of our future world in this regard. In the hundreds of schools and many intercultural centers the Gülen Movement tries to establish a common language for better understanding.

Conclusion

It is now an accepted fact that the last two centuries have brought people together to communicate more actively. This formation is known today as globalization. Because of incredible development in various fields in our modern world, everybody has to take the notion of globalization seriously. On the Muslim world, the Gülen Movement represents one of the best examples in this regard. Being aware of the importance of globalization, they also prepare themselves against the danger of fallacies in the understanding of globalization. Thus they are not reactionaries to any global or modern development and equally they are not passive on easily influenced under the dominant nature of global activities.

As summarized briefly above, the middle way is the main characteristic of the Gülen Movement. The Movement is aware of global issues and problems and they believe sincerely that these problems can be solved only by global cooperation. Here, they try to develop a sense of culture based on Turkish Islam and Anatolian Sufism to preserve their own identity, but at the same time they are ready and open to new changes. At this juncture, education, moral development, spirituality and tolerance-dialogue play a significant role. A lack of any of these concepts may lead a very civilized movement to power or tyranny. Unfortunately, many authoritarian programs could not bring peace and material-spiritual developments to the societies. Systems which recognize no ethical values and depend solely on power have nothing to contribute to the global progress of all humanity. Continuing wars at the beginning of the third millennium have shown that it is impossible to control people by killing or suppressing them. Thus what is needed is the development of a global movement which covers or surrounds a person's every dimension. To do so, there is no instant solution. Gülen and his followers have chosen education and intercultural gatherings in the formation of a new man and woman (ideal human/*al-insan al-kamil*). This is not a rigid educational movement. Laying prime stress on representation (*tamthil*), teachers in the Movement expend great effort on showing students how to internalize values of morality and tolerance. Because lack of faith and ethical values are the cause and root of every conflict and problem in the world, Gülen Movement's *raison d'être* is to establish an environment where the student's heart and mind are simultaneously satisfied. So the Movement tries to domesticate excessive positivism with emphasis on the inner and spiritual dimensions of Islam. But this is not an exclusivist approach though it takes its power from Islamic faith. As regards globalization, their motto 'Because we love the Creator we love all His creatures'[43] is the starting point and every Muslim is considered a religious brother and representatives of other faiths are considered as brother in creation. So the number of sister schools and dialogue centers in more than one hundred fifty countries, together with various interactions, are the best way to serve the citizens of the globe. They are practicing globalization vividly and contributing to contemporizing and modernizing Muslims without losing their faith in any detail and without any hidden political or ideological agenda. Because human beings are potentially respected creature and they are able to achieve, the Gülen Movement is very optimistic for the future of the globe. As long as we preserve a civil, just and free atmosphere to pave the way for the education of advantaged and disadvantaged people, there is no barrier to transforming the world into paradise.

---

[43] Ergene, 2005:17.

Muslim-Christian Dialogue: *Nostra Aetate* and Gülen's Philosophy of Dialogue[44]

Salih Yücel[45]
Monash University, Australia

Introduction

At a time when half of the Ottoman Empire's lands were occupied by Russia, Italy, England, and France, Said Nursi proposed dialogue and collaboration between Muslims and Christians before a congregation of over 10,000 Muslims, including 100 prominent religious scholars, in the Umayyad Mosque, Damascus.[46] The strength of Nursi's proposal comes from his foresight when other Muslim thinkers were on the defensive against the invading colonial forces. Nursi held this approach even after the Ottoman Empire had collapsed after a turbulent conflict between the Empire and Europe.

Nursi strongly believed that the source of international aggression is materialistic philosophy. The problem was not East vs. West or Christian vs. Muslim, but the philosophy that he regarded as 'the evil of civilization.' For Nursi, there are two types of Europe: 'the first follows the sciences which serve justice and activities beneficial for the life of society through the inspiration it has received from true Christianity.' The second is 'corrupt, through the darkness of the philosophy of naturalism...

[44] This article was first published in *Australian eJournal of Theology*, Vol. 20/3, December, 2013. I would like to thank the editor of the Journal for his kind permission for the republication of this article.
[45] Dr Salih Yucel is Senior Lecturer in Islamic Studies at Centre for Religious Studies, Monash University, Australia.
[46] Nursi, *Hutbe-i Şamiye: Damascus Sermon* (trans. Şükran Vahide), 18.

which has driven humankind to vice and misguidance.'[47] This philosophy drives people to greed, which then causes major conflicts from individual to global levels. This was the reasoning behind his call for unity and collaboration between followers of the two major faiths, namely Muslims and Christians. Both have common enemies, such as the problems of poverty, ignorance, and enmity. 'Believers should now unite, not only with their Muslim fellow-believers, but with truly religious and pious Christians, disregarding questions of dispute and not arguing over them, for absolute disbelief is on the attack.'[48] Nursi faced imprisonment, political exile, and home arrest during the second half of his life, making him unable to put his vision in practice.

It was over half-a-century after Nursi's proposal when the Second Vatican Council declared *Nostra Aetate*, 'The Relation of the Church to Non-Christian Religions' in 1965. The declaration was originally intended to deal with the Catholic theological standing towards Judaism. It was not until Arab Catholic, Maronite, and Coptic bishops argued that a statement that ignored Muslims was not politically viable that Muslims were included in the declaration.[49] *Nostra Aetate* is a significant document that challenges Roman Catholics as well as Protestant Churches to open up, rethink their attitudes towards other religions, and reflect on the fact that all human beings are 'but one community.'[50]

Nostra Aetate has been considered one of the most important turning points in the history of Catholic-Muslim relations.[51] In the words of Pope Benedict XVI in 2005, *Nostra Aetate* is the *Magna Carta* of the Catholic Church in terms of Muslim-Christian relations.[52] Since 1967, the Popes

---

Nursi, *Lemalar: The Flashes* (trans. Şükran Vahide), 161.

48 Ibid., 204.

49 Kail Ellis, O.S.A, 'Vatican II and the Contemporary Islam' *New Catholic World*, 269ff; Edward Idris Cardinal Cassidy, *Ecumenism and Interreligious Dialogue: Unitatis Redintegratio, Nostra Aetate*, 127.

50 Ataullah Siddiqui, *Christian-Muslim Dialogue in the Twentieth Century*, 34.

51 Scott C. Alexander, 'We go way back: The history of Muslim-Catholic relations is one of both confrontation and dialogue.' *U.S. Catholic*, February.

52 John Borelli, *'Interreligious Dialogue as a Spiritual Practice,'* Georgetown University international conference proceedings, *Islam in the Age of Global Challenges: Alternative Perspectives of the Hizmet Movement Conference.* Available at en.fgulen. com/conference-papers/gulen-conference-in-washington-dc/3100–interreligious-dialogue-as-a-spiritual-practice.

have congratulated Muslims on *Eid al-Fitr* after the month of Ramadan. In 1974, the Vatican formed the Commission for Religious Relations with Muslims (CRRM). In 1976, the Vatican co-organized the Christian-Islam Congress in Tripoli with the World Islamic Call Society (WICS). In 1990, the Vatican established the *Nostra Aetate* Foundation. In 1994, the Pontifical Council for Interreligious Dialogue (PCID) led a conference with the Muslim World League, the Organization of the Islamic Conference, and the Muslim World Congress in Cairo. In 1995, the Muslim-Christian Liaison Committee was set up with four international Muslim organizations. The Permanent Committee for Dialogue set up a joint committee with al-Azhar University's Monotheist Religions Committee in 1998 with the signing of an agreement in Rome.

In 2001, the late Pope, John Paul II, visited the Umayyad Mosque as the first pope to visit a mosque, 1363 years after Caliph 'Umar ibn Khattab (586–644) who visited the Church of the Holy Sepulchre in Jerusalem. 2007 was the year 138 Muslim scholars and leaders signed an open letter called 'A Common Word between Us and You' to Pope Benedict XVI as a response to the Pope's remarks at the University of Regensburg lecture. In 2008, the PCID and the Centre for Inter-religious Dialogue of the Islamic Culture and Relations Organization made a joint declaration in Iran. In February 2009, the Vatican and al-Azhar University's Joint Committee for Dialogue signed a declaration promoting a culture of peace. In Catholic archdioceses in many countries, there is a committee devoted to interfaith relations. These are all fruits of the *Nostra Aetate* declaration.

Gülen's View of Dialogue

Fethullah Gülen is aware that the theology of dialogue between Christians and Muslims precedes this declaration by centuries. Dialogue between the two communities, in fact, goes back to the beginning of Islam, and the Qur'an itself invites Christians to dialogue 'with fair words' in order to adore the one God (Qur'an 3:64) and invites Muslims to converse with Christians in a courteous manner.[53] However, this fact, together with historical and current Muslim-initiated dialogue activities is not as well publicized as *Nostra Aetate* due to the lack of a religious hierarchy in Islam.

---

[53] Khaled Akasheh, 'Nostra Ateate: 40 Years Later,' *L'Osservatore Romano* (Weekly Edition in English), 28 June (2006), 8.

Therefore, Muslim leaders attempt to 'offer authoritative statements based on scholarly and sectarian credentials.'[54]

Leading Muslim thinker and the spiritual leader of a global movement, Fethullah Gülen, studied Nursi's approach to other religions, specifically Christianity, and applied Nursi's philosophy beyond *Nostra Aetate*. In 1986, Gülen asked his followers to engage in dialogue with people from all the diverse segments of Turkish society, from the left to the right wing, and the secular to the agnostic or atheist. He inspired his followers to establish the Journalists' and Writers' Foundation in 1994 and other dialogue centers with this aim,[55] thereby becoming the first leading person behind the institutionalization of dialogue in the Turkish context.

Gülen has been called 'one of the most persuasive and influential voices in the Muslim community' calling for dialogue.[56] Gülen regards interfaith cooperation as 'compulsory for Muslims to support peace'[57] relying on the basic Islamic sources to affirm this point.[58] Enes Ergene, a pupil of Gülen's study circle, writes that Gülen does not rely on theological sources alone. 'These two concepts [tolerance and dialogue], first developed on a small scale, have turned into a search for a culture of reconciliation on a world scale.... Gülen strengthens this search with religious, legal, and philosophical foundations.'[59] In his view, a human being is related to every-

---

[54]   Turan Kayaoğlu, 'Preachers of Dialogue: International Relations and Interfaith Theology,' international conference proceedings, *Muslim World in Transition: Contributions of the Hizmet Movement*, 521.

[55]   In the US alone, there are over 50 interfaith dialogue centers whose establishment was inspired by Gülen. Thomas Michel, SJ, 'Fighting Poverty with Kimse Yok Mu' Georgetown University international conference proceedings, *Islam in the Age of Global Challenges: Alternative Perspectives of the Hizmet Movement Conference*. (Now it is more than 200 hundreds throughout the world).

[56]   Thomas Michel, SJ, 'Two Frontrunners for Peace: John Paul II and Fethullah Gülen,' en.fgulen.com/content/view/1944/13/ accessed May, 19, 2009.

[57]   Zeki Sarıtoprak, 'An Islamic Approach to Peace and Nonviolence: A Turkish Experience,' *The Muslim World*, 423.

[58]   İsmail Albayrak, 'The Juxtaposition of Islam and Violence' in Hunt and Aslandogan, op cit., 127; and M. Hakan Yavuz, 'The Hizmet Movement: The Turkish Puritans' in M. Hakan Yavuz and John L. Esposito, *Turkish Islam and The Secular State. The Hizmet Movement*, 19–47.

[59]   Enes Ergene, *The Hizmet Movement, Dialogue, and Tolerance*, 5 Aug 2008, www.fethullahgulen.org/about-fethullah-gulen/an-analysis-of-the-gulen-movement/3022–the-gulen-movement-dialogue-and-tolerance.html, accessed May 20, 2009.

thing in the cosmos; to engage in dialogue with other related beings is therefore part of human nature. Another of Gülen's students, Mehmet Şeker, posits that Gülen has two aims for interfaith and intercultural dialogue. Firstly, he seeks a world in which civilizations do not clash. Secondly, he pictures a world where religious, cultural and linguistic differences are not denied or repressed, but rather expressed freely in the form of a civilization of love. He dreams of a world without conflict and enmity. In such a world, people avoid hurting or annoying each other.[60]

From the establishment of the Republic of Turkey up until around 1990, the meeting of Muslim and non-Muslim leaders was considered unacceptable. However, Gülen broke this unwritten rule and met with the Chief Rabbi of Turkey David Pinto, the Armenian Patriarch Mesrob Mutafyan, Sephardic Chief Rabbi of Jerusalem Eliyahu Bakshi-Doron, Greek Orthodox Patriarch Bartholomeos in İstanbul, and former Vatican Representative Monsignor George Marowich, who then arranged Gülen's meeting with Pope John Paul II at the Vatican in 1998. During his meeting with the Pope, Gülen proposed the establishment of a joint school of Divinity in Urfa (Old Edessa), Turkey, the birthplace of Abraham, to disprove the idea of 'a clash of civilizations.'[61] While such meetings may be welcomed today, it was almost taboo during the 1990s in the political and religious atmosphere in Turkey. The meetings, especially with the Pope, were harshly criticized by ultra-secularists and some Islamists. A group of young Islamists argued that Gülen should not have humiliated himself to the extent of going to the Vatican and meeting with the Pope. Gülen, however, responded to this kind of reductionism by saying that humility was an attribute of Muslims.[62]

In 1999, Gülen travelled to the US to seek medical attention, and remained there due to the political conditions in Turkey. His followers in the US have been active in realizing his vision, especially after 9/11. With

---

[60]   Mehmet Şeker, *Müsbet Hareket*, 80 .

[61]   Loye Ashton and Tamer Balcı, 'A Contextual Analysis of the Supporters and Critics of the Gülen/Hizmet Movement,' Georgetown University international conference proceedings, *Islam in the Age of Global Challenges: Alternative Perspectives of the Hizmet Movement Conference*, 84, available at en.fgulen.com/conference-papers/gulen-conference-in-washington-dc/3123–a-contextual-analysis-of-the-supporters-and-critics-of-the-gulen-movement.

[62]   Zeki Sarıtoprak and Sidney Grifith, "Fethullah Gülen and the People of the Book': A Voice from Turkey for Interfaith Dialogue," *The Muslim World*, 329–341.

his encouragement, over 50 dialogue centers were established in North America by his followers and supporters. Although no official count has taken place, it is possible that the number exceeds 100 in the Americas, Europe, and Australia. Other Muslim organizations or groups have put effort into interfaith relations, but Gülen's followers and supporters have actually established dialogue centers, and have given more time, funds, and efforts to this sector.

One reason for the success of the Gülen Movement is the universal nature of Gülen's vision, exemplified by his nonviolent and tolerant approach during a time marked by fear of religious extremism. Based on personal examination of some of these center's activities via the Internet, it is evident that these dialogue centers do not engage with the religious segment alone. Besides the usual dialogue activities such as dinners, seminars, and conferences, these centers organize joint projects, such as food drives, interfaith education curriculum design, and trips to holy sites in İstanbul, Jerusalem, Rome, and London. They have entered the academic sector and published articles, magazines, and books. Through high school and university student exchange programs, these centers are reaching out to the younger demographic in order to achieve their aim of the cultural acceptance of dialogue.

Over the course of time, the activities of the Movement eventually gained more attention through public relations works and general publicity. It attracted the attention of the academic world which slowly began studying its global projects and productions. After some years of study, Gülen's followers and admirers, both Muslim and non-Muslim, founded tertiary institutes devoted to the study and research of interfaith relations, faith, and spirituality. Among these are the Nursi Chair in Islamic Studies at John Carroll University in Ohio, the Fethullah Gülen Chair in the Study of Islam and Muslim-Catholic Relations at the Australian Catholic University in Melbourne, Australia, the Fethullah Gülen Chair at Syarif Hidayetullah Islam University, Indonesia, Gülen Institute at the University of Houston and the Fethullah Gülen Chair for Intercultural Studies at Catholic University of Leuven in Belgium.

The Institutionalizing of Dialogue

In *Christian-Muslim Dialogue in the Twentieth Century*, Ataullah Siddiqui analyses the definitions and methods of prominent Muslim scholars in the case of interfaith dialogue. Dialogue is understood as meeting and com-municating with other faiths, sharing thoughts and exchanging views, and reaching mutual understanding and respect through focusing on com-mon ground.[63] However, Gülen goes beyond this understanding of dia-logue. Interfaith dialogue needs to be institutionalized and collaboration must take place through joint projects for there to be any effectual dia-logue in the current atmosphere of skepticism. Dialogue programs occur at a local level with small projects on the part of other Muslim organiza-tions, but larger-scale programs and projects that attract public atten-tion are needed.[64]

It is for this purpose that during his meeting with the Pope, Gülen proposed the establishment of a joint divinity school, student exchange programs between divinity schools, and joint trips to holy sites. There was no response from the Vatican, possibly due to political conditions in Turkey. If this project had become a reality, it would have been a first and original institution, serving as a model in the world. The silence from the Vatican did not discourage Gülen since he was aiming for more than a Turkey-Vatican dialogue. When Samuel Huntington's wrote about 'the clash of civilizations,' Gülen put forth his ideas on the cooperation of civiliza-tions. Gülen is working for an inter-civilizational dialogue,[65] one that trans-gresses beyond faith. This point is another significant difference in Gül-en's understanding of current dialogue activities. He bases dialogue not entirely on the grounds of faith, but on *muhabbet*, love. Gülen's social phi-losophy revolves around the idea of serving humanity, and institutions should serve this purpose. Institutes formed by one group will not be all-embracing, but those formed by a coalition of groups, such as inter-faith groups, will serve a greater population.

Analysis and Criticism

Nostra Aetate was the first step in promoting the culture of dialogue with Muslims. Despite the mention of shared values between the two faiths and the urge to promote social justice and moral welfare, there are no

---

[63] Siddiqui, *Christian-Muslim Dialogue,* 163–169.

[64] Mahmoud Ayoub, "Christian-Muslim Dialogue: Goals and Obstacles" *The Muslim World*, 313–320.

[65] Sarıtoprak, and Grifith, 'Fethullah Gülen,' 329–341.

specifics in terms of collaboration and institutionalization. Most of the joint declarations and committees with Muslims after *Nostra Aetate* could not bring interfaith collaboration into institutionalized dialogue with other Muslim groups apart from the Hizmet Movement. However, it is observed that all Muslim-Christian dialogue has so far achieved is the recognition of the Abrahamic roots of the two faiths.[66] Not all Muslims and Christians embraced the declaration of *Nostra Aetate*. In 1970, evangelicals convened in Frankfurt, Germany, and signed a declaration called the *Frankfurt Declaration*, underlining the mission of Christ, and harshly criticizing organized dialogue as a 'betrayal of the universality of Christ.'[67] In both the *Dialogue and Mission* statement by the Secretariat for non-Christians in the Vatican in 1984 and in *Dialogue and Proclamation* in 1991, dialogue is placed within the mission of the Church, the building of God's kingdom,[68] thereby evoking apprehension on the part of Muslims.

Nonetheless, it should be stated that Muslim thinkers often brought polemics to the table, asking that they be resolved before genuine dialogue takes place. In his response to Pope Paul VI's letter regarding Peace Day, Abu Ala Mawdudi (1903–1979), founder of the Islamic revivalist party in Pakistan, Jamaat al-Islami, asked that the Pope use all his influence to remove that which poisons the relations between the two faith groups, such as the attacks on Prophet Muhammad, peace and blessings be upon him, and the Qur'an made by Christian scholars. When the Second Vatican Council was discussing the idea of forgetting the historical troubles between Muslims and Christians, French-Indian Muslim leader Professor Muhammad Hamidullah in France responded with a letter to the Pope, requesting that the Vatican officially disavow the Church's past unjustifiable and anti-Islamic resolutions of Councils and Synods. One viewpoint among Muslim thinkers is that forgetting the past is 'a way of getting us to disarm ourselves.'[69]

Other major thinkers, such as Isma'il Raji al-Faruqi (1921–1986), Mahmoud Ayoub, Hasan Askari, Khurshid Ahmad, Mohammed Talbi, and

[66] Liyakatali Takim, 'From Conversion to Conversation: Interfaith Dialogue in Post 9–11 America,' *The Muslim World*, 343–357.
[67] Yvonne Haddad, and Wadi Haddad, *Christian-Muslim Encounters*, xiii.
[68] Edward Idris Cardinal Cassidi, *Ecumenism and Interreligious Dialogue: Unitatis Redintegratio, Nostra Aetate*, 148–150.
[69] Siddiqui, *Christian-Muslim Dialogue*, 55.

many other Muslim scholars, placed some conditions before dialogue. There was skepticism regarding dialogue, and fear that it would be used as a missionary tool and carried political agendas. Khurshid Ahmad posited that the West did not view Islam as a religion or civilization, but 'merely as a rival political power,'[70] thus making dialogue unbalanced. In the basket was the general mistrust of Muslims due to the negative reputation of missionaries in Muslim lands and the double-standards of the West. For example, Ahmad points out how the West accepts everything from the 'bikini to the evening dress' as natural, but sees the *hijab* (head scarf) as unnatural and threatening local culture. In 2005, the rector of al-Azhar University, the most prestigious religious institution in Muslim world, asked the Vatican to apologize for the Crusades.[71]

Looking at the most prominent Muslim leaders and thinkers of the 20th century, we see Said Nursi and Fethullah Gülen, each of whom put sincere interfaith dialogue and collaboration at the forefront, along with the condition of leaving polemics behind and focusing on common points.[72] For Nursi and Gülen to come out with the request for unconditional dialogue is remarkable and bold. If dialogue is institutionalized, it is possible that it will thereby reduce mistrust and criticism. The establishment of many interfaith dialogue and cultural centers and academic institutes created skepticism and received criticism in Turkey and abroad. Some opponents accuse the Hizmet Movement of concealing a political agenda to change Turkey as a secular republic while others see the Movement as an American project to use soft Islam to control the Muslim world. These opponents range from the ultra-nationalists, radical political Islamists, and ideological leftists in Turkey and some Evangelists and neo-conservatives in the US and around the world.

According to Paul Stenhouse, Gülen seems to be promoting tolerance, understanding, peace and interfaith dialogue, but in reality, he is secret-

---

[70] Ismail R. Al-Faruqi, 'Common Bases between the Two Religions in Regard to Convictions, and Points of Agreement in the Spheres of Life,' *Seminar of the Islamic-Christian Dialogue* (1976). Tripoli: Popular Office of Foreign Relations, Socialist Peoples Libyan Arab Jamhariya, 1981, 243 as cited in Ataullah Siddiqui, *Christian-Muslim Dialogue in the Twentieth Century*, 130 .

[71] Robert Spencer, 'A Vatican Apology for the Crusades?' www.frontpagemagazine.com, March 22, 2005.

[72] Gülen, *Essays, Perspectives, Opinions*, 34.

ly establishing a caliphate. On the establishment of the Fethullah Gülen Chair of Islamic Studies and Interfaith Dialogue, within the Centre of Inter-Religious Dialogue at the Australian Catholic University in Melbourne, Stenhouse raised questions about Gülen, and implied that the Hizmet Movement is a 'group that is *ex professo* dedicated to promoting an Islamist ideology.'[73] However Greg Barton[74] and David Tittensor [75] have dismissed these claims. Barton, in his responses to Stenhouse, also confined the debate to the realms of discourse. Reporting in *The Australian* newspaper, Barton dismissed Stenhouse's article as 'not particularly well argued' and further stated, 'Father Stenhouse conflates this quiescent Sufism with some of the rare examples of Sufi militantism'. Former Vatican Representative in İstanbul Monsignor George Marowich, who has known Gülen for over a decade, bears a special admiration toward Gülen for his pioneering efforts in dialogue. 'He is the Mawlana (Rumi) of our age,' he would say.[76]

While Gülen is accused of being Islam's Trojan horse in the Western Christian World, in the Turkish world, he is paradoxically accused of being the Pope's Trojan Horse.[77] Gülen and his followers have also been accused of being 'bad representatives' of Islam, and 'cater(ing) to' Jews and Christians.[78] Mehmet Şevket Eygi, syndicated columnist for *Milli Gazete,* a publication aligned to former Prime Minister Necmettin Erbakan's Welfare Party, questioned Gülen and his followers on their dialogue activities and

---

[73] Doğan Koç, "Strategic Defamation of Fethullah Gülen - English vs Turkish,' *European Journal of Economic and Political Studies*, 189–244.

[74] Jill Rowbotham. Catholic hits Islamic chair, *The Australian*, 16 January,2008. www.theaustralian.com.au/higher-education/catholic-hits-islamic-chair/story-e6frgcjx-1111115325 accessed on July 23,.2013.

[75] David Tittensor, "The Hizmet Movement and the Case of a Secret Agenda: Putting the Debate in Perspective" *Journal of Islam and Christian-Muslim Relations*, 163– 179.

[76] 'Claims and Answers,' en.fgulen.com/press-room/columns/3280–a-lonely-man-in-a-rest-home acessed July 21, 2013.

[77] Koç, *Strategic Defamation of Fethullah Gülen,* 189–244.

[78] This was by two opponents, Haydar Baş, Turkish academic, leader of a small religious community, and politician associated with the Independent Turkey Party (BTP), and Şevki Yılmaz, former parliamentary representative of former Prime Minister Necmettin Erbakan's Welfare Party in Turkey. In Loye Ashton and Tamer Balcı, *A Contextual Analysis of the Supporters and Critics of the Gülen/Hizmet Movement*, Georgetown University international conference proceedings, *Islam in the Age of Global Challenges: Alternative Perspectives of the Hizmet Movement Conference*, 105.

representation of Muslims. He did not approve of the activities as it opened the doors to missionaries, and went as far as calling interfaith dialogue un-Islamic and unlawful based on religious texts. Despite such accusations, Gülen's continuation of dialogue is admirable. In his message at the Parliament of the World's Religions Gülen wrote that dialogue with the adherents of other religious traditions is an integral part of an Islamic ethic that has been long neglected. [79] Şeker argues that Gülen's dialogue work is not un-Islamic or something new to Islam, but is rather based on the spirit of the *Medina Charter*, an agreement drawn up between the Muslims and non-Muslims (Jews and pagans) in Medina that granted rights and respect towards non-Muslims. Şeker adds that Gülen also draws from the spirit of the final sermon of Prophet Muhammad peace and blessings be upon him. [80]

The important issue these criticisms raise is one that fails to receive enough attention: that there is no body or institution representing Muslims all over the world, nor is there any agreement on who should represent the adherents of this faith.[81] Interfaith dialogue by Muslims is carried out by government-appointed scholars who are limited in their approaches, leaders of spiritual groups, or small groups and individuals.[82] This makes it difficult for Christians, because it leaves them to engage in dialogue with a variety of Muslim nations, institutions, groups, and spiritual leaders. Moreover this draws criticism from Muslims who feel that the Christian world is not engaging with the right organization or person. In order to overcome this missing link of representation, Muslims and Christians need to establish joint institutions and social welfare organizations.

In 1993, Pope John Paul II in Rome appealed for peace in Bosnia-Herzegovina and called for a special prayer day at Assisi. 42 delegates, including two Bosnian Muslims, attended the prayer service for Christian, Jewish, and Muslim participants.[83] It is possible that this and similar services inspired the cooperation in 1996 when a group of Catholic and Mus-

[79] Gülen, 'The Necessity of Dialogue,' www.fethullahgulen.org/about-fethullah-gulen/messages/972–the-necessity-of-interfaith-dialogue-a-muslim-approach.html accessed January 6, 2009.
[80] Şeker, *Müsbet Hareket*, 83.
[81] Yvonne Haddad; Wadi Haddad, *Christian-Muslim Encounters*, xv.
[82] Siddiqui, *Christian-Muslim Dialogue*, 52.
[83] Cassidi, *Ecumenism and Interreligious Dialogue*,142.

lim religious people met to discuss how they could support the building of a new water system that would serve both the Muslim community in Fojnica and the Croatian community of Kiseljak, two cities that experienced major violence during the Muslim-Croat fighting in 1993–1994. However, due to lack of local personnel and expertise to supervise volunteers, this project was never realized, despite the genuine interest and efforts of local clergy.[84]

Conclusion

We have yet to witness another prominent Muslim leader pronouncing dialogue as an 'obligation' like Gülen, who holds that dialogue is the duty of Muslims in the struggle to make our world a more peaceful place.[85] Gülen believes that dialogue is among the duties of Muslims on earth because of what it contributes to the promotion of peace and safety in our world. Both the declaration of *Nostra Aetate* and the vision of Gülen have pushed religious persons to open their doors to each other. Yet, it is only when theories and ideas are applied that they gain credibility and give benefit. Interfaith dialogue faces boundaries of mistrust and skepticism, especially among radical religious people, due to historical relations between the East and West, a lack of credibility and results, and political imbalance between the two sides.

Nostra Aetate was a commendable step. Yet, it was declared over 48 years ago. Vatican and Muslim organizations need to take steps in order to remove the perception of interfaith dialogue as a twentieth-century fashion[86] and 'a clubby brotherhood.'[87] For any Vatican or Christian initiatives to be successful, Muslim leaders and participants in dialogue need to leave behind historical grudges when engaging in dialogue, even if they do not wish to forget the past. Both Christians and Muslims are equal partners, and not opponents, in dialogue. In addition, the issue of repre-

---

[84] David Steele, 'Contributions of Interfaith Dialogue to Peacebuilding in the Former Yugoslavia' in *Interfaith Dialogue and Peacebuilding*, Ed. David R. Smock, 85.

[85] Sarıtoprak and Grifith, 'Fethullah Gülen,' 329–341.

[86] John Borelli, 'Interreligious Dialogue as a Spiritual Practice,' Georgetown University international conference proceedings, *Islam in the Age of Global Challenges: Alternative Perspectives of the Hizmet Movement Conference*, 147.

[87] Thomas Michel, SJ, *Toward a Dialogue of Liberation with Muslims*, www.sjweb.info/dialogo/index.cfm, accessed 20 May, 2009.

sentation on behalf of Muslims must be addressed, possibly by forming a pluralist council where members are democratically elected, representing every nation of the *ummah*, the Muslim community. While this may not be applicable in current global political, social, and religious conditions in the Muslim world, it is a feasible possibility that could be politically and culturally accepted.

In order to clear the air of hidden agendas, leaders on both sides of the dialogue need to undertake theological reasoning to reduce the concept of the 'dialogue mission' and 'dialogue *da'wah*'—that is, the use of dialogue for covert proselytism. While it is not possible to completely erase concealed intentions, whether they may be religious, political, or cultural, it is necessary to decrease these and continue the dialogue by focusing on and building from common ground. For Muslims, engaging in dialogue evokes hope and arouses fear at the same time.[88] This needs further study in order to understand the roots of this issue.

Institution-oriented dialogue grants opportunities for adherents of different faiths to see the world and each other from different windows. This is one aim and meaning of dialogue: creating a common base to combat materialistic philosophy and aggressive secularism, and working together for social welfare and justice projects. The more this is implemented beyond declarations and discussions, the greater will be its cultural acceptance. This move to institutionalizing dialogue will gain trust once the joint projects produce visible and measurable results that go beyond the common desire for peace. The goal of interfaith dialogue and collaboration between different peoples is the exploration of new dynamics that will benefit all humanity.

---

[88] Haddad and Haddad, *Christian-Muslim Encounters*, xiv.

Islamic Radicalism and Gülen's Response

Salih Yücel
Monash University, Australia

Introduction

The language employed in contemporary debates over religious issues has often been exaggerated, and in many cases provocative. Moreover, as the literary editor of *The New Republic* Leon Wieseltier aptly said, 'No faith has suffered more at the hands of this improper usage than Islam'.[89] Over the last century, especially from the late 70s there have been Muslim groups, communities, leaders and individuals who have responded in a reactionary and sometimes violent manner towards events or actions that seem to be debilitating to Islam and Muslims. Methods of response have included various acts in the guise of Islamic behavior, such as the repetition of Islamic slogans during protests and demonstrations, and attempts at so called military jihad. When publicly displaying their reactions, some Muslims have made radical speeches, burned flags and effigies, and condemned entire nations. Sometimes these acts have become violent, or have led to violence. Such acts have been viewed as a religious obligation, or a defensive holy struggle, and therefore a necessary display of Muslim power in defense of Islam and Muslims. Thus, Islam has been presented as a form of human-made, revolutionary ideology operating under the flag of Divine religion. Other Muslims saw these acts as a means to speak out against injustice, and to protect or obtain their rights. Muslims who refuse to participate in such acts

---

[89] Leon Wieseltier, 'The Jewish Face of Fundamentalism,' in *The Fundamentalist Phenomenon: A View from Within, a Response from Without* (ed. Norman J. Cohen), 192–196.

are viewed by some of the radical protestors as pacifists, cowards and even traitors. During the turmoil or crisis in the Muslim world, while most of the great Islamic leaders and scholars have focused on internal factors, extremists and reactionary groups have instead placed the blame on external factors as the cause of the problems.

The most controversial and reaction-provoking events have been the occupation of Palestine, the Islamic Revolution in Iran, the wars in Afghanistan, Bosnia and Iraq, the clashes in Kashmir, Salman Rushdie's *Satanic Verses*, the Danish cartoon controversy and the recent *Innocence of Muslims* movie. Reactions to these events have ranged from protests, and have even gone as far as violent acts, some of which have caused innocent deaths. These types of events have led to the coining of the terms 'radical Islam' or 'Islamism' after the revolution in Iran.

The word Islamism appeared in the late 19th century and was used mainly by Western Orientalists[90] and it has no place in the Islamic tradition at all.[91] Radical Islam was almost unknown in the Western world before 1979. Prior to that there was barely a reference to Islamic fundamentalism, either in the academic literature or in the mass media. David Harrington Watt found that until 1979, the word 'fundamentalism' was used almost exclusively in reference to the beliefs and practices associated with Protestant Christians such as Jerry Falwell and Curtis Lee Laws.[92] From 1978 to 2010, the catalogue of Harvard University's library contained more than 1,300 records for texts on Islamic fundamentalism that had been published after 1978. Academic Search Premier Database listed over 1,600 such references while JSTOR listed over 5,000. Washington Post index gave over three thousand references to 'Islamic fundamentalists' in articles published between 1979 and 2010 while the *New York Times* gave records for over four thousand.[93] While the topic has been covered from a number of different angles, especially political, there has been little attention paid to the religious legitimacy of the activities of radical Muslims. The bulk of this coverage, including media reports and scholarly articles, has touched upon verses of the Qur'an superficially, but has

---

[90] M. Şükrü Hanioğlu, 'İslamcılık Üzerine,' *Sabah*, 2/9/2012.

[91] Gülen, *Fasıldan Fasıla-3*, 191.

[92] David Harrington Watt, *Muslims, Fundamentalists, and the Fear of the Dangerous Other in American Culture*, V. 12 (2010), 1–13.

[93] Ibid.

rarely gone in depth into their interpretation. Still less have those cover-
ing these matters debated whether the actions of extremists were legitimate in the light of the classical tradition.

The 'Islamicness' of these reactionary methods—that is to say, their
supposed foundation in sacred texts—is not certain, and is therefore
considered controversial. Such acts are recent in the history of Muslims.
Their rise coincided with the period during and immediately after the
collapse of the Ottoman Empire. Colonization of the Muslim world and
the divide-and-rule policy by European powers spurred a natural reactionary pose by Muslims. The Muslim world was influenced, too, by the
French Revolution and the *Communist Manifesto,* both of which unhinged
Europe. Some Muslims have adopted similar methodologies as those
employed in revolutionary Europe, as a means to obtain their rights, but
have done so under the banner of Islam. In the same way that groups
rose to support a pure Communist state, Muslim groups also rose to support a pure Islamic state. Europeans called for democracy, while Muslims
called for theodemocracy.[94] Just as Communists wanted a socialist economic system, and Capitalists wanted a free market, so too Muslims wanted an Islamic economic system to solve the woes of their own nations. In
both trends, a defeatist psychology plays an important role in spurring
reactions. The President of the Ministry of Religious Affairs in Turkey,
Mehmet Görmez, holds that these reactions bear the weight of a 200–
year wounded mentality. The head of the Tunisian *al-Nahda* Movement
Rashid al-Ghannushi views Islamic radicalism as a project to create chaos
and divide Muslims.[95] There are other causes and factors that could be
explored, but this is out of the scope of this article. The majority of published work so far has focused on the actions of extremist and violent
Muslim groups, but has not investigated primary sources and prominent

---

[94] This notion was first proposed by Abul Ala Mawdudi. Fore more information, see:
Abu'a Ala al-Mawdudi. in *Political Theory of Islam* edited by Khurshid Ahmad; *Islam
and Its Meaning and Message,* Islamic Council of Europe, London , 1976, 160–162,
Seyyed Vali Reza Nasr, "Mawdudi and the Jama'at-i Islami: The Origins, Theory and
Practice of Islamic Revivalism" in *Pioneer of Islamic Revival* (ed. Ali Rahnema),
98–123.

[95] Rashid Gannusi, 'İslam diyalog dini, radikalizm ise fitne ve kaos çıkarma projesidir,'
Zaman, www.zaman.com.tr/gundem_islam-diyalog-dini-radikalizm-ise-fitne-cikar-
ma-projesidir_2082413.html retrieved 25.4.2013.

scholars' interpretations of sacred texts[96] for the religious legitimacy of these groups.

This article will explore the methodology, style and language used by some radical Muslims, and whether or not it contradicts with two primary sources: the Qur'an, and the tradition of Prophet Muhammad, peace and blessings be upon him. This article will also examine the views of two prominent contemporary Muslim scholars, Said Nursi (1877–1960) and particularly Fethullah Gülen (1941–), in relation to the reactionary methods of some extremist Muslims who indiscriminately condemn entire nations or all the adherents of a faith. Such extremist methods might take the form of burning a country's flag or an effigy of a country's leader, or calling for the complete destruction of a country. The tendency in these cases is to stereotype or generalize the targeted religious group or nation, painting that particular group with the same dark brush. Gülen always avoids such slogans, and he is generally against what might be called 'sloganic' Islam.[97] He states that radicalism conflicts with the very essentials of Islam.[98]

Qur'anic Anti-dote to Violence

Although Islam is considered as a way that does not neglect any aspect of life[99], providing guidelines from social relations to personal hygiene, it is nevertheless not an ideology.[100] It has provided guidelines for Muslims

---

[96] The Arabic source is *www.altafsir.com*, English and Arabic website, and certified, accurate Qur'anic text from the Ministry of Religious Affairs of the Hashemite Kingdom of Jordan and its reliability has been approved by Al- Azhar University. Arabic and the Turkish sources used for this article were translated by the author.

[97] Margaret Coffey, interview with Zeki Sarıtoprak from John Carroll University on ABC Radio National's Encounter, 'Fethullah Gülen,' en.fgulen.com/press-room/news/2412–fethullah-gulen-on-abc-radio-nationals-encounter, retrieved 25.04.2013.

[98] Mehmet Kalyoncu, 'Civilian Response to Ethno-Religious Terrorism.' This paper was presented at *Muslim World in Transition: Contributions of the Hizmet Movement* at SOAS University of London, House of Lords and London School of Economics on 25–27 October, 2007 en.fgulen.com/conference-papers/contributions-of-the-gulen-movement.

[99] For detail of this issue, see Sayyid Abu'l Ala Mawdudi, *The Islamic Way of Life*, Marakzi Maktabi Islami, (Delhi, 1967).

[100] Coffey, 'Fethullah Gülen.'

on ways of responding to aggression and injustice, and has methods for presenting the truth and righteousness, preserving collective and individual rights, and ensuring justice. It has made clear that dealing properly with non-Muslims is just as important as dealing with Muslims.[101]

In the last two decades, particularly after the 9/11 terrorist attacks, prejudice and abuse directed towards Islam and Muslims have risen sharply. Some marginal Muslim groups and individuals have reacted to this prejudice with 'un-Islamic' behavior, meaning actions that are not based on the sacred sources of values and universal principles, and include reactionary responses such as violent protests. These reactions mar the reputation of Muslims, especially those who live in non-Muslim countries. Muslims will naturally feel disturbed when Prophet Muhammad, peace and blessings be upon him, or any other Prophet, is abused in any way, since it is a principle of Islam to love Prophet Muhammad (pbuh) and follow his example. Islamic principles also set a method of response based on the Qur'an and life of Prophet Muhammad (pbuh). These two sources set rules on responding to physical aggression against Muslims and non-physical aggression and abuse against the sacred values of Islam. This chapter will focus on examples of Prophets from the Qur'an and life of Prophet Muhammad (pbuh) in order to define how Muslims should deal with offences against Islam, in ways based upon religious values in general. The Prophet is the role model for all Muslims as the Qur'an states (33:21).

Just like other faiths, Islam is no stranger to suffering assaults. The Qur'an refers to the struggle between those who believe in *tawhid*, One God, and those who are sternly against it, exemplified particularly in the epic stories of Adam and Eve and Satan, Jonah and his tribe, Moses and Pharaoh, and Prophet Muhammad (pbuh) and the Meccan polytheists. The Qur'an explains that those who were against *tawhid* used every act and tool in order to inflict harm and persecute the believers in one God. According to Muslim theologians, Prophets occupy a spiritual station higher than the angels. From this, Muslims must draw the lesson that they should speak well of the members of other faiths, even towards those who commit acts of injustice against God and Muslims.

---

[101] Gülen, *Fasıldan Fasıla-5*, 84–85.

The first humans as mentioned in the Qur'an, Adam and Eve, were deceived by Satan to eat fruits from the banned tree.[102] This caused their expulsion from Paradise. Although they had no evil intention when eating the forbidden fruits, Adam and Eve turned to God in repentance immediately. 'They said (straightaway), 'Our Lord! We have wronged ourselves, and if You do not forgive us and do not have mercy on us, we will surely be among those who have lost!' (Qur'an:7:23). They could have cursed Satan, and asked God to punish him. According to Qur'anic exegete al-Tabari (838–923), Adam and Eve did not blame Satan, but pointed the finger at themselves.[103] They did not rebel against God like Satan, but instead sought forgiveness and mercy from God. For contemporary Muslims, this example depicts the ideal reaction: to criticize oneself before blaming others. Before launching diatribes against those who portray Islam in unfavorable colors, Muslims need to turn to themselves, reflect on their methodology, their presenting style, how well they have represented their faith, and then subsequently seek forgiveness from God for not reflecting their faith properly.

The story of Prophet Abraham in the Qur'an was revealed when Prophet Muhammad (pbuh) faced death threats, persecution and harsh treatment at the hands of the polytheists of Mecca. Abraham's story was to serve as an example to the Prophet and his Companions on how to carry themselves when dealing with aggression and injustice.[104] Abraham told his polytheist father that he had indeed received revelations from God, knowledge which his father did not possess (19:43) and told him that belief in God would grant him immense rewards in both this life and the hereafter. Abraham concluded his preaching by warning Azar of the grave punishment he would face if he did not mend his ways (19:45). When Abraham offered his father the guidance and advice of God, he rejected it, and threatened to stone him to death (19:46). Despite such a threat

---

[102] According to Islamic theology, Prophets are infallible, but may commit minor mistakes unintentionally. Adam was a Prophet who made a minor mistake out of good intention.

[103] Muhammed ibn Jarir al-Tabari, *Jami al-Bayan an Ta'wil Ay al-Qur'an* www.altafsir. com/Tafasir.asp?tMadhNo=0&tTafsirNo=1&tSoraNo=7&tAyahNo=23&tDisplay= yes&UserProfile=0&LanguageId=1, retrieved 2.8.2013.

[104] Fakhr al-Din al-Razi, *Tafsir al-Kabir,* www.altafsir.com/Tafasir.asp?tMadhNo=1&t TafsirNo=4&tSoraNo=19&tAyahNo=47&tDisplay=yes&UserProfile=0&LanguageI d=1 retrieved 1.2.2013

from his polytheist father, Abraham was still kind in his speech and treatment towards him. (19:47).[105] In Tabari's exegesis, Abraham's response to his father's threat was 'Even if you stone me, I will not harm you.' Ibn Kathir (1301–1373) extends this further, adding 'I will not harm, insult or even disrespect you'.[106] Abraham even asked God to forgive him. It was only because of a promise that he had made earlier to him. When it became clear that Azar's unrelenting hatred towards pure monotheism would never be fought, Abraham dissociated himself from him (9:114).

The coverage and mention of the story of Moses and Pharaoh is the most frequently referenced narrative in the Qur'an. Pharaoh is mentioned as an extreme tyrant who committed all kinds of evil and injustice, from the killing of male children to the oppression of the Israelites. He went as far as declaring himself to be a god. Despite this, God commanded Moses and his brother Aaron to speak gently with Pharaoh. '... But speak to him with gentle words, so that he might reflect and be mindful or feel some awe (of me, and behave with humility)...' (20:43–44). All prominent classical and contemporary exegetes of the Qur'an agree that the two Prophets followed this order, even when Pharaoh killed more of the believers and the Children of Israel. Qurtubi (1214–1273) interprets the command to mean speak gently, implying that Moses should not use any word implying hatred or animosity. He goes on to state that this is a general rule to be applied by those who seek to enjoin good and forbid evil.[107] Al-Qushayri (986–1072) extends this rule to cover not only a person's speech, but also their demeanor.[108] In another verse, believers are instructed to '...speak kindly and well to the people...' (2:83). Tabari interprets this verse as explaining the proper way—which is to say, the way that pleases Allah—to communicate with others. This includes speaking gently, using kind

---

[105] al-Tabari, *Jami al-Bayan.*

[106] Ismail ibn Umar ibn Kathir, *Tafsir al-Qur'an al-Karim,* www.altafsir.com/Tafsir.a sp?tMadhNo=1&tTafsirNo=7&tSoraNo=19&tAyahNo=47&tDisplay=yes&UserPro file=0&LanguageId=1 retrieved 2.27.2010.

[107] Abu Abdullah al-Qurtubi, *Al-Jamiu li-Ahkam al-Qur'an,* www.altafsir.com/Tafsir. asp?tMadhNo=1&tTafsirNo=5&tSoraNo=20&tAyahNo=44&tDisplay=yes&UserPr ofile=0&LanguageId=1 rerieved 8.10.2011.

[108] Abd al-Karim ibn Hawazin al-Qushayri, *Lata'if al-Isharat bi Tafsir al-Qur'an,* www. altafsir.com/Tafsir.asp?tMadhNo=3&tTafsirNo=31&tSoraNo=20&tAyahNo=44 &tDisplay=yes&UserProfile=0&LanguageId=1 retrieved 8.10.2011.

words, not being harsh, and maintaining the best of manners.[109] Razi (1149–1209) stated that this verse makes it a requirement for all believers to speak gently.[110] Ibn Kathir went further to say that the overall approach to others should be gentle and non-provoking.[111]

When commenting on this verse, Fethullah Gülen says, 'God commanded Moses [and Aaron] to treat kindly and speak gently to Pharaoh who oppressed, persecuted and killed Moses' people for decades. Therefore, even if before you there is a Pharaoh who has for years killed your people, you must treat him with gentle words and a mild demeanor. The meaning of this command is to show that the other party may listen if spoken to gently, but if dealt with harshly, the other party will neither listen nor care.'[112] This implies that even if the unjust party is as evil as Pharaoh, there is still a proper method in which to deal with them. Moreover, he also comments that even rightful anger deserves a suitable method of expression that is not harsh.[113] This is because the key for opening a heart is soft words and soft manner.[114]

Prophet Jonah is another leading example in the Qur'an, who is well known for his total submission and prayer to God during his most difficult and testing times. He had invited his people to believe in God, but was rejected continuously by them. After years of rejection, he decided to leave the city. He boarded a ship which later faced a dangerous storm in the midst of a turbulent sea. According to many exegetes of the Qur'an, those on the ship believed that someone amongst them had committed a wrong and they were being punished with the storm. Prophet Jonah then confessed that he had made the mistake of leaving his people and was subsequently tossed into the sea and swallowed by a whale. Inside the whale, he begged God to be his savior and made the famous prayer, [115] 'There is no god other than You, Glory be unto You! Indeed, I was among the wrongdoers' (21:87). Instead of accusing his disbelieving people, he

---

[109] al-Tabari, *Jami al-Bayan.*

[110] al-Razi, *Tafsir al-Kabir.*

[111] Ibn Kathir, *Tafsir al-Qur'an al-Karim.*

[112] Gülen, *Prizma-1*, 41.

[113] Gülen, 'Tatlı Dil ve Firavunlar,' www.herkul.org/index.php/krk-testi/kirik-testi-arsiv/2647–Tatl%C4%B1%20Dil%20ve%20Firavunlar retrieved 1.27.2013.

[114] Gülen, 'Fitne Zamanı ve Çekirdek Toplum,' herkul.org/index.php/bamteli/bamteli, retrieved on May 22, 2013.

[115] al-Tabari, *Jami al-Bayan.*

took himself to account. It was after this reflection that God saved Jonah miraculously.[116] Another example of oppressed believers turning to God is that of a group that lived before Prophet Muhammad's time. Non-believers had persecuted them and their Prophet had been killed by an army.[117] The Qur'an says of them, 'What they said (when they encountered the enemy) was, 'Our Lord! Forgive us our sins and any wasteful act we may have done in our duty, and set our feet firm, and help us to victory over the disbelieving people!'' (3:147). According to Razi, this group of believers held themselves responsible for their sins, defects and misfortune, asked for forgiveness from God and pleaded to God for victory.[118] 'So God granted them the reward of this world as well as the best reward of the Hereafter. Indeed God loves those devoted to doing good, aware that God is seeing them' (3:148).

The Qur'an charts the recommended course of action beginning with: (1) seeking forgiveness; (2) reflecting on past deeds, and ending with; (3) sincere prayer for help while; (4) keeping steadfast on the path of religion. In this way, those who repent may find the internal causes or factors for their negative situations and losses,[119] which in turn gave them victory over the enemy. Whether in politics or in social situations, a Muslim needs to respond to aggression with the four actions of this praised group of believers in the Qur'an. However, the actions and words of radical and reactionary Muslims do not conform to the prescribed or recommended manner of dealing with aggression outlined in Islam's sacred texts. The Qur'an often addresses all people as 'O humankind'. Qur'anic exegetes explain that every human being falls into this category, including polytheists, hypocrites, Muslims and non-Muslims alike. Zamakhshari (1075–1144) views this address as referring to polytheists only since verses that begin with 'O humankind' were revealed during the Meccan period of revelation.[120] Razi expounds that although polytheists commit the greatest sin of associating partners with God, and it was a group of

[116] Ibn Kathir, *Tafsir al-Qur'an al-Karim*.
[117] al-Tabari, *Jami al-Bayan*.
[118] al-Razi, *Tafsir al-Kabir*.
[119] al-Tabari, *Jami al-Bayan*.
[120] Mahmud ibn Umar al-Zamakhshari, *Al-Kashaaf*, www.altafsir.com/Tafasir.asp?tMadhNo=1&tTafsirNo=2&tSoraNo=2&tAyahNo=21&tDisplay=yes&UserProfile=0&LanguageId=1.

polytheists who persecuted and killed the early Muslims, they are not being differentiated in this address.[121] Qurtubi states that while verses beginning with that address serve as warnings, the term of address in itself is kind.[122] Said Nursi referred to those who committed injustice against Islam and Muslims as 'people who are devoted to this world or worldly' instead of calling them infidels, heathens, oppressors or devils. Gülen has followed the same path, and even used the Turkish term of respect 'bey' (gentleman) towards aggressors, including those who slandered him and accused him or heresy and betrayal.[123]

Radicals and reactionaries do not respect the values of those considered as 'enemies,' whether they are political, religious, or economic. The Qur'an orders Muslims to refrain from insulting even the polytheists and their idols. 'And do not (O believers) revile the things or beings that they have, apart from God, deified and invoke, lest (if you do so) they attempt to revile God out of spite, and in ignorance..'(6:108).[124] Qushayri stated not to argue with the non-believers because the carnal soul can dominate the argument, which in turn will lead to more harm and wrongdoing.[125] Qurtubi commented on this verse as being timeless and an order not to offend others on account of their beliefs or harm a place of worship.[126] Ibn Kathir views defamation towards other faiths as a cause of disorder.[127] Razi commented in a similar vein, saying that even if the enemy insults Islam, a Muslim is not permitted to respond in the same manner, because this will open the door to more insults. If a Muslim speaks ill of the idols, the polytheists will speak ill of God.[128] A prominent Shiite exegete Tabatabi (1892–1981) points to the etiquette put forth by this verse, stating that it is contrary to Islamic ethics to attack or insult the sacred values of others.[129]

---

[121] al-Razi, *Tafsir al-Kabir*.

[122] al-Qurtubi, *Al-Jamiu li-Ahkam al-Qur'an*.

[123] Gülen, *Fasıldan Fasıla-3*, 103.

[124] Ali Ünal, *The Qur'an with Annoted Interpretation in Modern English*.

[125] al-Qushayri, *Lata'if al-Isharat bi Tafsir al-Qur'an*.

[126] al-Qurtubi, *Al-Jamiu li-Ahkam al-Qur'an*.

[127] Ibn Kathir, *Tafsir al-Qur'an al-Karim*.

[128] al-Razi, *Tafsir al-Kabir*.

[129] Muhammad Husayn Tabatabai, *Tafsir al-Mizan*, www.altafsir.com/Tafsir.asp?tM adhNo=4&tTafsirNo=56&tSoraNo=6&tAyahNo=108&tDisplay=yes&Page=3&Size =1&LanguageId=1 retrieved 11.9.2012.

Referring to this verse, Gülen comments that it is a believer's duty neither to respond with curses or bad language, nor to hurt the other party's feelings or dignity, regardless of that person's status or background.[130] The role model for humanity, Prophet Muhammad (pbuh), never spoke about an error or sin committed by any person, group or tribe openly or privately. He would speak about the error in a general way to many people.[131] Gülen states that it is a Muslim's duty not to abuse or insult anyone, speak inappropriately, or offend anyone. He takes this concept further and says that by insulting a religion or a leader, a person insults all the followers of that religion or the leader. Moreover, calling someone 'infidel' or using that term is not a sunnah of the Prophet. A person who uses this label does so to satisfy his or her own desire and will not benefit from it.[132] Gülen goes as far as saying that to call someone an 'infidel' in some situations is sinful. The Qur'an explains how Muslims ought to behave in the face of mistreatment or misconduct. 'The (true) servants of the All-Merciful are they who move on the earth gently and humbly, and when the ignorant, foolish ones address them (with insolence or vulgarity, as befits their ignorance and foolishness), they respond with (words of) peace (without engaging in hostility with them)' (25: 63).

Tabari interprets this verse as meaning that God's merciful subjects act kindly towards those who are ignorant and do not fall down to their level.[133] Razi adds that the believers should either respond with silence or act justly.[134] Qurtubi states that even towards those who hate the verses where God orders people to worship Him as the Most Merciful One, a believer must act peacefully.[135] Ibn Kathir goes further to add that a believer not only avoids using harsh language, but also forgives the aggressive or wrong party for any mistreatment which they have caused. Qushayri even states that a believer should respond with praise of the other party's positive characteristics.[136]

---

[130] Gülen, Fazilet Ehlinin Dört Şiarı, www.herkul.org/index.php/bamteli/bamteli-arsiv/9176–fazilet-ehlinin-dort-siari retrieved 20.4.2013.

[131] Gülen, Uslup ve Hikmet, www.herkul.org/index.php/krk-testi/kirik-testi-arsiv/7905–%C3%9Csl%C3%BBp%20ve%20Hikmet retrieved 20.4.2013.

[132] Gülen, Fasıldan Fasıla-5, Nil Yayınları, 84–85.

[133] al-Tabari, Jami al-Bayan.

[134] Al-Razi, Tafsir al-Kabir.

[135] Ibn Kathir, Tafsir al-Qur'an al-Karim.

[136] Al-Qurtubi, Al-Jamiu li-Ahkam al-Qur'an.

There are verses in the Qur'an containing harsh words and strong criticism. However, Gülen says these are aimed not so much at the individuals or groups in question, but rather at the wrong beliefs or actions committed by them.[137] Prophet Muhammad (pbuh) knew of these verses, but nonetheless he still acted kindly towards people. Just as there are verses in the Qur'an which criticize Christians, Jews and others, there are also verses which praise them. Gülen interpret this as the Qur'an judging groups by their actions and attributes and not by their religion, affiliation or any other defining factor.[138]The Qur'an refers to the Jews and Christians as *Ahl al-Kitab*, or People of the Book, a title of honor since a book implies civilization and enlightenment. Gülen also supports Nursi's view.[139]

No one can be claimed to be as evil as Pharaoh, and no one, including Muslims, can be as pious and gentle as Moses and Aaron. In the Qur'an, God commands Prophet Moses and Aaron to speak gently to Pharaoh, who committed all types of evil and even declared himself as a god. (20:44).

Also in the Qur'an, when Luqman, who is considered as a Prophet or a great saint in Islam, advises his son, who was a polytheist, 'O my son, do not associate [anything] with Allah. Indeed, association [with him] is great injustice. (31:13)'. Although associating partners with God is the greatest sin in Islam, Luqman still refers to his son as *ya bunayya*, my sweet little darling son, in loving terms. Prophet Muhammad (pbuh) exemplifies and embodies such a desirable trait in a believer. He did not curse those who persecuted him and the believers, nor did he directly blame anyone. Out of many examples, this article will focus on three examples from the Prophet's life. It was during the most difficult years of his life in Mecca when Prophet Muhammad (pbuh) sought the leaders of the sister town of Ta'if for protection. Having lost his chief protector and uncle, Abu Talib (549–619), as well as his supporter, his beloved

---

[137] Gülen, 'Tatlı Dil ve Firavunlar,' www.herkul.org/index.php/krk-testi/kirik-testi-arsiv/2647–Tatl%C4%B1%20Dil%20ve%20Firavunlar retrieved 12.13.2012.

[138] Zeki Sarıtoprak, 'Said Nursi's Teachings on the People of the Book: a case study of Islamic social policy in the early twentieth century,' *Islam and Christian-Muslim relations*, 11:3, 321–332.

[139] Zeki Sarıtoprak and Sidney Griffith, 'Fethullah Gülen and 'the People of the Book': A Voice from Turkey for Interfaith Dialogue,' *The Muslim World*, 329–340.

wife Khadijah (d.619), the Prophet needed a secure place for the persecuted Muslims. He travelled to Ta'if with hope, and sincerely addressed
the leaders and people of Ta'if for ten days. They mocked him, disbelieving that he was a Prophet, and ran him out of the city pelting him with
stones. Bloodied and weary, he took refuge under the shade of a tree out
of the city limits. According to Islamic historians, an angel appeared
before him asking him if he wished for the city of Ta'if to be destroyed.
However the Prophet preferred that the city might be saved, out of the
hope that even one person might turn out to be an ally and seek the
truth.[140] He continued, 'My Lord, I complain only to You of my weakness,
powerlessness and my being despicable to the people. If you do not have
anger against me, then I do not mind the suffering, misfortunes and difficulties that I faced.'[141] Towards the polytheist leaders who persecuted
and killed the Muslims and harmed the Prophet through assassination
attempts, direct assaults and heavy insults, the Prophet's response was
only to raise his hands and say, 'O Lord, I leave these to You.'[142]

Prophet Muhammad (pbuh) did not call curses upon or ask for the
destruction of those who caused him suffering, or who killed people from
amongst the community of believers and members of his family. He later
forgave all those who had trampled his individual rights when he conquered Mecca.[143] If this is how the prime role model of Islam reacted to
those who threw stones at him, then this is how Muslims should also react
against those who throw words of slander and accusations towards the
Prophet. In both his actions and reactions, the Prophet was extremely
patient, going through all proper courses of action (i.e. dialogue and
diplomacy) and never turning to violence unless it was ordained by God.

The traits of showing patience, and adopting appropriate actions in
the face of aggression, characterize all Prophets. Joseph remained patient
towards his siblings even after they left him at the bottom of the well
and sold him into slavery (12:15–19). He did not curse them or harm

---

[140] Narrated by Bukhari and Muslim.
[141] Ibn Sa'd, *Al-Tabaqat al-Kubra*, 1/211–212; Ibn Hisham, Al-Sirat al-nabawiyya.
Cited in www.herkul.org/kiriktesti/index.php?article_id=7075 'Uslupta
istikamet.' Retrieved 10.8.2012.
[142] Müslim, III, 418, Bayhaqi, Dalail al-Nubuwwa, II. 280, Zahabi, 217, Abu al-Fida,
III.44, 45, Halabi, I.470. cited in M. Asım Köksal, *İslam Tarihi*, I, 359–366.
[143] Tabari, III, 120, Ibn Athir, II, 252 in M. Asım Köksal, *İslam Tarihi*, VI, 424–427.

them when the opportunity came. On the contrary, he helped them when they came to seek aid (12:59) and, just like his father Jacob (12:98), he forgave them (12:92). Other Prophets were known and praised for their clemency and their forgiving and non-aggressive nature against the non-believers. The only exception occurs in the story of Noah. It was after years of warning his people and inviting them to believe in one God (71:5), both in public and private (71:8–9), and imploring them to remember God's blessings upon them (71:11–20), with the kindest of words and best manner for 950 years (29:14) that he eventually sought justice in regard to their misdeeds.[144] Not only did they not listen, they rejected him and conspired against him in many ways.[145] Finally, Noah supplicated for the destruction of the disbelievers amongst his tribe (71:26). The 19th Century exegete Mahmud Alusi stated that Noah felt sorrow over his people's conditions and would weep heavily. His constant crying leads to him being called Noah, which means the one who cries a lot. Noah's original name was Abd al-Ghaffar,[146] meaning 'The Servant of the Oft-Forgiving'. Qurtubi states that towards the end of his life, Noah was ordered by God to pray for the destruction of his people who rejected and harmed him and Noah followed the order.[147]

When Prophet Muhammad (pbuh) received a wound in the face by a non-believer during the Battle of Uhud, he pleaded to God, 'My Lord, forgive my tribe. They do not know what they are doing.'[148] Even against Abu Jahl, the most aggressive oppressor of Muslims, and other polytheist leaders, Prophet Muhammad (pbuh) said, 'O God, I leave them to you.'[149] God may guide them to become good people, or punish them as He sees fit. He forgave those polytheists who had persecuted him, killed his companions, and expelled him and Muslims from Mecca.[150] The Prophet's strat-

[144] al-Razi, *Tafsir al-Kabir*.

[145] al-Tabari, *Jami al-Bayan*.

[146] Cited in Elmalılı Muhammed Hamdi Yazır, *Kur'ani Kerim Tefsiri*, www.kuranikerim.com/telmalili/nuh.htm retrieved 5.10.2012.

[147] al-Qurtubi, *Al-Jamiu li-Ahkam al-Qur'an*.

[148] Bukhari, Anbiya, 54; Muslim, Jjihad, 104–105 cited in Gülen, *Muhammad: The Messenger of God*, 77.

[149] Ibn Seyyid al-Nass, *Uyun al-Athar*, www.risaleforum.net/islamiyet-72/resulullah-aleyhisselatu-vesselam-90/117592–allahim-sen-kavmimi-bagisla.html and cited in www.herkul.org/kiriktesti/index.php?article_id=3471 retrieved 2.4.2011 .

[150] Gülen, *The Messenger of God: Muhammad*, 247.

egy was to bring people close to Islam and gain more allies instead of challenging those who were against him. Taking a lesson from Prophet Muhammad's clemency and examples from the Qur'an, saints and other righteous Muslims did not act impulsively, but patiently endured and sought help from God in order to build relationships with the immediate and wider community.

Great Muslim figures throughout history have adopted the patience and clemency of the Prophets. Throughout history, successful Muslim leaders were those who engaged in reflection and were critical of themselves. They focused on serving and reforming their communities instead of laying the cause of failure in others. Examples include Umar ibn Abd al-Aziz (682–720), Nur al-Din Zangi (1118–1174), Salah al-Din Ayyubi (1138–1193), Nizam al-Mulk (1018–1092) and Imam Rabbani (1564–1624). Imam Rabbani lived in India during a time of spiritual crisis. Mughal Emperor Akbar Shah persecuted Imam Rabbani and jailed him. Imam Rabbani's students wanted to revolt, but he did not allow them. Instead, he sought for an audience with the Emperor and saw that the Emperor's advisors affected the Emperor's views on Imam Rabbani. The Imam chose to solve this problem through the power of persuasion, despite all the unfair treatment and imprisonment.[151] Said Nursi, a contemporary Muslim scholar, was also abused, imprisoned, exiled and poisoned unjustly. However, in spite of this, he never sought revenge, made curses upon those who mistreated him, nor did he engage in any extreme behavior out of anger. The persecution he underwent led him closer to desiring God's love and forgiveness. He would offer prayer for hours through invoking God's names and repeating Prophet Muhammad's supplications. Even on his death bed, he forgave those who had made his life miserable.[152]

All these examples from the Qur'an and history provide Muslims with a guide on how to respond to misfortune, abuse, oppression, and calamity. In such situations, there are four things which should be done. Firstly, Muslims must beseech God more than ever, through various means such as ritual prayer, supplication, recitation of the Qur'an, the invocation of God's names, and extra prayers, as well as prayers for the unjust individuals or groups to be guided. Secondly, they should repent from wrongdoings and beg for forgiveness. Thirdly, they should forgive those

---

[151] Imam Rabbani, *Mektubat* (trans. Hüseyin Hilmi Işık), 2–6.

[152] Suat Yıldırım, 'Vefatından Elli Yıl Sonra Bediüzzaman İle Helallaşma,' *Yeni Ümit*.

who have violated their personal rights. And finally, they should focus on internal factors and call themselves to account first, reflecting on their own deeds, sins and shortcomings. The final rule is the most significant: a Muslim should be patient and proactive. Part of reflecting on past deeds is considering whether the individual or group in question has taken the necessary and suitable actions to allow good causes to arise, or has taken measures to prevent an atmosphere of hate and discrimination. To judge any action, an individual or group must consider that act in light of guidelines laid down in sacred texts and civil laws. Actions that provoke people and stir feelings of distrust need to be discontinued. Muslim communities must reach out beyond their own sphere and build relationships that would strengthen the general community and enhance feelings of security. It is not an individual or group responsibility to physically defend Islam, but a duty of the Muslim countries' governments.

An individual has to act in the light of these rules and be instructed by rational thought. When dealing with problems, a Muslim has to think long-term and globally and react positively. Instead of reacting impulsively, a Muslim needs to take planned steps towards solving the problem, while keeping in mind how those steps will affect other Muslims both locally and globally. In place of accusing and blaming others, Muslims need to present the preferred action or communicate the right information. Finally, a Muslim should turn to God, asking Him to enlighten those who misunderstand Islam, guide those who misrepresent Islam, and direct Muslims to the right actions and thoughts. As God says in the Qur'an, '(O human being!) Whatever good happens to you, it is from God, and whatever evil befalls you, it is from yourself...' (4:79). Tabari[153] and Ibn Kathir[154] state that calamities and evils that befall believers are due to their wrong actions. Muslims should think, 'Had we done what was necessary and suitable on time, perhaps this evil may not have befallen us?' One who accuses his soul sees its faults. And one, who admits his faults, then seeks forgiveness for them. And one, who seeks forgiveness, takes refuge with God. And one who takes refuge with God, is saved from Satan's evil. Not to see his faults is a greater fault than the first fault. And not to

---

153 al-Tabari, *Jami al-Bayan*.
154 Ibn Kathir, *Tafsir al-Qur'an al-Karim*.

admit to his faults is a serious defect. If he sees the fault, it ceases to be a fault. If he admits it, he becomes worthy of forgiveness.[155]

Another trait of reactionaries is the act blaming others as the cause of one's own misfortunes, or accusing them of being responsible for social and religious problems. By contrast, in the Qur'an, when the Muslims were almost defeated at the Battle of Uhud, God warned the Muslims and commanded them to call themselves to account instead of condemning the polytheists (3:140–143–155). Gülen adds that it is inappropriate to lay blame only upon aggressors, occupiers, tyrants and unjust governments. Even more importantly, it is necessary to call the individual self or community to account, and search for weaknesses, mistakes and shortcomings. When a person, community or nation fall victim to oppression, the victim must not look outward for the source of the problem first, but should turn inward to search for what could have been done to avoid the problem.[156]

Gülen views reactionaries as indicative of backwardness or a lack of progress, and saw lack of proactivism as a spiritual weakness.[157] Reactionism does not solve problems; rather, it aggravates them and causes further disorder. It gives an advantage to the opposing forces, by providing material to the sensationalist mass media which can then be used against Islam and Muslims.[158] Nursi considers providing such damaging material, which appears to be prejudicial to Islam, as a betrayal of the faith. It opens the door to tolerance for any interpretation, and unsound things have become mixed with sublime Qur'anic truths. This has led some unfair critics, and those who tend to go to extremes to accuse the Qur'an and the Prophetic Tradition of containing certain fallacies.[159] Even if reactionary individuals' or groups' actions uphold legitimate values and causes—such as expressing anger over insults towards the religion—the inappropriate methodology and manner in which they respond make them seem the unjust party or lead to more tension and misconceptions.

---

[155] Nursi, *Flashes*, 124.
[156] Gülen, www.herkul.org/kiriktesti/index.php?article_id=8785 retrieved 23.4.2013.
[157] Gülen, *Fasıldan Fasıla-2*, 135.
[158] Gülen, *Fasıldan Fasıla-3*, 246.
[159] Nursi, *The Reasonings: A Key to Understanding the Qur'an's Eloquence*, 20.

Yelling at protests or making radical speeches does not further the cause of Islam or bring people closer to it, contrary to what some reactionaries and radicals might think. Nor does it solve problems.[160] In order to cause change, and seek rights and freedoms, persuasive speaking and diplomatic action based on the situation is the most effective way. Gülen states we must neither be hostage to our reactionary instincts, nor must we remain completely silent in the face of the systematic defamation of our values and beliefs.[161] Gülen sees Muslims as lacking in this area and believes they need to develop in this respect. Gülen agrees that it is natural for those who are active in Islamic work or dedicated to serving Muslims to be disturbed greatly when the sacred values of Islam are under attack or insulted, such as when Prophet Muhammad's image was defiled through the Danish cartoon. In reacting to such incitements, a Muslim should not sway from the proper middle path. Many correct forms of response can be found by appealing to the collective conscience of society and to the international community.[162] In such situations, Gülen believes Muslims should be even keener to act appropriately and work harder to present that which is right.[163] This will be the most effective means to reform, influence, or at least maintain a positive image. First of all, a person, group or people should be aware of his/her/their rights and hold onto them. However, if these rights are usurped or taken away, then laws and diplomatic situations should be applied to regain that which was lost. Through such means, the person or group seeking to regain rights will earn the respect and even influence those who took the rights away.

Islam cannot be conveyed through shouting at protests, and loud voices, and in an atmosphere of hate, because in that atmosphere, even the truth receives a negative reaction.[164] It is not right to condemn people for their faults. All our relations must take the path of leniency and tolerance. If we continue to act gently towards those who are aggressive

---

[160] Gülen, *Prizma-1*, 42.

[161] Gülen, *Violence is not in the tradition of the Prophet*, Financial Times, 20.09.2012.

[162] Ibid.

[163] Gülen, Toplumun İleri Gelenleri ve Gönüllerin Fethi, herkul.org/index.php/krk-testi/kirik-testi-arsiv/8785–Toplumun%20%C4%B0leri%20Gelenleri%20ve%20G%C3%B6n%C3%BCllerin%20Fethi, retrieved 25.4.2013.

[164] Gülen, *Fasıldan Fasıla-5*, 178.

and unjustly critical towards Islam and Muslims, then Gülen believes that there will be a day when a majority of them will become most sincere friends.[165] One common trait shared by Nursi and Gülen is their preference for positive and proactive responses to political injustice, rather than the use of force. They believe that just as political diplomacy uses soft power, hearts and minds can be conquered through a similar soft power. The characteristics of this soft power are the uses of persuasion over force, proactive responses over aggressive reactions, peace over disorder, conquering hearts over force, mildness over harshness, forgiving personal rights over seeking revenge, establishing common grounds over differences, getting along over quarrelling and constructive criticism over destructive criticism. For Gülen, the use of force was seen as a method which could once be used to convince others during a particular historical period, but one which time has since abrogated. In today's world, civilized people are won over by persuasion.[166]

Gülen's views of criticism

Gülen sees criticism as a path to the ideal state. To criticize in a constructive manner and to be open to constructive criticism is fundamental to general and scholarly learning.[167] Elderly, experienced and professional people should use their wisdom as a way to encourage good and be examples.[168] However, this does not mean that the aforementioned people should speak as they see fit. Criticism should have its code of conduct:

- Those who offer criticism should avoid rude gestures, tasteless acts, prideful remarks, boasting and arrogance, and other acts which displease God, as well as avoiding acts that injure hearts and leads to reactionism.
- Not every truth should be spoken at every moment, especially if it will lead to conflict and division.
- A person's manner of communication reflects his or her character. Therefore, towards friends or foes, we must act the same. To

---

[165] Gülen, *Fasıldan Fasıla-1*, 104.

[166] Gülen, *Prizma-1*, 41.

[167] Gülen, *Teknit Adabı ve hakka hürmet*, www.herkul.org/bamteli/index.php?article_id=5244 Retrieved 10.3.2013.

[168] Ibid.

those who curse, defame and insult him, Gülen still refers to them as 'bey,' 'efendi' (sir or gentleman) as he refers to his close friends because this is the manner of a believer. 'If we compromise our values, we will fall to a very low position.'[169]

- Even the humor we use to criticize should be gentle, soft and constructive. Criticism should be as objective as possible, the truth should be valued, and strong bias should be avoided as much as possible.[170] The one criticizing should propose an alternative. Otherwise, the criticism could be harmful, not insightful.

When speaking, or just reacting, a person or group should speak or react according to the manners, etiquette and social and political conditions of the time and place. Gülen views reactionary protests and speeches as counterproductive because the manner in which they are carried out does not do any favors for the message it is trying to convey. It may harm the message or lead to misunderstandings. Moreover, it devalues and disrespects what it is trying to protect. Gülen refers to a personal example in order to explain this. When he was arrested in 1972 during the military coup in Turkey, he stayed in the same block as the communists and extreme left-wing students. Gülen said something about Karl Marx (1818–1883) which offended a Communist. The Communist, in return, said, 'Would you like it if I cursed your Prophet?' This terrified Gülen. He experienced such a deep regret and understood further the manner and methodology of speaking that Islam has prescribed.[171] He publicly apologized in 1999 and again in 2005 for some of his statements which caused offence to some people. He states that a Muslim must be respectful and tolerant towards others, but this does not mean a Muslim should passively accept other people's wrong actions or a denial of his faith.[172] After referring to Islamic primary texts, Gülen goes on to quote from Mawlana Jalaluddin Rumi (1207–1273), who was accused of being embracing of Christians and Jews and even welcoming of sinners, which, it was alleged, in turn made him dishonor and devalue Islam. The person accusing him called him a 'zindiq' and stated 'even Hell will not accept you'. In

[169] Gülen, Fasıldan Fasıla-3, 103–104.
[170] Gülen, Teknit Adabı ve hakka hürmet, www.herkul.org/bamteli/index.php?article_id=5244 Retrieved 10.3.2013.
[171] Gülen, www.herkul.org/kiriktesti/index.php?article_id=7905 retrived 10.10.2010.
[172] Gülen, Fasıldan Fasıla-2, Nil Yayınları, (İstanbul 2008), 86.

response to this, Rūmi wrote, 'Come! I have a seat for you in my heart as well.'[173] Gülen goes on further to say that a consistent use of gentle and suitable speech over time could lead to improved relations and even friendships amongst most people, including those who were once enemies.[174] Responding to mistreatment or aggression in a similar form or manner does nothing to mitigate the problem. On the contrary, it only aggravates it even further. A believer must refrain from speech or actions that provoke enmity or hatred. By doing this, it is possible to ease hatred and other negative feelings in an atmosphere of gentleness and tolerance.

Due to such views as these, Gülen has been accused by some scholars and radical political Islamist groups of being tolerant of infidels/disbelief. They argue that being tolerant means compromising the religion. Gülen responded to such criticisms with the aforementioned verses and examples from Prophet Muhammad's life regarding tolerance in Islam.

Conclusion

Politically, Muslims in the twentieth century have been more reactionary than proactive. Instead of taking a critical approach to their weaknesses, understanding the root of their problems and taking progressive action accordingly, they have tended to resort to the easier path of reactionism. Although they may claim to be acting in the name of Islam, often their reaction has been influenced by the current political climate, such as the rise of Communism and Capitalism. Moreover, they have also neglected to look at and understand their own history when Muslims have dealt with large-scale issues and crises. Turning religion into a political tool, or using religion as a cover for politics or as a means for pursuing ulterior objectives, is against Islamic principles. Historically, this has been a cause of failure for Muslims, whereas strong and sustainable Muslim civilizations and leaders, such as Umar ibn Abd al-Aziz (682–720), Abd al-Rahman I (731–788), Salah al-Din Ayyubi, Osman Gazi (1258–1326) and many other great rulers were led by religious principles. They held themselves accountable first, and worked to improve the conditions of their people before pointing blame at external factors. Contemporary extremist groups,

---

[173] Gülen, *Fazilet Ehlinin Dört Şiarı*. www.herkul.org/index.php/bamteli/bamteli-arsiv/9176–fazilet-ehlinin-doert-siar reterived 25.03.2013.

[174] Gülen, *Fasıldan Fasıla-3*, 104.

on the other hand, have worsened both the condition of Muslims and the public image of Islam by wasting efforts on unfruitful acts, causing disorder and even creating chaos. Ghazali's (1158–1111) statement, 'A hundred years of injustice are better than a day of chaos,'[175] still holds true for today's Muslims. Some individuals and groups act as vigilantes and use their powers against injustice and oppression without the majority support of their community or nation. This leads to further tension and even chaos. Revolting against an unjust government with force has caused the death of tens of thousands Syrians, mostly civilians, the displacement of four million people, and economic destruction which will affect the country for many years to come.

Regrettably, these attention-seeking extremist groups do not question the validity and results of their actions, nor do they call themselves to account. One should scrutinize the possible ramifications of each and every action, and seek the wisdom of the collective judgment.[176] Unreflective action is against the core Islamic principle of struggling with one's self. A faith that does not count even the blaming Satan as an act of worship, should not view blaming others as rewarding. Despite the suffering they lived through, including imprisonment, exile, persecution and threats to life to them and their followers, Nursi and Gülen did not react with anger, violence or even negative criticism towards their aggressors. Moreover, they forgave those who harmed them greatly. Their patience was not passive; rather it is proactive. It was the regular call for self-accounting and self-blaming in the leaders and literature of the Hizmet Movement that made it successful. Their chosen distance from politics, and their focus upon internal factors, have attracted millions of followers.[177] Nursi is the most influential contemporary Muslim scholar, while the Hizmet Movement inspired by his works is one of the largest faith-based movements in the world. For Gülen, the future will not be built on hatred, grudges, violence and wars, but on love, tolerance and accepting and respecting each other.[178] This either will, or will not, come true. Only time will give the answer.

[175] Mimat Hafez Barazangi, M. Raquibuz Zaman and Omar Afzal , *Islamic Identity and the Struggle for Justice* , 25.

[176] Gülen , *Financial Times*, 20.9.2012.

[177] 'A Farm Boy on the World Stage' *The Economist* (March 6, 2008). Available online at www.fethullahGülen.org/press-room/news/2851–a-farm-boy-onthe-world-stage.html. retrived 2.3.2010.

[178] Gülen, *Fasıldan Fasıla-3*, 129.

Challenges in Inter-Religious Dialogue: Initiatives and Activities of the Gülen (Hizmet) Movement in Turkey

İsmail Albayrak
Australian Catholic University/Sakarya University

Introduction

No one would claim that inter-religious dialogue was initiated by the Gülen/Hizmet (GH) Movement in the Muslim world in general and in Turkey in particular. Before the Movement was founded there were many attempts and meetings aiming to foster inter-religious dialogue in various Muslim countries including Turkey. Nevertheless, it is not wrong to say that the involvement of the GH Movement in dialogue activities accelerated the growth of such events and facilitated their acceptance in many circles. Previously, at least in the Turkish context, dialogue initiatives had been limited to a few Divinity faculty lecturers and had never gained any legitimacy among the people, and so dialogue activities at the institutional level were generally unknown and unheard. However, the Movement's involvement in dialogue has not been limited to Turkey, and it is now global. So it is no exaggeration to say that although the Movement is not the only dialogue organization in the world it is certainly one of the most powerful and influential. Furthermore, it makes a strong connection between its dialogue activities and its transnational educational institutions. Thus teaching the value of differences and encouraging the young generations to appreciate shared values and think about such contemporary issues as human rights and dignity, intercultural dialogue, gender equality, women's and children's rights, poverty, the dangers of racism, the need for clean water, environmental awareness, the problem of illiteracy, war, and democratic values are the main concerns of these activities. In this article, we consider first the relationships and tensions between majorities and minorities, and the perception of Muslims as a minority in the Western world. We then move to discuss the claim that Muslims give priority to engagement in inter-faith dialogue only in the Western world or only in non-Muslim societies while neglecting such initiatives in nations where the Muslim population is numerically and culturally dominant. The validity of this claim will be assessed by examining the inter-religious and cultural activities conducted by the GH Movement in one of those nations, the Republic of Turkey. Finally, in order to judge the movement's sincerity in these activities, criticisms raised by various Muslim individuals are discussed; this will allow a deeper understanding of the conditions and challenges faced by the movement.

Majority and Minority Relations in General

The word 'minority' is generally used in the technical sense, meaning a group numerically smaller than the majority population in terms of racial, ethnic, political, economic, sexual, physical, cultural, or theological differences, though today some prefer to use the term 'historically excluded groups.'[179] Relationships between minority and majority groups are very complicated. Bearing in mind that over 90 percent of the world's nation-states are poly-ethnic,[180] it is clear that this issue is very important. In addition, the increase of immigration for various internal and external reasons in our globalizing world means that we will see more— and new—minority groups in the near future. The existence, sometimes the absence, of multicultural and immigration policies in many states

---

[179] Peter C. Phan and Jonathan Y. Tan, 'Interreligious Majority-Minority Dynamics,' *Understanding Interreligious Relations,* (eds.) David Cheetham, Douglas Pratt, and David Thomas, Oxford: Oxford Press, 2013, 219; Ondřej Valenta, 'Relationship Between Minority and Majority Population Groups: Examining Factors of Spatial Concentration of Ethnic Minorities,' www.postemoderne.net/ondre/centrum/skola_soubory/Prirodoveda/rocnikovka.htm, accessed on 5 May 2014.

[180] Berlin accommodates more than 360 religious communities; Basel and Zurich are known to house more than 370 different religious groups (Herman L. Beck, 'Beyond Living Together in Fragments: Muslims, Religious Diversity and Religious Identity in the Netherlands,' *Journal of Muslim Minority Affairs,* 33 (2013), 112; Valenta, 'Relationship Between Minority and Majority Population Groups,' 16).

together with varying perceptions of the implementation of those policies complicate the matter further.[181] These relationships are worsened by tragic events such as 9/11, the London and Madrid bombings and so on. Clearly, people are quick to perceive the diversity and presence of minorities at times of crisis and insecurity as fragmentation and separatism.[182]

Majority and Minority Relations

At this juncture, it is worth summarizing some assumptions regarding the power relations between majorities and minorities. Nations are built around core ethnic majority groups, whose level of attachment and loyalty to the state/nation tends to be higher than that of the minorities. This high level of national identification gives the majority a special privilege: to represent the society as whole and enjoy their higher status as the real owners of society's values, norms and attributes.[183] Sometimes, this privilege empowers the majority to the extent of absolving them of

---

[181] Valenta states that different historical experience of nation-state formation plays a significant role in this different performance of immigration policy. For instance, he mentions France, whose immigration policy most resembles the assimilation model. Nevertheless, there are other countries which have switched the assimilation model of their immigration policy to the pluralistic model (Valenta, 'Relationship Between Minority and Majority Population Groups, 5–7). Staerklé and others draw attention to the progressive aspects of nationhood and ethnocultural attachment which evolve and take on different forms and meanings over time. (C. Staerklé-J. Sidanius, E.G.T. Green, L. Molina, 'Ethnic Minority-Majority Asymmetry and Attitudes Towards Immigrants Across 11 Nations, *Psicologia Politica*, 30 (2005), 24).

[182] One interesting example of this is Australia, a nation of immigrants, which is supposed to adopt a more tolerant attitude towards its minorities than many other nations which receive very little immigration. Michàlis argues that right after 9/11, greater anxiety was voiced about the relevance, meaning, and value of multiculturalism in Australia (Michàlis S. Michael, 'Framing Interfaith Dialogue in Australia's Multicultural Setting: Mounting an Interfaith and Intercultural Network in Melbourne's Northern Region,' *Religion, State and Society*, 41/1 (2013), 38); When it comes to religious groups, as Waardenburg says, a similar reflex can be observed: 'Christians and Muslims, be they majorities or minorities, behave as monolithic blocks only in situations of confrontation that is to say in crisis situations'. (Jacques Waardenburg, 'Between Baghdad and Birmingham: minorities-Christian and Muslim,' *Islam and Christian-Muslim Relations*, 14/1 (2003), 13).

[183] Staerklé and others, 2005:10.

the need to justify their attitudes towards minorities. Minorities, however, feel the obligation to justify themselves and convince the majority through their actions.

Minorities, especially newcomers to host societies, are sometimes seen by the majority as the main obstacle to social cohesion, shared values and norms, even public security. Since the immigrants do not share a common past with the receiving society, their sense of belonging to their new home is always questioned by the majority group. When the minorities are viewed and evaluated from the majority's perspectives, they are seen as a threat to the existing order and the majority ascribes to them many undesirable and negative characteristics and an inferior social position.[184] Many researchers find a positive correlation between a high level of xenophobia against immigrants and minorities and the majority's sense of exclusive ownership of and identification with the state and the dominant culture. In addition, a frequent discourse used by the majority to the effect that minorities take jobs, cause unemployment, are a burden on health care, education, and housing services and so on, worsen the relationship further. In brief, the majority views its space as not to be commonly shared. As Nick Hopkins and others underline, there are majority and minority spaces, but any common space must be built on equality between the participants.[185]

When we look at the same issues from minority perspectives, we see a different picture. Minority consciousness implies some degree of fear, alienation, exclusivism and marginalization. They feel that they are excluded from the mainstream of economic, political, and social life. This ranges from gaining national citizenship to benefiting from labor markets. They strongly believe that as the dominant culture of the majority group sets the stage for any contact between them, they are disadvantaged. Some even consider this contact a vehicle to undermine their collective identity and impose gradual assimilation in the absence of a healthy

---

[184] Waardenburg, 2003:18; Valenta, 'Relationship Between Minority and Majority Population Groups, 3.

[185] Nick Hopkins, Ponni Michelle Greenwood, Maisha Birchall, 'Minority understanding of the dynamics to intergroup contact encounters: British Muslims' (sometimes ambivalent) experiences of representing their group to others,' *South African Journal of Psychology*, 37/4 (2007), 695.

relationship between the two groups.[186] This occurs especially when an insecure minority meets an insecure majority. As a result, we find that many people prefer to live in their ghettos and avoid mixing with majority groups to save themselves from assimilation. On the other hand, healthy multicultural and intercultural contacts take place when both majority and minority groups feel secure.[187] Nor should we forget the diversity present in majority and minority groups. Because of this diversity, each majority and minority group finds various ways of solving the tension, depending on location, time, ability to adapt and change and so on.[188]

It should be noted that the relationship between majority and minority is not always negative. Societies which internalize real pluralism, understand the richness of differences and value many similarities can manage the shift from monoculture to multiculture by building bridges among the various strata of society and thus achieving real social harmony. In other words, there can be mutual and positive interactions and influences. Serge argues that a consistent minority exerts influence at both latent and manifest levels.[189]

Critical Western Perceptions of the Presence of Muslim Minorities

When speaking of Muslim minorities in the West, it is safe to assume that the general discussion about power relations between the above-mentioned majority and minority is also applicable to them. Since the power relations between majority and minority groups are unequal, many assume that Muslims have embraced inter-religious and cultural dia-

---

[186] Hopkins, Greenwood and Birchall, 2007:684. There is no doubt that any newcomer in the host society will gradually weaken their ties to their native cultural profile and values and subsequently adopt the cultural norms of the host society. One can even speak about the melting-pot model, when ethnic minorities gradually melt into the host society. Valenta draws attention to structural assimilation: 'when structural assimilation (intermarriage etc.) has occurred, all of the other types of assimilation will naturally follow. Particular prejudice will decline (if not disappear), and the minority's separate identity will wane' (Valenta, 'Relationship Between Minority and Majority Population Groups, 6).

[187] Valenta, 'Relationship Between Minority and Majority Population Groups, 9.

[188] Phan and Tan, 2013:231.

[189] Serge Moscovici and Elisabeth Lage, 'Studies in social influence III: Majority versus minority influence in a group,' *Europe Journal of Social Psychology*, 6/2, 151.

logue wholeheartedly post 9/11. Some go so far as to claim that Muslim minorities use dialogue or the language of tolerance tactically to avoid insecurity and fragmentation.[190] When it comes to their own majority countries, they deny their own diversity and overlook minority consciousness, which serves to create serious exclusivism and isolation.[191]

Thus there is a growing tendency among people in the West to see Islam and Muslims as a threat the preservation of their own identity. Since Muslims, in contrast to many other minorities, constitute a visible minority, many treat this identity as a massive, uniform, monolithic block[192] and see them a real threat to social norms and cohesion of Western societies.[193] Beck remarks that the debate on minorities and multiculturalism has become Islamized, which may be the reason the policy of multiculturalism implemented in Germany, France, Holland and many other Western countries is considered to have failed.[194] Although the growing Muslim presence in Europe (and the United States) is certainly not the result of a well-designed strategic plan to conquest, some people who have a strong influence on the decision-making process have voiced their concern and want leaders to take measures to limit immigration from Muslim countries.[195] Many disregard the socio-economic factors behind the immigration and focus on the assumed inability of Muslims to cope with European values and ways of life. On the basis of some terrorist activities, they conceive Islam to be a militant, violent, terrorist, expansionist, misogynist, intolerant, inflexible religion. Fearing

---

[190] Roger Boase (ed.), *Islam and Global Dialogue: Religious Pluralism and Pursuit of Peace,* England: Ashgate, 2005, 236; Waardenburg talks about this attitude as a common characteristic of majorities: 'those who are in a majority position or simply have power, have only very occasionally been interested in taking initiatives for dialogue, except for the sake of law and order or for diplomatic reasons' (Waardenburg, 2003:17).

[191] Boase, 2005:29.

[192] It should be noted that intra-religious tension is stronger than inter-religious tension.

[193] Beck, 2013:120; Valenta, 'Relationship Between Minority and Majority Population Groups, 10.

[194] This is the view of many political leaders and right-wing people in the West. Beck says that there is more attention is being paid to religious diversity now, but usually and mistakenly associated with the Muslim presence in the Netherlands (Beck, 2013:117, 119).

[195] Ibid., 112.

encroaching Islamization, they urge the restriction of expression of Muslim culture without recognizing that this attitude contradicts their own 'Western' values. Some go so far as to call for a ban on Islamic clothing and the building of new mosques or minarets while others make it very clear that as Islamic identity is incompatible with Western norms if Muslim minorities want to stay in Europe they should give up their faith.[196]

Although there are some who are skeptical about Muslims' presence in the West, others continue to support multiculturalism and value the contribution of Muslims to their society. Moreover, it would be wrong to put the responsibility for all these misunderstandings on the shoulders of Westerners. It should be noted that Muslims can also fail to act as proper believers should, and their everyday contact with their non-Muslim neighbors contributes little to improving those neighbors' understanding of Islam and Muslim identity.[197] We can now turn to the contribution of the GH Movement to multiculturalism, with special reference to their activities in Turkey.

Minority and Majority: the Perspective of the Hizmet Movement in Turkey

Interfaith dialogue activities in Turkey began as far back as the late 60s and early 70s. Pope Paul VI's visit to Turkey in 1967 was followed by that of John Paul II in 1979, which initiated inter-religious dialogue officially. Nevertheless, it is striking that there were no significant and genuine activities among the Turkish public before the 1990s.[198] A few dialogue events occurred at the academic level but these had no effect on Turkish society at large or on minority groups. The memorandum of understanding between Ankara University Divinity Faculty and the Gregorian University of Rome is a good illustration of this. In fact, as Yücel rightly says, until the 1990s the meeting of Muslims with non-Muslims

---

[196] Beck puts it very neatly by saying that a few people therefore think that, with the Muslims residing here, the Trojan horse has been let in. He also notes that Dutch people's fear of Islam is founded on not only the Islamization of their country but also the introduction of sharia law (Beck, 2013:119–120).

[197] Hopkins, Greenwood and Birchall, 2007:693.

[198] Mahmut Aydın, *Dinlerarası Diyalog: Mahiyet, İlkeler ve Tartışmalar*, İstanbul: Pınar, 2008, 292, 314.

was unacceptable at the community level in Turkey.[199] Thus it is safe to assume that the involvement of GH Movement in interfaith dialogue activities in Turkey mark a new beginning. Gülen broke this long-lived unwritten rule and in İstanbul met with Chief Rabbi of Turkey, David Pinto; the Armenian Patriarch, Mesrob Mutafyan; the Sephardic Chief Rabbi of Jerusalem, Eliyahu Bakshi-Doron; the Greek Orthodox Patriarch, Bartholomeos; and the former Vatican representative in İstanbul, Monsignor George Marovitch, who then arranged Gülen's meeting with Pope John Paul II at the Vatican in 1998.[200] According to Gülen, genuine dialogue can only be achieved by the engagement of both majority and minority religious and secular groups in mutual relationships at the grassroots level. Thus he does not stop at interfaith dialogue but advocates intercultural dialogue which welcomes those who have no religious faith. In a country where people have suffered greatly from internal division, Gülen's initiative has been warmly received by many representatives of groups both large and small and even by some marginal groups.

Gülen begins by accepting the existence and diversity of Turkey's own minorities, and their values and norms. This is his way of beginning to engage actively and constructively with those varied groups. We should note that Turkish minorities and their diverse sub-minority groups, are generally not recent immigrants or new asylum-seekers, although some are newly arrived from Africa, Central Asia and the Middle East. Rather, they are historical minorities who have participated jointly with Turkish people in their shared history, experience, suffering and happiness. This openness and engagement with a variety of groups and views is actually part of the Seljuk and Ottoman legacy, which is being re-activated by the Movement. The Muslim Turks lived alongside Greek Orthodox, Armenian Orthodox, and Assyrian Christians, and Jewish neighbors for centuries under Ottoman rule. The Ottoman *millet* system, Aslandoğan notes, granted certain autonomies to religious minorities, establishing what were for that time relatively favorable conditions. However, with the decline of the Ottoman state, some minority groups sought independence with the support of British and other Western powers. Upon finding their former

---

[199] Salih Yücel, 'Muslim-Christian Dialogue: Nostra Aetate and Fethullah Gülen's Philosophy of Dialogue,' *Australian eJournal of Theology*, 20/3, (2013), 200.
[200] Ibid., 200.

neighbors taking up arms against them, Turkish Muslims began to doubt the loyalty of non-Muslim minorities.[201]

Be that as it may, today we are living in a different situation, and to understand others we have first to deconstruct first our previous understanding.[202] Since globalization tends to aggravate tensions among different groups, we are now more in need of and dependent on each other. The Qur'an gives this global and responsible role to human beings.[203] Since Gülen has a strong faith in his own tradition, he believes that religions have a positive impact on our societies and that in the near future religions will play a significant role in changing societies for the better.[204] His suggestion during his meeting with Pope John Paul II that a joint Divinity Faculty be established in Urfa is one result of this conviction. Common points between these three religions (Islam, Christianity and Judaism) and their shared responsibility to build a happy world for all God's creatures make dialogue among them necessary.[205]

Since dialogue involves the confirmation of differences, Gülen wants every group (whether majority or minority) to live their faith and ideals in the utmost freedom and peace without societal disapproval. He emphasizes the separate character of different groups and believes that there is divine wisdom in these dissimilarities. As Roy expresses it, local differences and particularities play a significant role in creating a unique cultural constellation.[206] Of course, this should be done jointly, otherwise it is very hard to achieve the desired result. Gülen sincerely wishes to end the social exclusion of religious and other minority or marginal groups (such as leftists, Alevi, secularists, Kurdish groups etc.) and encourages

---

[201] Yüksel A. Aslandoğan, 'Historical Background of Turkish Democratization and Gülen/Hizmet Movement's Contributions,' (unpublished article), 13.

[202] İbrahim Özdemir, 'Promoting a Culture of Tolerance through Education: with Special Reference to Turkey,' *Teaching for Tolerance in Muslim Majority Societies,* (eds.) Recep Kaymakcan and Oddbjørn Leirvik, İstanbul: DEM, 2007, 82.

[203] Amer al-Roubaie-Shaifiq al-Alvi, 'Globalization in the Light of Bediuzzaman Said Nursi's Risale-i Nur,' *Globalization, Ethics and Islam: The Case of Bediuzzaman Said Nursi,* (eds.) Ian Markham and İbrahim Özdemir, USA: Ashgate 2005, 138.

[204] Niyazi Öktem, *Çağımız Hıristiyan Müslüman Diyalog Önderleri,* İstanbul: Selis, 2013, 188.

[205] Helen Rose Ebaugh, *The Gülen Movement: A Sociological Analysis of a Civic Movement Rooted in Moderate Islam,* London-New York: Springer, 2010, 39.

[206] Oliver Roy, *Globalised Islam,* 2004, 74–75.

them to engage and participate in joint activities. This is not a call for empty dialogue but for a serious paradigm shift in inter-religious and cultural relations. In other words, he urges people to shift from dialogue to collaboration and partnership on agreed universal values. Partners should work for the happiness of all instead of just their own. Following Said Nursi's (1887-1960) philosophy, Gülen believes that conflict in society stems from ignorance, ambition for personal advantage and profit from the vested interests of particular groups. Religion neither approves nor condones such qualities and motives.[207]

Gülen's key question may be summarized as: Why not work together for the betterment of all people?' His philosophy sees no need to marginalize any group. He has always attempted to find a middle way between minorities and the majority and take action to integrate minority groups without pushing them into assimilation or ghettoization. His call for dialogue does not merely involve passive tolerance of minorities, or ignoring what they have to say or accepting their existence reluctantly, or turning a blind eye to their activities. As Beck rightly states, active tolerance is, rather, a moral concept that implies a particular attitude towards groups and accepts their differences as those of equals.[208] Gülen's understanding of dialogue is that it does not merely pay lip service to these minorities and act so as to temporarily please them while privately disagreeing with them. He is convinced that dialogue initiatives are not only a moral but a religious duty. His dialogue activities (visiting their places of worship, joint dinners, iftar dinners, joint prayer, seminars and conferences on certain interfaith topics) give Turkish religious minorities the opportunity to express themselves clearly. Cooperation is the only way to remove fear, mistrust, suspicion, intolerance, hostility, violence, and so on. Gülen invites minorities to introduce themselves to Turkish society. He believes that to overcome prejudice bias, communities should work together. Although we find some inspiration in the classical Islamic sources, today the classical notion of *dhimmitude* (protected people)

---

[207] Joshua D. Hendrick, 'The Regulated Potential of Kinetic Islam: Antitheses in Global Activism,' *Muslim Citizens of the Globalized World: Contribution of the Gülen Movement,* Robert A. Hunt and Yüksel A. Aslandoğan, New Jersey: Light, 2006, 24.

[208] Beck, 2013:115.

status whereby minorities ask for protection from the majority needs a new interpretation.

The Hizmet Movement's educational and dialogue activities are insep-arable. On the one hand schools, currently operating in more than 150 countries, contribute to intercultural and inter-religious dialogue immense-ly; on the other hand institutions including the Foundation of Journalists and Writers, Dialogue Central Asia/Euro-Asia, Intercultural Platform, and Abant Platform serve as an antidote against theories such as the clash of civilization and the end of history. For the Movement and in Gülen's phi-losophy, one of the prime functions of education is to foster intercultural understanding. Failure to take the diverse nature of society in education feeds the homogeneous and monocultural dominance in many host cul-tures. Denial or disregard of the diversity which already exists in society leads to misrepresentation of others. This partisanship is the root of every turmoil and social conflict. In a world becoming more and more global-ized, one has to know who will be one's future next door neighbor. Fur-thermore, like neighbors, nations also need each other in a global scale. One of the most important factors here is to eliminate causes that sepa-rate people, such as discrimination based on color, race, belief and eth-nicity. Education, Gülen says, can uproot these evils.[209] In this regard, edu-cation is considered an island of unity. Teaching differences and giving an accurate picture of the unfamiliar other give opportunities to move on. Gülen thinks that this is a key for the improvement of relationships among the world's nations. Religiously speaking, in the understanding of Gülen, what is good for all is also good in Islam (and other religions).

In the Gülen Movement schools in Turkey, tolerance education is being practiced energetically although most students have a Turkish Muslim background. Outside Turkey, diversity is part of the movement's school-ing system. For example, in Bosnia, Croatian and Serbian students, though few in number, study peacefully alongside Bosnian students, in spite of the brutal war. This is a powerful indication that the Gülen Movement's schools have succeeded in establishing a non-sectarian atmosphere in their educational system while respecting cultural and religious differ-ences. It is also worth mentioning the nature of current religious text-books in Turkish schools, where there has been a marked change in atti-

[209] Ali Ünal and Alphonse Williams, *Fethullah Gülen: Advocate of Dialogue*, Fairfax: The Fountain 2000, 330.

tude towards the teaching of Christianity, Judaism and other world religions. Previously, school had taught that these two religions were originally, like Islam, among the revealed (heavenly) religions, but with the passage of time they were corrupted by their followers. There was also no mention of the living (contemporary) nature of those religions in Turkish Religious Education textbooks. From the early 2000s, however, the textbooks were occasionally revised and today these religions are presented in textbooks that are more representative than earlier editions which focused on mainly Muslim perspectives. Hizmet dialogue activities in Turkey played a significant role in this transition, in cooperation with other partners.[210]

Secondly, Prof. Suat Yıldırım, a close associate of Gülen, has produced an outstanding Turkish Qur'an translation, in which he uses extensively many Biblical passages which are presented as parallel to the Qur'anic verses. Despite many criticisms (some of which are not criticisms but open insults),[211] the Hizmet Movement is promoting this translation to pave the way for textual dialogue. What Yıldırım did is not new in Islamic tradition but it represents significant step in the Turkish context by demonstrating that there are similarities as well as differences in the two scriptures. That some quotations do not correspond directly to the Qur'anic verses does not diminish great effort Yıldırım made to find some significant similarities. Moreover, he has never promoted the idea that the Qur'anic verses and Biblical passages are the same.

It is also important to note that the involvement of the Hizmet Movement in dialogue activities has made a positive contribution to

---

[210] Recep Kaymakcan is the first Turkish academic to draw attention to this issue. According to his research, non-Islamic religions are generally externalized as religions due to the explicit influence of the confessional approach in Turkish religious education. See Recep Kaymakcan, 'Christianity in Turkish religious education,' *Islam and Christian-Muslim Relations,* 10/3 (1999), 279–293.

[211] For instance, Yıldırım is accused of promoting claims to pluralistic truth through his translation. It is claimed that by explaining Qur'anic verses using Biblical passages, Yıldırım is denying the notion of the distortion of the Biblical texts and confirming their authenticity. Some even say that his translation is not a scholarly accurate work (Mehmet Bayraktar, *Dinlerarası Diyalog ve Başkalaştırılan İslam,* İstanbul: Kelam, 2011, 128–130; Bayram Sevinç, *Diyalog ve Korku: Postmodern Bir Dilemma,* İstanbul: İz, 2012, 93; Yümni Sezen, *Dinlerarası Diyalog İhaneti: Dini, Psikolojik, Sosyolojik Tahlil,* İstanbul: Kelam, 2011, 21).

institutionalized interfaith dialogue in Turkey. For instance, the Director of Presidency of Religious Affairs (the Diyanet) had for many years been sent a celebratory letter of Ramadan and Sacrifice days festive greetings by the Vatican, but only recently has begun to reply. As Yıldırım points out, the Diyanet wrote back after the GH Movement became involved in dialogue.[212] Clearly, the GH Movement is playing the role of a catalyst to facilitate interfaith dialogue in Turkey. Aydın notes that the Diyanet accelerated its dialogue activities after Hizmet's involvement. For instance, he mentions that the Diyanet organized a second religious consultation meeting in 1998 and one commission out of three was dedicated to inter-religious matters. Consequently, the Diyanet established a dialogue department.[213] In addition, immediately following Gülen's visit to the Pope, the Director of the Diyanet also made an official visit to the Vatican, after which some important interfaith events were included in the Muslim calendar, although some severely criticized this initiative.[214] As Öktem points out, Gülen's visit made dialogue international but many came late to an understanding of its importance.[215]

Today's global discourse teaches us that one's happiness depends on the other's happiness, and many crises in the global context can be overcome only by the promotion of tolerance and dialogue. Gülen often stresses the importance of forgoing revenge for past injuries,, disregarding polemics, and eliminating hatred from one's vocabulary. Gülen asks his followers to see their own mistakes clearly and be blind to the mistakes of others.[216] There is a need of need serious engagement with minorities to foster healthy integration. This is only way to overcome our ignorance about many religious minorities, their teachings, and the way of life they promote. In questioning the limits of diversity, we have to understand first that achieving social harmony in diversity is a ceaseless process. Ongoing dialogue activities are the sole remedy for fragmentation. Thus for Gülen, engaging in dialogue and focusing on commonalities are not a luxury but a religious commandment.

---

[212] Sevinç, 2012:89.

[213] Aydın, 2008:82.

[214] Sezen, 2011:41.

[215] Öktem, 2013:195.

[216] Gülen, *Key Concepts in the Practice of Sufism*, New Jersey: Light, 2004, I.98.

In summary, it is safe to say that the Hizmet Movement and its activities are currently supported by almost every segment and stratum of Turkish society. Equally, their activities, especially the intercultural and the inter-religious, are being criticized, sometimes severely, by various individuals and groups. Nevertheless, since the Movement active involvement in dialogue activities began, it has been evident that they have never taken a backward step, no matter how harsh the criticism. This is a clear evidence of their sincerity and faith in inter-religious dialogue activities and their desired results, such as a commitment to the common good and to benefits for all, both within and outside Turkey. In order to understand the difficulties and challenges the movement faces, we will now summarize some of the criticisms levelled at the GH Movement.

Major Criticisms raised by Other Muslims and Secular Groups Against Hizmet Movement

In this part we will list and try to evaluate the various criticisms raised by different groups against Hizmet movement's dialogue activities to point out that these activities are no easy option but difficult and challenging in the modern Turkish context. There is no doubt that this kind of objection is not unique to Turkey and it is possible to find similar criticisms voiced by academics, religious groups, nationalists, leftists, and even free-thinkers in many Western countries, especially those where some political leaders and intellectuals frequently insist that multiculturalism as a policy is dead. Nevertheless, because of the differences within religious traditions, Muslims' objections to dialogue also vary. Some of these criticisms seem theologically motivated while others appear to be ideologically oriented. It is therefore not surprising to see polemics, distortions of discourse and misinterpretation based on mere refutation. To have some idea of the opposition, it is enough to consider the titles of books written in order to reject or blame dialogue activities in Turkey: 'the trap of dialogue,' 'the betrayal of dialogue,' 'dialogue and fear,' 'the door opened with unbelief (*kufr*): inter-religious dialogue' 'dialogue which never begins,' 'the disease enters the body when it becomes very weak: be careful, the missionaries are coming,' 'the other face of inter-religious dialogue,' 'inter-religious dialogue as an act of distortion,' and 'a lesson for those who are Christianizing Turks and eliminating Islam' are typical examples. Alongside many anti-dialogue works, however, there are also many pro-dialogue publications in Turkey. Here we will mainly focus on the concerns of the anti-dialogue discourses, especially on those that associate dialogue uniquely with the Hizmet Movement. These criticisms can be classified into two main categories: theological and political.[217]

Some theological/dogmatic issues:

Misuse of the Qur'anic and Prophetic data for interfaith dialogue

Although Gülen makes it very clear that 'If the world changes fifty times, our attitude towards dialogue activities will be the same and we share the same view in relation to interfaith dialogue because our sources do not allow us to do the opposite'.[218] Dialogue, according to Gülen, is not innovation but the revival of the long-neglected dimension of Islam. For the critics of dialogue, however, the Qur'anic verses and Prophetic examples used as evidence are not compatible with these dialogue activities. They hold the view that the readings of the Qur'anic verses and Prophetic reports made by Gülen and others in the Hizmet Movement are one-sided, selective and taken out of context.[219] It is interesting to find that sometimes the same verses or anecdotes are used by different people for opposite purposes. Consequently some question how one verse can be read as both pro- and anti-dialogue. Clearly, they oppose the way Gülen approaches these sources with the aim of forming a generation ready to embrace and promote dialogue.[220] Some even imply that Gülen's approach to the Qur'an is not Islamic but conjectural and based mainly on the teach-

---

[217] It should be noted that there are also other groups and people in different parts of the world who oppose the Hizmet movement's dialogue activities. Their major concern is completely different from that expressed in Turkey: while Turkish critics accuse the movement of being tools in the hands of Christians, Jews, and many other imperialist powers, critics in the West believe that the movement is trying to Islamize/shariatize the West. The article written by Father Stenhouse is a good illustration of this criticism. See Paul Stenhouse, 'Islam's Trojan Horse? Turkish Nationalism and the Naqshibandi Sufi Order,' *Quadrant Magazine Religion*. December 2007, LI/12.

[218] Gülen, 'Hoşgörü Sürecinin Tahlili,' www.herkul.org/kirik-testi/hosgoru-surecinin-tahlili, accessed on August 19, 2014.

[219] Sevinç, 2012:65; Bayraktar, 2011:168–170.

[220] Sevinç, 2012:65.

ing of Nursi.[221] By this critical evaluation, they reject not only Gülen's reading of the Qur'an but also Nursi's.

Many criticisms of Gülen's reading of the main sources of Islam are ideological and one-sided, and those critics also read Gülen's writings partially, not as a whole. Consequently, they express their dissatisfaction with almost every single interpretation Gülen has made of Islamic sources in relation to inter-religious dialogue. For instance, Gülen, like Nursi, regards the Qur'an as the book of *dhikr* (reflection), *fikr* (contemplation), *shukr* (thanksgiving), *ibadah* (worship), *shari'ah* (law) and so on, and he also finds in it many verses which encourage Muslims to engage in dialogue with other Muslims, non-Muslims and indeed the whole universe. He never limits the Qur'anic function to inter-religious dialogue. However, he states several times that this aspect is also an original contribution of the Qur'an. Rejecting Gülen's views, his critics unanimously object that the Qur'an did not initiate a dialogue; it is a book not of dialogue but of *da'wah* (calling people to Islam).[222] Gülen has never denied this aspect; his *İrşad Ekseni* and *Tebliğ ve İrşad* clearly show where he stands on this question. Islamically speaking, both are very important but dialogue is different from *da'wah.* Nonetheless, it seems that his critics' academic integrity does not allow them to look at without prejudice these works or at his general views.

It is also interesting to note that there have been concerted efforts by some Turkish scholars to disregard many anecdotes from the life of the Prophet which are used by Gülen to support dialogue activities. Although there are others whose approaches are very close to Gülen,[223] his critics hold the view that reports on the Medina Charter, the immigration to Abyssinia, the letters or messengers sent by the Prophet to some tribes and leaders of the region, the Prophet's efforts to communi-

---

[221] Yümni Sezen, *Dinlerarası Diyalog İhaneti Dini, Psikolojik, Sosyolojik Tahlil,* İstanbul: Kelam, 2011, 176.

[222] Sezen, 2011:228.

[223] There are those who say that until Gülen published his dialogue discourse we had not been aware that there are so many verses in the Qur'an encouraging inter-religious dialogue and cooperation (İhsan Yılmaz, 'Ijtihad and Tajdid by Conduct: The Gülen Movement,' in *Turkish Islam and the Secular State: The Gülen Movement*, (eds.) M. Hakan Yavuz and John L. Esposito, New York: Syracuse University Press, 2003, 232). There are some intellectuals who read these verses, reports and anecdotes with reference to dialogue and intercultural engagement (See Sevinç, 2012:78).

cate with people in markets during the early years of Islam, the Huday-biya pact, the farewell speech of the Prophet, and the Prophet's meeting with Christians from Najran are nothing to do with dialogue. For them, people like Gülen are guilty of exaggeration in connecting these events with inter-religious dialogue.[224] Since these events happened in a differ-ent socio-historical context, I do not think that Gülen himself applies them only to today's dialogue activities. Nevertheless, if these narratives are studied carefully, it will be seen that they contain many hints as to future dialogical engagement with others. If the Muslim immigration to Abyssinia is evaluated only in the asylum-seekers context, it is easy to miss the point of what Gülen is trying to do;[225] however, if one considers the dialogue between Ja'far b. Abi Talib and the King of Abyssinia (the Negus), the Muslims' long sojourn there, their relations with the native people, and so on, it becomes clear that there are dialogical aspects in this process. Gülen's difference from many other contemporary Turkish Muslims lies in his deep knowledge of *siyar* (the genre of the life/biogra-phy of the Prophet) and making this knowledge relevant to the contem-porary world. A similar comment can be made about almost every single event. While Gülen does not claim that this is the only way to read the *siyar* literatures, I would argue that many critics misuse and abuse his writings to justify conclusions they have already reached.

Problematizing the usage of the term 'Abrahamic religions'

Many critics have raised this issue. They believe that the concept of 'Abrahamic Religions' (for some this is just a fabricated story or legend)[226] was first used deliberately by Louis Massignon, a French Catholic orien-talist. Instead of adopting an obviously negative attitude towards Mus-lims, Mehmet Bayraktar claims, Massignon prefers to use this umbrella term to reshape Muslims into the form he wishes.[227] For others, as this con-cept does not exist in the Qur'an and Prophetic tradition, the main aim of this deliberate and constant usage is to separate Muslims from the Prophet Muhammad. Some go further and argue that the people who use it are denying the importance of *tawhid* (Oneness of God) and trying to

---

[224] See Sezen, 2011:88–89, 95; Aydın, 2008:302–315.
[225] Sezen, 2011:89.
[226] Sevinç, 2012:84–85.
[227] Bayraktar, 2011:67.

unite these three different religions under the name of Abraham.[228] They also note that when people accept the so-called sameness of these three religions, they become insincere and lazy towards religion.[229] In other words, indifference to the particular nature of their own religion gradually alienates people from their religious practices and turns them into mere secularists; thus the idea of Abrahamic religions has sown serious doubts and confusions in the mind of many Muslims.[230] Obviously, for those who hold this view, the notion of Abrahamic religion does serious damage to Muslim identity. Other critics concentrate on the notion of Prophethood in these different religious traditions and conclude that the gap between the Islamic understanding of Prophethood and that of the others cannot be closed; for each religion, the understanding of the status of Abraham is different. For instance, Oruç says that the great Prophet Ibrahim as we know him in Islam is very different from Abraham, who is a simple tribal leader in the Biblical text.[231]

There are others who find this term very problematic and argue that the notion of Abrahamic religions will lead the diverse religious traditions to create one universal religion or faith. One result of this would be to swallow Islamic identity in this universal pot.[232] For instance, Bayraktar considers the book written by a Palestinian-American priest and entitled *al-Furqan al-Haqq,* which brings Biblical and Qur'anic verses together, an attempt to manipulate and distort both the Qur'an and Islam.[233] So, to seek a common essence, universal ethics and a way to general peace in various religious traditions by creating one universal religion is to undermine the very concept of religious differences. One critic goes so far as to claim that the GH Movement's attempt to make a synthesis of these religions will result in, among other disasters, the legitimization of usury and of alcohol consumption, the abrogation of marriage act and the promotion of illegitimate sexual activities.[234]

---

[228]   Sezen, 2011:32, Bayraktar, 2011:180.

[229]   Sevinç, 2012:28.

[230]   Mehmet Oruç, *Dinlerarası Diyalog Tuzağı ve Dinde Reform,* İstanbul: Arı, 2004, 81.

[231]   Ibid., 47.

[232]   Bayraktar, 2011:37.

[233]   Ibid., 41.

[234]   Sezen, 2011:173.

It is very difficult to justify such claims from an Islamic perspective, and I think it is equally difficult to justify them from a non-Islamic perspective. Proactive people in dialogue and especially the Hizmet Movement use the concept of Abrahamic religions for practical reasons and disregard its heavy dogmatic implications. Thus the claim that advocates of dialogue are bringing these three religions under the umbrella of Abraham and forcing them to become one is a slander. None of the participants in dialogue activities has such a heinous aim. Gülen himself has stated many times that interfaith dialogue is not theological compromise. As noted above, he insists that the strength of the participants lies in their differences. Moreover, although this concept was used by participants from different religious traditions for time, inter-religious dialogue is not a static activity but changes and progresses constantly, and so during the last five years at dialogue events held in different parts of world the term 'Abrahamic religions' was rarely used. A similar refutation can be made of the accusation of seeking to create a universal religion. Differences are reality, factual fact; nobody considers them as a problem, and denying them against the nature of dialogue. Hizmet people insist that our differences enrich our societies, and so we should come together and collaborate sincerely. They never promote cultural, religious, or social homogeneity. Aydüz puts it unambiguously: 'inter-religious dialogue is not to produce a new religion, melt all religions in one pot but a means to know each other and to be known in the atmosphere of tolerance'.[235]

The misuse of inter-religious dialogue

Some hostile writers accuse the Hizmet Movement of extensively misusing the term inter-religious dialogue.[236] For them, religions cannot engage in dialogue; only their adherents or followers can do this. These critics believe that inter-religious dialogue is a barrier to the propagation of Islam, and so argue that people in the GH Movement are directly or indirectly helping non-Muslims to stop the spread of Islam. As Bayraktar puts it, the notion of inter-religious dialogue is used as a disguise to bring about the defeat of Islam from within. This use of the concept is the final

---

[235] Davut Aydüz, *Tarih Boyunca Dinlerarası Diyalog*, İzmir, 2005, 20–22.
[236] Bayraktar, 2011:26, 204.

stage of the ongoing orientalist project in the Muslim world.[237] Why the critics are so allergic to this expression is a long story, but it is very clear that their main aim is to find something with which to criticize the Hizmet Movement. Years ago, Gülen himself elaborated on this expression and made it very clear that although the term 'inter-religious dialogue' is conveniently used, dialogue actually takes place among the followers of these religions in question; everybody knows that religions cannot engage in dialogue but their followers can. People opposed to this expression justify their criticism on the basis of polemic rather than offering serious analytical discussion. For instance, Sezen insists that for Muslims there is only one religion, not religions. This one religion is Islam. The very concept of inter-religious dialogue thus creates a type who comes and goes between two religions, namely Islam and Christianity.[238] In other words, for Sezen, inter-religious dialogue is a means to confuse the truth with error because religiously Muslims have nothing in common with Christians.[239] However, the GH Movement uses expressions such as inter-religious and cultural dialogue for practical rather than theological purposes; thus, such criticisms in this context are unjust.

The notion of salvation

Critics attack Gülen and Hizmet on the ground that they are in a great hurry to put all the People of the Book into paradise, thus transferring the monopoly on granting entry to paradise from God to the GH Movement. Consequently, people in the Movement rush to declare that many Western leaders are secret Muslims.[240] According to such critics, since Islam exclusively possesses the power of absolute salvation, interfaith dialogue and discourse on commonalities among various religions can serve to dilute the distinctiveness of the Islamic faith. Oruç states that interfaith dialogue is a means to induce Muslims to give up the belief that 'my reli-

---

[237] Bayraktar, 2011:41; Bayraktar holds the view that inter-religious dialogue is also very dangerous to the other religious traditions. (Bayraktar, 2011:45).

[238] Interestingly, Turkish critics of dialogue reiterate that dialogue is generally conducted between Muslims and Christians, and not with any other religious groups. For instance, Jews are very reluctant to participate in dialogue. When they do take part, it is always indirectly. (See. Bayraktar, 2011:75; Oruç, 2004:114).

[239] Sezen, 2011:36, 85, 179, 207.

[240] Bayraktar, 2011:143–145.

gion is the last one and the most authentic'.[241] These critics are certain that the promotion of the 'common word' in dialogue makes *tawhid* (Oneness of God) and *tathlith* (Trinity) equal.[242] Bayraktar goes so far as to claim that interfaith dialogue is an attempt to make Muslims abandon the community of Muhammad for the community of Jesus.[243] Sezen remarks that Hizmet people believe that the difference between Islam and Christianity is as thin as a cigarette paper, and concludes that for Hizmet, being a moral person is an unconditional requirement but being a Muslim is not. Elsewhere he says that there is a deep humanity and human love in the GH Movement but deep love of Islam is always absent.[244] Sezen recognizes no religious or moral criteria or scholarly norms in his evaluation of the GH Movement and so can easily blame them in whatever way he wishes. Aydın is, however, more cautious and scholarly than others, and observes 'it is almost impossible to claim that both Muslims and Christians believe in the same God; nevertheless, we do not claim that the concept of God is the same in all Christians' understanding'.[245]

Regarding the notion of salvation, the critics go into great detail in discussing about Gülen's and Hizmet's approach to the acceptance or rejection of the Prophet Muhammad by non-Muslims. They are indeed extremely critical, alleging that Gülen and his followers are working very hard to abrogate the second part of the Islamic formula of faith, *kalima al-tawhid* (There is no god but Allah, Muhammad is His messenger). According to them, Gülen promotes the idea that there will be salvation for those who do not approve the Prophethood of Muhammad.[246] To support this view, they generally quote Gülen's statement about 'approaching with compassion the people who only say `there is no god but Allah` and do not say `Muhammad is His messenger`' which appears in his book *Fasıldan Fasıla.* Unfortunately, many critics do not study the context of this comment enough. Gülen's original talk has nothing to do with the salvation of non-Muslims or disregarding the second part of the declaration of the faith. Gülen does not say that there are no differences between

---

[241] Oruç, 2004:21.

[242] Bayraktar, 2011:182.

[243] Ibid., 126.

[244] Sezen, 2011:157–158, 209.

[245] Aydın, 2008:323.

[246] Bayraktar, 2011: 105, 124, Sezen, 2011:131, Oruç, 2004:31.

Islam and Christianity or that the differences which exist are not signifi-
cant. For him, there are indeed important differences between the two.
Nevertheless, the serious criticism of both Christians and Jews in the
Qur'an, Gülen says, needs to be viewed in its historical context.

This historical reading, according to Gülen, will allow Muslims to re-
establish healthier relationships with other communities, both religious
and non-religious. He is against the partial reading of the Qur'an and
says that some people are unable to comprehend the route the Qur'an is
indicating. Consequently, they derive some conclusion which is not compatible with the Qur'anic text. For instance, a claim of salvation outside
the *tariq Ahmadiyya* (the footpath of Prophet Muhammad) is one of
these partial readings because if the verses in the Qur'an are investigated carefully, it becomes evident that the Qur'an is trying to build bridges
for the People of the Book and is showing them various doors so that
they may find a correct way. According to Gülen, the Qur'an should be read
holistically otherwise it cannot be understood clearly. So the main issue
is the *tadrij* (step by step) and the Qur'an indicates frankly where and
how one should begin.[247] Obviously, the starting point in Gülen's understanding is belief in One God, which is the central and normative basis of
all moral values. In several places in his writings Gülen deliberately
avoids talking about salvation in the hereafter and points out cautiously
that because salvation is in the hand of God and we can only learn it in
the hereafter, no Muslim has a guarantee of salvation in this world. Surely someone who holds this view would never say that non-Muslims will
be saved just by saying *La ilaha illallah*. To depict Gülen as a man who is
seeking to establish some kind of theological comprise is to draw an
incorrect theological picture of him.

In reality, Gülen's emphasis is on the cultural and social aspects of
pluralism rather than on the dogmatic ones. Anyone who is familiar with
his writings must acknowledge his love of the Prophet and confirm that
he never separates the second part of the *kalima al-tawhid* from the first,
nor is there any relativism or pluralism regarding the truth in his understanding. Nevertheless, for Gülen, real salvation is found not only in avoid-

---

[247] See. Selçuk Camcı-Kudret Ünal, *Hoşgörü ve Diyalog İklimi*, İzmir: Merkür, 1999,
156; *Fasıldan Fasıla*, İzmir: Nil, 1995, II.170; Gülen, *Kur'an'dan İdrake Yansıyanlar
I-II*, İstanbul: Feza Gazetecilik, 2000, I.109–113.

ance from sin but also in active engagement in improving the world.[248] In addition, he does not accept the view of those who say that 'interfaith dialogue with non-Muslims is impossible because Muslims accept all the Prophets but non-Muslims do not accept the Prophet Muhammad'.[249] If non-Muslims accept the Prophet Muhammad, they become Muslims and the meaning of interfaith is not Muslims meeting with Muslims. Dialogue is accepting differences and trying to find a common ground on which to work together. Finally, it is worth noting that Gülen does not accept that 'the People of the Book' is a socio-legal description rather than a religious community. As many Qur'anic usages of this expression are related to dogmatic and theological matters, seeing them only as a socio-legal community[250] is a very reductionist approach. Reducing them to the category of unbeliever (kafir) is also not justifiable from the Qur'anic perspective.[251] There are others who reiterate their accusation that the GH Movement wants to unite the religions in the context of the notion of salvation,[252] but there is no need to open new page about this baseless claim.

Joint Iftar Dinners

The Hizmet Movement is also criticized for its joint iftar dinner organization. For some critics, this is an open insult to non-Muslims. Others think that interfaith dialogue should not include the participation of different religious groups in each other's worship. To invite a person who is not fasting to an iftar dinner forces non-Muslims in return to organize an iftar dinner for Muslims. This is not the appropriate attitude.[253] Similarly, joint prayer, participation in each other's funeral ceremony, and visiting each other on festive days[254] are considered by some critics an abuse of interfaith dialogue. They argue that these kinds of activity are outside

---

[248] M. Hakan Yavuz, 'Islam in the Public Sphere: The Case of the Nur Movement,' in *Turkish Islam and the Secular State: The Gülen Movement*, (eds.) M. Hakan Yavuz and John L. Esposito, New York: Syracuse University Press, 2003, 25.

[249] Oruç, 2004:385.

[250] Bayraktar, 2011:172–173.

[251] Bayraktar condemns Ahmet Kurucan, a close associate of Gülen, for making this remark (Bayraktar, 2011:175). Nonetheless, we would argue that Kurucan's remark is clearly based on the Qur'anic text.

[252] Sezen, 2011:148–149.

[253] Aydın, 2008:322.

[254] Oruç, 2004:87, 104.

the scope of inter-religious dialogue. There are others who see them in a more constructive way and believe that togetherness helps people to understand each other. For instance, Niyazi Öktem praises the prayer of peace held in İstanbul with the participation of religious leaders such as those of the Catholic, Greek Orthodox, Syriac and Armenian Churches, and the Chief Rabbi, and Grand Mufti of İstanbul on 15 January 2004.[255] If such a prayer were theologically and ethically wrong why would the Mufti of İstanbul, Mustafa Çağrıcı, have accepted such an invitation? From Gülen's perspective, if an activity is compatible with basic disciplines of Islam, gives people the opportunity to come together rather than force them to avoid each other, and paves the way for reconciliation and harmony, it is worth trying. It should also be noted that these kinds of activities are not limited to Turkey, but are being held in many other countries. By attending an iftar dinner non-Muslims learn the content of Muslim fasting; when Hizmet people outside Turkey invite non-Muslims to share their iftar dinners, these guests visit a Muslim home and witness at first hand the Muslim way of life. Prejudice created by the media can only be broken by coming together amicably and the iftar dinner is one of the best opportunities for this. Finally, this kind of visit allows non-Muslims to witness the hospitality and generosity of Muslims. This is a unique way of showing the beauty of Islam.

Political issues

Inter-religious dialogue becomes Hizmet dialogue

Another important issue raised by many critics is that of representation and monopoly in dialogue activities. How can one be sure that in dialogue both sides are intellectually, institutionally, financially and influentially equal? In contrast to Christians, there is no strong organizational body, very well-established hierarchy, and means to promote dialogue in Muslim communities. Furthermore, many critics believe that since Muslims have not often initiated the dialogue activities, they are generally passive receivers rather than independent contributors to this process. Aydın mentions another aspect of this issue, one which affects Muslims negatively, namely the use of a common language (English) in dialogue meetings. Since many Muslims are not native speakers, they feel at

---

[255] Öktem, 2013:197.

a disadvantage and do not express themselves very well.[256] In other words, on the one hand there are very well-trained Christians and on the other there are rather diffident Muslims. For many, this format does produces not a dialogue but a monologue.[257] So the main question to be answered is 'who will participate in dialogue?'. For some critics, lay Muslims who take part in these activities with Christian theologians or priests are engaging not in dialogue but in missionary work as prospective converts.[258] Here the anti-dialogue advocates' main concern is that these unequal encounters make Muslims vulnerable to outside influence; some see such meetings as posing a significant risk. It is also important to note that some critics make a distinction between institutional and individual dialogue: although many believe that any dialogue initiative carried out by the Church is simply missionary activity, very few deny that individual dialogue may contribute to the solution of common problems.

Be that as it may, anti-dialogue campaigners in Turkey constantly ask the same question: does the GH Movement represent all Muslims?[259] Some even go so far as to claim that this Movement, which has, according to them, been trying to monopolize religion for a long time, now wants to control all dialogue activities too.[260] Although these accusations are baseless, it is very clear that some people are angry and disconcerted by the Movement's dialogue activities. Seeking any opportunity to criticize, they question why Gülen should visit the Pope; Since the Vatican is a state, does Gülen have any official position that would justify the visit? How does he compose a letter to the Pope? Some interpret this visit as Gülen's assuming a leadership status above even that of the Presidency of Religious Affairs of the Turkish Republic. Gülen is also criticized for his visit to the Patriarch of the Greek Orthodox Church in İstanbul. Some hardcore nationalists and secularists consider it an attempt to undermine the sovereignty of the Turkish state. Their criticisms are not limit-

---

[256] Aydın, 2008:30.

[257] Oruç, 2004:44; Aydın, 2008:33, 300.

[258] Sezen, 2011:233.

[259] Bayraktar, 2011:119.

[260] Sezen, 2011:13. Sezen says, characteristically, that the movement puts itself in the place of religion (Sezen, 2011:17). Sezen seems unable to be moderate and says that the movement replaces religious consciousness with the consciousness of the leader of the movement (Sezen, 2011:176).

ed to the above-mentioned points; for them the main issue is the prob-lem of representation: put simply, the GH Movement represents neither Islam nor Muslims. Some even question the nature of the religious beliefs held by people in the Movement. They regard the Movement as a secret religious order or cult, operating like Masonic and Messianic movements, or like communists; its methods in dialogue are un-Islamic.[261] Moreover, the Western description of Gülen as an advocate of dialogue and the West's support of the GH Movement[262] are enough to cast suspicion on his dia-logue activities.

First of all, Gülen and his followers never claim to be the sole patrons of dialogue and representing all Muslims. For them, to encourage dia-logue is to fulfil the Qur'anic command 'compete in goodness,' and so they open the door of dialogue to everyone. In fact, the critics' main con-cern is not dialogue itself but their dissatisfaction with Hizmet's involve-ment in dialogue. In other words, *la li ḥubb 'Aliyy wa-lakin li bughḍ 'Umar* (Not through love of 'Ali but from hatred of 'Umar) is the main motiva-tion here. Secondly, Gülen is not the only person who has met with Pope without holding any official title; moreover, he did not act independent-ly but sought the advice of the Turkish authorities before the meeting. He has inspired a world-wide global movement and has earned the right to exchange ideas with other religious and political leaders, but no one should assume that his meeting with the Pope signaled any loss of adher-ence to Islam. He is very well aware of changes in the world, common problems and the importance of collaboration, and insists that the arena of interfaith activities is open to everyone. Gülen strongly believes that dialogue is a vital, but to describe dialogue activities of the movement as an obsession,[263] a way to please the West, the EU and the USA, eradicat-ing the synthesis of Turkish-Islam, and promoting secularization[264] can-not be justified. To see the Movement's dialogue activities as supporting the interests of Israel, the Vatican, the USA and its various centers in the Muslim world and Africa rather than sincere attempts at collaboration is to indulge are actually fantasies.

---

[261] Ibid., 166–167.
[262] Ibid., 165, 169.
[263] Ibid., 164.
[264] Ibid., 170–171.

Some critics assert that immediately after Gülen's move to America, inter-religious dialogue became Hizmet Movement dialogue,[265] meaning that the initiative passed from the Vatican to the USA, and thereby implying that Hizmet is now a tool the Americans will use for the benefit of the USA. To support this view, Bayraktar and Sezen urge their readers to examine Gülen's discourse and see how he praises the USA.[266] Critics habitually connect the Movement's dialogue activities with outside powers. Some allege that since there is no hierarchy in Islam, the CIA trains its own Muslim scholars in various Muslim lands using bribery, threats and so on,[267] one implication being that because the GH Movement teaches English in its schools it must be part of this project. According to some, the dependence of Gülen and his followers on foreign governments in their struggle with their own state is clear evidence of their close collaboration with outside powers;[268] others argue that behind Gülen's excessive emphasis on dialogue lies his commitment to protect the Hizmet schools and the activities of the Movement outside Turkey.[269] These two positions see a different form of pragmatism in Hizmet's activities but both display a markedly reductionist understanding of the GH Movement's vision of dialogue.

Finally, it is important to note that many critics believe that only the Diyanet has the authority to conduct dialogue activities Gülen used to be a part of this institution and retains a great respect for it. Nevertheless, many critics miss the point that official and institutional dialogue is different from private and individual dialogue. Because they fear that some participants in dialogue are insincere they wish to keep dialogue activities at the level of experts and official institutions. If any organization other than the Diyanet takes part in dialogue, its activities can be divisive and uncontrollable.[270] Despite such arguments, the GH Movement sees the world as *dar al-hizmet* (the land of service);[271] consequently their activi-

---

[265] Bayraktar, 2011:74.

[266] Ibid., 110; Sezen, 2011:179.

[267] Oruç, 2004:26.

[268] Sezen, 2011:164, 176.

[269] Aydın, 2008:317.

[270] Sezen, 2011:182, 230.

[271] Sezen expresses his dissatisfaction with this term and criticizes hizmet by replacing the notions of *dar al-harb* (abode of unbelief) and *dar al-Islam* (abode of belief) with the concept of *dar al-hizmet*.(Sezen, 2011:170).

ties go beyond the Turkish border and are not limited to religious people but include non-religious, atheists, secularists, free-thinkers and so on. It should be remembered that Hizmet is a civic movement and works for the common good. Its members have a strong religious conviction that informs what they do but they refrain from emphasizing this constantly. Also, here are things that official bodies do best and there are activities best performed by civic. So the Hizmet movement never seeks to hold the monopoly in dialogue and indeed does not accept that there should be any monopolies. Some critics who condemn the movement for monopolizing dialogue fall into the same trap they set for Hizmet. A few critics argue that the GH Movement should engage in dialogue with other Muslims rather than non-Muslims, because if someone fails to engage in dialogue with their co-religionists, inter-religious dialogue is rendered meaningless. They also assert that intra-religious dialogue is harder than inter-religious dialogue.[272] I think these critics forget Gülen's numerous letters to many Muslim leaders both within Turkey and outside Turkey on various occasions, few of whom have ever responded. It is also important to note that Gülen encourages his close friends to support other groups' activities and not criticize any of them.

Light Islam

An interesting discussion in relation to the Movement's dialogue activities concerns its alleged promotion of light or moderate Islam. Curiously, its critics in this regard include secularists and ultra-nationalists, who do not practice Islam. As mentioned above, many ordinary supporters of the Movement are devout Muslims who are very sensitive to any issues related what is to lawful and unlawful in Islam. Their aim in dialogue is not to domesticate the Islamic faith or reduce it to empty philosophical conceptualization, although Sezen claims they are guilty on both counts.[273] Critics have a strong belief that the GH Movement is helping outside powers to realize their project of breaking Muslims' resistance by promoting light Islam; but 'what is light Islam? For them, light Islam is a weak kind of faith that adapts to every kind of environment, sacrifices its fundamental principles, never gets involved in political and social issues,

---

[272] Aydın, 2008:28, 49.
[273] Sezen, 2011:161, 194.

and displays an excessively obedient character. Light Islam is inspired not by Islam itself but by outside influences which promote a simple, cheap and lawless religion.[274] Thus Bayraktar regards dialogue activities as a spring-board to create light Islam,[275] and many hold the view that the USA is using the GH Movement as an instrument to foster moderate Islam in the Middle East as part of its greater plan in the region.[276] For this plan to succeed, the USA needs to soften Islamic principles and the Movement is an appropriate tool for this purpose. Another critic claims that donations made to some Islamic studies in Western countries are intended to enrich and empower light Islam.[277] These are the critics' personal views expressed to insult the Movement, rather than a scientific investigation of its activities. I worked for nearly six years in one of its institutions and do not remember myself or any other person in the movement sacrificing any principle we valued. On the contrary, you are only valuable in dialogue if you preserve your own identity and convictions. Unfortunately, many narrow-minded people believe that dialogue must involve compromise. Definitely not! Diversity and differences are the main strengths of dialogue. Critics seem not to want to understand that others can learn from you and you learn from others only through dialogue and serious engagement. People in the Movement practice their faith in dialogue organizations in all conditions. It should be noted that people who live with Gülen know their religious life very well and are sensitive to the minutest details of the religious commandments. If their religious life is light, I do not know what to call that of others'.

Cities for dialogue

One of the major concerns reiterated by some critics is the selection of Turkish cities for dialogue activities. Bayraktar draws attention to the importance of these cities for Christians, and mentions some that used to be centers of Christianity: İstanbul, İzmir, Hatay (Antioch), Mardin, and Urfa.[278] Sezen makes the same insinuation and implies that the GH Move-

---

[274] Oruç, 2004:386; Sezen, 2011:210.

[275] Bayraktar, 2011:124.

[276] Aslandoğan, 'Historical Background of Turkish Democratization and Gülen/ Hizmet Movement's Contributions,' 17.

[277] Sezen, 2011:191.

[278] Bayraktar, 2011:150.

ment is trying to reconnect these cities with their Christian heritage.[279] In reality, the Hizmet Movement's dialogue activities are not confined to these cities but are organized in other cities in Turkey and in other countries. In addition, the GH Movement has never denied the importance of these cities to Muslims, Christians and many other minorities. Even today, outside the GH Movement, similar meetings are held by different groups in these places but no one criticizes them. The GH Movement also organizes dialogue meetings in London, Cambridge, Paris, Rome, Washington, Chicago, Melbourne, Sydney, Sarajevo, Cairo, Jakarta and many other cities; there is no need to look for hidden agendas in this selection.

Missionary Activities

In the Turkish context, when people talk about inter-religious dialogue, the first thing that comes to mind is the Vatican and their missionary activities.[280] Thus, some suspect the motives behind dialogue activities and some find the collaboration with missionaries very sinister.[281] For Turkish critics, the aim of inter-religious dialogue is to Christianize the Turks; when the period of colonialism and imperialism ended; Christian missionaries invented the concept of dialogue to support their missionary activities.[282] In this context, many critics refer to the role played by missionaries in the collapse of the Ottoman state[283] and argue that a similar fate is awaiting present-day Turks in the Turkish Republic, and in other Turkish countries in central Asia.[284] For others, the Movement for inter-religious dialogue is similar to the reformist movement, Wahhabism or Salafism, which they contend, aims to destroy Islam from within. The missionaries' method, according to the critics, is simple: first devalue Islam in the eyes of Muslims, and then convert them to Christianity.[285]

Again, there is a strong conviction among the critics that participants in dialogue do not know its real face and content. Muslims are passive participants and dialogue is steered by Westerners and Christians

[279] Sezen, 2011:219.
[280] Aydın, 2008:293.
[281] Oruç, 2004:404.
[282] Ibid., 6–7.
[283] Ibid., 137.
[284] Sezen, 2011:208, 216.
[285] Oruç, 2004:121, 142.

to the detriment of Muslims. Sezen asks an interesting question 'Does Turkey solve all its problems except interfaith dialogue issue?' In other words, despite the fact that people in Turkey have many problems, why do we focus on interfaith issue?[286] It seems that critics in Turkey (and it is not clear whether they know the content of the various dialogue activities) are obsessed with the fear of missionary intervention. We do not claim that no mission-oriented people are engaged in dialogue, but it is wrong to see these countless events as tools of Christian missionaries. We must admit that some of the post-Vatican II documents issued by the Papal office and Catholic Christians such as Dialogue and Mission (1984), Redemptoris Mission (1990), Dialogue and Proclamation (1991), and Dominus Jesus (2001) make it clear that, for some, dialogue and mission are inseparable.[287] Moreover, the Frankfurt declaration issued by Lutheran Christians, which rejects dialogue and insists on the sole authenticity of Christianity,[288] and the various home or secret churches[289] established by different Protestant groups in the Muslim world constitute a serious obstacle to dialogue. Nevertheless, it is difficult to argue that every Christian who engages in dialogue seeks to convert Muslims to Christianity.[290] The number of Muslims converting to Christianity, which is reported in Turkish media and used by critics does not, however, reflect the actual fact.[291] There are also many Christians who oppose interfaith dialogue and express similar excuses to those used by Turkish critics. Rather than make ceaseless efforts and invest in the young generations' education and religious upbringing, Turkish critics prefer to accuse others and discuss protective measures which are losing their importance in this century of mass communication technology. Seeing interfaith dialogue as detrimental to the notion of *amr bi al-ma'ruf wa nahy an al-munkar* (enjoining good and forbidding evil)[292] is also a typical reflex of this protective mind-set. There are limitless ways of doing good and one of these is engaging in interfaith dialogue activities.

---

[286] Sezen, 2011:152, 235.

[287] Aydın, 2008:91, 279.

[288] Mustafa Köylü, *Dinlerarası Diyalog*, İstanbul: İnsan, 2007, 147.

[289] Oruç, 2004:134.

[290] Aydın says that missionary agendas are very strong in Protestant Christian circles (Aydın, 2008:94).

[291] Oruç, 2004:117.

[292] Ibid., 36.

Death of Dialogue

Many Muslims, who participate actively in dialogue, were disappointed by the remark made by Pope Benedict XVI at the University of Regensburg on 12 September 2006. After this speech, Pope Benedict invited Muslim ambassadors to the Vatican and reiterated the importance of inter-religious dialogue, and it is important to note that after this speech, there were many Muslim-Catholic dialogue initiatives in various parts of the world. Nevertheless, people in the Hizmet Movement, including Gülen, criticized the Pope's remark, as did some Catholics. Moreover, many anti-dialogue writers regarded the Pope's comment as marking the end of inter-religious dialogue, and some believed that it was evidence of the bankruptcy of institutionalized dialogue activities.[293] They asked whether or not the GH Movement would continue its dialogue with Roman Catholics. Since 2006, there have been many major and minor dialogue activities between Muslims and Catholics, which show that people from both religions believe that dialogue must continue. This is not an attempt to justify what Pope Benedict said, but the praxis in both Catholic groups and the GH Movement indicates that people's dedication to dialogue has not been disturbed by his remark. Even the Pope himself continued to engage in dialogue with other religious groups.

Conclusion

The relationship between majority and minorities is a difficult one. Because of the constant influx of immigration from war zones, economic deprivation, epidemic disease and so on, it seems that this discussion will preserve its vitality for a long time. The GH Movement is aware of global issues and problems and believes sincerely that these problems can be solved only by glocal cooperation. Here intercultural and tolerance education together with inter-religious dialogue play a significant role. If these are lacking, cultural intolerance may lead even very civilized people to commit injustice and show a complete disregard of others. The GH Movement has been working very hard to develop this active cooperation between various faith groups. Hizmet people are not doing this because of the pressure on Muslims applied immediately after 9/11 but because they believe that the future prosperity of human

---

[293] Aydın, 2008:279–280, 286–287.

beings depends on the mutual and collective efforts of all groups. In addition, as we explained in this article, they put their ideals and beliefs into practice wherever they live, no matter whether they belong to the majority or a minority. Gülen believes that Islam is theologically and historically a very tolerant religion and he wants to re-activate most neglected aspect. He asks his followers to engage proactively and positively with the contemporary world to establish permanent peace, security and a prosperous future for all (both minorities and majorities). Thus the Gülen/Hizmet movement acts consistently in both majority and minority positions despite the serious criticisms and allegations raised against it. For instance, as Salih Yücel points out, while he is accused of being Islam's Trojan horse in the Western Christian world, in the Turkish world he is paradoxically accused of being the Pope's Trojan horse. His followers accused of being bad representatives of Islam and of catering to Jews and Christians.[294] Although many appreciate the Hizmet Movement's activities everywhere, polarized views about Gülen and the movement abound among those on the left and on the right wing, among the religious and irreligious. I think the main reason for this polarization lies in the movement's consistent activities both within and outside Turkey, in education and dialogue, and in relief and health organizations.

---

[294] See for details Yücel, 2013:197–206.

The Concepts of Jihad and Terror from the Perspective of Fethullah Gülen[295]

İsmail Albayrak
Australian Catholic University/Sakarya University

Introduction

I slam and terror are now generally debated together. Regrettably, it is extremely common to identify terrorism with Islam—as if the two were natural allies—thus we feel that we are under an obligation to bring these two different terms together in this article. The aim of this article is to show that this association is not very relevant due to the subject matter of the discussion. To do this we focus mainly on the questions: what is the meaning of terror? We examine what Islamic teachings say about terror; what is the relationship between the notion of *jihad* and Islam; what status does Islam confer on suicide attacks; and with a focus on the false justification of war in the modern world, which can only pave the way for more terrorist actions. We will address these issues from the perspective of the distinguished and eminent Turkish scholar and thinker Fethullah Gülen. At the end of the article, I will conclude with a summary of the positive effects of the interfaith/cultural dialogue meetings that Gülen has initiated both inside and outside Turkey in order to promote national and international tolerance, peace and mutual understanding.

---

[295] The first version of this article is published in *Muslim Citizens of the Globalized World: Contribution of the Hizmet Movement* (eds. Robert A. Hunt-Yüksel A. Aslandoğan). I would like to thank editors for their kind permission.

What is terrorism?

Although terrorist activities are defined with great difficulty today, terrorism's cruel and ruthless disregard of laws and ethics was shown by the attacks of 9/11. In addition, terrorists or their organizations potentially have access to chemical, nuclear and biological weapons, making the possibility of killing large numbers of innocent people and the causing of mass destruction to a frightening extent. Now everybody is vulnerable to a terrorist attack and many live in a continual state of fear. Today we know very well that these crimes are perpetrated across borders and cause global unrest and create anarchy, fear and uncertainty. Unfortunately, it is observed that the terrorists, who have unleashed this global calamity against all humanity, do not see themselves as guilty. Furthermore, their attacks on innocent people only serve to increase their internal solidarity, resistance, unity and conviction of their own righteousness. Consequently, these organized activities produce in our modern world polarity between 'us' and 'them'. It is a great pity that, similarly to the terrorists, some media members, scholars, politicians, strategists and other institutions must be held responsible for this polarization. We see sadly that in recent years people easily associate our common problem, namely violence and terrorism, with Islam and Muslims, and thus Muslims are quickly categorized as 'them'. The approach of Fethullah Gülen to this complex problem is extremely important due to the difficulty of formulating and sustaining a balanced view. Gülen's approach to terror stays away from easy emotionalism and prejudice and seeks to embrace all humanity.

Islamic principles against the violence and terror

As noted above, Islam and terror are nowadays indissolubly linked together; nonetheless, when we carefully analyze the Islamic sources and tradition acutely it will be seen that there is no relationship between terror and Islam. In fact, there is no religion in the world which condones terror. Religions actually aim to promote peace, happiness and prosperity, both in this world and the next, therefore, violence and terror are incompatible with basic religious tenets. It is therefore not reasonable to attribute a terrorist act to the religion of a particular terrorist. The terrorist may be a Muslim, a Christian or a Jew, but this does not mean that his or her act is an Islamic, a Christian, or a Jewish act. Therefore, people of good intention must avoid generalizations about terms such as 'Islamic terror'. To speak in such terms, is an insult to pious, sincere and innocent Muslims all over the world. A small percentage of uneducated, discontented, misled, deceived, brainwashed fanatics should not be taken to represent countless sincere believers.

Clearly the association of Islam—which is etymologically derived from the Arabic root s-l-m meaning 'peace,' 'submission,' 'deliverance' and 'safety'—with terrorism is a grievous mistake. From the Qur'anic perspective, attention should also be paid to the relationship between the concept of sulh (peace) and the concept of amal salih (good deeds). Salih, like sulh, comes from the same root and means 'to cleave to peace or move towards peace.' Gülen holds that this peace is a result of tawhid (Unity of God/Oneness of God) and that Islam, being a religion of Unity (tawhid), ensures universal unity, equality, peace and cooperation among humankind.[296] Briefly, Islam is a religion of peace and safety and 'Muslim' means a trustworthy, peaceful and reliable person. Thus when Prophet Muhammad describes the Muslim he says that the people are safe from his hand and tongue.

It should first be emphasized that one of the greatest sins in Islam is to kill an innocent person. Allah says in Surah Nisa (4:93) 'If one kills an innocent person intentionally, his reward is Hell forever. Allah's wrath is against him and He has cursed him and prepared for him an awful doom.' The eminent companion Abdullah ibn Abbas interprets this verse to mean that the repentance of those who kill innocent people purposefully will be denied, and they will be doomed to eternal Hell.[297] In fact the Qur'an promises not only the punishment of the killer in the hereafter but also the reward and punishment of the smallest (good and bad) action in the hereafter: 'Whosoever does an atom's weight of good shall see it, and whosoever does an atom's weight ill shall see it.'[298] Interestingly, when we look at the Qur'an, we see that killing of innocent people is mentioned alongside associating partners or other gods with Allah.[299] If the Qur'an

---

[296] Davut Aydüz, 2005:227.
[297] Ibn Jarir al-Tabari, Jami al-Bayan an Ta'wil Ay al-Qur'an, IV, 295; Ergün Çapan, 'Suicide Attacks and Islam,' An Islamic Perspective: Terror and Suicide Attacks, 2004, 82.
[298] Zilzal, 99:7–8.
[299] Furqan, 27:68.

and the life of Prophet Muhammad are examined deeply it will be seen that both offer a strong condemnation of violence and terrorism, which is the most catastrophic calamity facing humanity today.

Also, while killing a person is considered a mortal sin in Islam, Islam also strictly prohibits suicide. According to Islamic law, one has no right to end one's own life or damage one's body. Therefore, the argument that one is the owner of one's life or body is erroneous. The reason for this lies in the Qur'an: 'Verily We have honored the children of Adam. We carry them on the land and the sea, and have made provision of good things for them, and have preferred them above many of those whom We created with a marked preferment.'[300] The Qur'an, thus, gives honor and glory to all humankind equally, and considers the killing of one innocent person equal to killing the whole of humanity.[301] This point is crucially important because it demonstrates that Islam considers killing to be a crime committed against not only Muslims but also all of humanity. Moreover, the Qur'an places great emphasis on the virtue of peace.[302] Peace is actually one of God's names (53:23) and thus the Qur'an forbids a person from responding to an evil deed with one which is worse; instead, it says 'Repel the evil deed with one which is better...'[303]. Sound reason also suggests this teaching. Injustice should not be resisted by sowing the seeds of revulsion and hatred among the people. The Qur'an and the life of the Prophet show us various peaceful methods in the solution of this problem.

The concept of *jihad* in Islam

Another important Islamic concept is *jihad*. Islam regards human life as most honorable and issuing many rules for the preservation of human happiness and dignity in this world and the hereafter. Islam acts with proper prudence to prevent war, terror, injustice and anarchy. Nevertheless, it is known that Islam allows Muslims to fight in particular situations, which, however, it regards as *arizi* (unnatural) and secondary. Peace, however, is essential in Islam. War is justified only to prevent chaos (which leads to

---

[300] Isra, 17:70.

[301] Maida, 5:32 (whoever kills a soul, unless it be for manslaughter or for mischief in the land, is like one who kills the whole of mankind; and whoever saves a life, is like one who saves the lives of all mankind).

[302] Nisa, 4:128 (...peace is better...).

[303] Fussilet, 41:34.

wars), anarchy, tyranny, mischief, rebellion and so on. The Qur'an explains this issue in Surah Baqarah (2:191) by stating 'tumult and oppression are worse than slaughter'. Thus, war is justified in these exceptional circumstances. Islamic law acknowledges that Muslims have the right to protect their religion, life, property, progeny, and their honor and sacred values. But Islam was the first religion in human history to codify regulations of war on the basis of rights and justice. In Surah Maida, Allah says 'O those who believe! Stand out firmly for God as witnesses to fair dealing and let not the hatred of others to you make you swerve to wrong and depart from justice. Be just; that is next to piety; and fear God for God is well acquainted with all that you do'. Attention should be paid to the issue that Islam allows war only to prevent anarchy; it does not sanctify war undertaken in order to compel people of other religions to convert to Islam or to bring the whole world under Islamic sovereignty, *Dar al-Islam*. In other words, Islam contains no concept of 'holy war' in this issue. If a Muslim country is secure, war is not obligatory. In addition, it is not legitimate to declare war against any people only on the basis of their belief or disbelief (*kufr*). There is also no claim in Islam to make the entire world Muslim.[304]

It is therefore a great pity that some Muslims and non-Muslims simplify the term *jihad* by associating it with war, offering shallow arguments concerning its meaning. Viewing Islam through the lens of *jihad* or continual mixture of *jihad* with terror and violence allows them to support the hypothesis that teachings of the Qur'an are fundamentally aggressive, has terrorism at its core and pose threats to peace rather than offering solution to conflict. The frequently used and abused term *jihad* has gained commercial attractiveness in the modern period: however this reductionist approach to the term narrows the comprehensiveness of the notion of *jihad,* because this key Qur'anic term is one of Islam's most important concepts, which embraces both the material and the spiritual life of humankind. Jihad does not mean simply a holy war. Although the word *jihad* and its cognates are repeated some 34 times in the Qur'an, only four of these usages relate directly to war.[305]

---

[304] Ali Bulaç, 'Jihad,' *An Islamic Perspective: Terror and Suicide Attacks*, 56.

[305] Tawba, 9:41, 73; Furqan, 25:52; Tahrim, 66:9. See Bekir Karlığa, 'Religion, Terror, War, and the Need for Global Ethics,' *An Islamic Perspective: Terror and Suicide Attacks*, 2004, 39.

Jihad, as Fethullah Gülen defines in general terms, is every kind of effort made by believers to obtain God's approval and to satisfy Him. There are various dimension of *jihad* (strife, endeavor and fighting). It is possible to categorize them as physical, psychological, spiritual, sociological, and intellectual *jihad*s. For instance, the Messenger of God equates those who work for widows and the poor with those who make *jihad* for God.[306] In another place the Prophet informs that the greatest *jihad* is a *jihad* made against one's self.[307] As Fethullah Gülen explains: Jihad is purification and seeking perfection to please God; it is a cleansing of the mind from false preconceptions, thoughts, and superstitions—by means of Qur'anic verses; it is an expelling of impurities from the heart through prayer; it is asking for forgiveness; austerity (*riyada*); and studying the Book, wisdom, and other knowledge with a purified heart and mind.[308] In brief, *jihad* for Gülen is a contemplative spiritual struggle; it is a ceaseless, continuous, conscious and affective struggle. Gülen draws attention to *jihad* as paving way for outer peace, which in turn leads to inner peace. Interestingly, the Prophet's description of war as a minor *jihad* shows clearly the object of the major *jihad*: in Islamic understanding *jihad* means an individual's struggle against Satan. In short, *jihad* is a form of worship, which embraces the material, and spiritual dimensions of humankind. War is limited to the external/physical aspect of this struggle and constitutes only a small part of *jihad*. Islam fixes the boundaries of both major and minor *jihad*s and it should be remembered that these boundaries and dimensions are not only legal but also humane and ethical.

Rules in war according to Islam

We should now examine the Islamic principles concerning the rules of war. First of all, Islam states clearly that individuals cannot start a war on behalf of Muslims. One cannot issue a *fatwa* (legal pronouncement) to fight against another country, nation, group or individuals. The reason for this is quite simple: according to Islamic law, the declaration or initiation of a war is the duty of a State in accordance with certain princi-

---

[306] Abu Abd Allah Muhammad b. Ismail al-Bukhari, *al-Jami al-Sahih*, Nafaqa, 1; Muslim b. Al-Hajjaj, *al-Jami al-Sahih*, Zuhd, 41; Karlığa, 2004:40.

[307] Muhammad b. Isa al-Tirmidhi, *al-Jami al-Sahih*, Fadail al-Jihad, 2.

[308] Fethullah Gülen, in an interview with the Italian Journalist Michele Zanzucchi, 2.

ples. No companion during the lifetime of the Prophet declared a war individually. When the state initiates a war it must obey certain principles.
According to Gülen, in war Islam defines the limits that constrain the treatment of the enemy. We see the best example of this at a time near the
death of the Prophet. When he was ill, news came that the Northern Arabs,
along with the Byzantines, were preparing an attack on Medina. The
Prophet ordered the preparation of an army under the command of
Uthama ibn Zayd, and gave the following instructions to Uthama: Fight
in God's way. Do not be cruel to people. Do not go against your covenant.
Do not cut down trees bearing fruits. Do not slaughter livestock. Do not
kill the pious who are secluded in monasteries, engaged in worship, or
children and women...[309] The instructions of the Prophet were enshrined
in Islamic legal literature, to the effect that the killing of non-combatants
such as women, children, the elderly, the disabled is expressly forbidden.[310] There is no Islamic text, which allows the killing of innocent civilians in war, because they are held to be not combatant (*muharib*). The
Qur'an states clearly 'Fight in the cause of God those who fight you (who
are liable and able to fight, and who participate actively in the fight) but
do not transgress the limits; for God loves not transgressors' (Baqarah
2:190). The Arabic verb *yuqatiluna* in the verse is of extreme importance. To explain this in grammatical terms, the mood (reciprocal form)
in Arabic denotes 'participation' which, in this sense, means 'those who fall
under the status of combatant'. Thus non-combatants are not to be fought
against. This must be obeyed rule in war and applies equally stringently
when war has not been declared. In addition to this, according to Islamic
law, Muslims may not start a war without informing their enemy, and if
the enemy calls on them to negotiate a settlement Muslim forces must
cease fighting.

Indeed, the Qur'an (Baqarah 2:190) warns Muslims not to transgress
the moral limits of war against the enemy. The meaning of 'transgression'
here is not to kill civilians, not to torture enemy's warriors, to respect
the dead bodies of the enemy, to meet the basic needs of the enemy and
to obey the rules of war. It is important to note that Islam prohibits

---

[309] Muhammad b. Umar b. Waqidi, *Kitab al-Maghazi*, III, 117–118; Hamza Aktan, 'Acts
of Terror and Suicide Attacks in the Light of the Qur'an and the Sunna,' *An Islamic
Perspective: Terror and Suicide Attacks*, 26.

[310] Tahawi, *Sharh al-Ma'ani al-Athar*, III, 224; Çapan, 2004:83.

reprisal. For example, if the enemy's soldiers rape Muslim women, Muslim soldiers should not rape the enemy's women; this prohibition also applies to the torture of captured warriors, to attacks on civilians, and so on. It is well known that when the Muslims in Andalusia (Spain) were expelled from the peninsula, some Muslims asked the Ottoman Sultan to expel his Christian subjects from İstanbul as retaliation for the Christians' attacks on the Andalusian Muslims. However, the Ottoman *Shaykh al-Islam* objected, arguing that this practice was against Islamic law concerning the rights of non-Muslim subjects.[311] In brief, Islam forbids reprisal and the frame of every action in war is defined by Islamic law, which nobody may transgress.

As stated above, Islam insists on the legal rights of the enemy soldier in war, even though it is difficult to maintain a balance in a combat situation. If the enemy warrior is protected by Islam, the civilian is protected even more stringently. No one may touch an innocent person; no one may be a 'suicide bomber' who rushes into crowds with bombs tied to his or her body; no one may kidnap innocent civilians and behead them, no matter what their religion. Moreover, just as it bans attacking civilians in war, Islam also considers attacking civilians in peace as a most grievous sin. The Qur'an, as has been mentioned above, equates killing innocent people with unbelief (Furqan, 25:68; An'am, 6:151). Thus those who attack the lives of innocent people in the name of religion will lose their happiness in this world and salvation in the hereafter. Islam is a true faith and it should be lived truly. As Gülen pointed out, faith cannot be attained by the use of untrue methods. In Islam, just as a goal must be legitimate, so must all the means employed to reach that goal. From this perspective it is clear that one cannot achieve Heaven by murdering another person.[312] Considering that human life is the most precious thing in Islam, the gravity of the present situation is obvious. Clearly, Islam rejects every kind of violent act unconditionally and discourages all kind of extremism. Gülen, who openly cursed the terrorists behind the attack of 9/11, calls upon everybody to curse the terrorists who are darkening the bright face of Islam, and to take collective action against them. As an Islamic scholar and an expert in this field, Gülen finds it unacceptable to associate Islam with terrorism. He declares that a Muslim must not be terrorist and a

---

[311] Bekir Karlığa, *Kültürlerarası Diyalog Sempozyumu*, 16.

[312] Fethullah Gülen, in an interview with the Italian journalist Michele Zanzucchi, 4.

terrorist cannot be a true Muslim.[313] As it is seen in his approach, Gülen is very critical of the instrumentalization of the religion in daily politics. The individuality of a crime is basic principle in Islam; whoever commits a crime is the only person to be called to account. As repeatedly stated in the Qur'an 'no bearer of a burden can bear the burden of another' (An'am, 6:164; Nahl, 16:15; Fatir, 35:18). Therefore it is not permissible in Islam to issue a *fatwa* allowing a crime against civilians to be carried out. It is obvious that such attacks are indiscriminate except in the sense that civilians rather than military personnel are deliberately targeted. Such indiscriminate attacks are totally incompatible with one of the general principles of Islamic law.[314] The proposition that any action is legitimate in order to achieve an undefined goal is contrary to Islam. The example used by Gülen is as follows: if there are nine guilty persons and one innocent on a ship, this ship should not be sunk; the innocent should not be sacrificed to punish the guilty majority.[315]

As we stated above, individual cannot declare war; only the state can do so. Today, those who carry out suicide attacks are acting contrary to the principles of their religion, and perpetrating irreligious acts in the name of religion. Gülen insists that Islamic principles should be tested by the consensus of the Muslim community (scholars). This shows his reliance on and trust in Islamic sources and the tradition, which has carried these sources and their interpretation from age to age up until today. Thus a few unqualified extremists' *fatwas* approving suicide attacks which are not confirmed by the Muslim community do not represent the view taken by Islam and its true followers. Having summarized the status of suicide attacks in Islam, we will focus on the causes of these activities,

---

[313] Rainer Hermann, Fethullah Gülen Offers Antidote For Terror, *Fethullah Gülen Web Site*, 1.

[314] Çapan, 2004:89.

[315] Gülen, *İnsanın Özündeki Sevgi*, (prepared for publication by Faruk Tuncer), İstanbul: Da Yay. 2003, 200. Said Nursi talked about this issue before Gülen and said that the wild principle of modern civilisation sacrifice the rights of the individual without hesitation for the sake of society. However, the pure justice of the Qur'an does not spill the life and blood of an innocent, even for the whole of humanity. The two are the same both in the view of Divine Power, and in the view of justice. But through self-interest man becomes such that he will destroy everything that forms an obstacle to his ambition, even the world if he can, and he will wipe out mankind.

their historical background and some solutions in the light of Fethullah Gülen's evaluations.

Gülen's critical re-evaluation of terrorist activities in the name of religion

At the beginning of this article it is noted that Gülen approaches the problem from various angles, considering religious, political, social, psychological and economic dimensions. At this juncture we place great stress on his critical re-evaluation of the approaches to terrorist activities adopted by both Muslims and non-Muslims. Gülen states that both Muslims and non-Muslims are responsible for the instability of the world today. Concerning Muslims, he argues that some thoughtless people who lack the power of discernment narrow the broad scope of Islam. For this reason Gülen argues that such people must first change the image of Islam in their mind. Because they have no comprehensive understanding of Islamic sources, they take as reference only some sections of the Islamic sources without exploring the Qur'an and the Prophetic tradition, or the understandings of prominent Muslim scholars. They read these texts literally and mostly out of context without examining what precede or follow them. The results are disastrous: they misinterpret their religious teachings and then put this mistaken understanding into practice; consequently they are misguided and they misguide others. Muslims should, Gülen says, begin to re-evaluate the *fatwas* of the people who claim that they represent Islam today, because today everybody experiences directly or indirectly the damage of the terror which directly results from this intolerance and misinterpretation. Furthermore, Gülen emphasizes the danger of the idea that carrying out terrorist acts against the innocent people of other nations under the pretense of 'representing the oppressed nations of the world'. This notion is by no means compatible with Islam. Terror does harm to Islam, to Muslims and to humanity at large. As an example, it is sufficient to look at the reports about 9/11 and the London bombings. These reports confirm that in the period immediately after the attacks, there was a sharp increase in faith-related hate crimes against Muslims across the globe. Unfortunately, this has resulted in many people, especially Muslims, fearing for their safety.

Moreover, Gülen thinks that a real Islamic world does not exist today, as Muslims are divided and scattered throughout the world. He means that there is no any Muslim country which follows all Islamic principles. Currently, Muslims are not able to maintain good relations with one another, and therefore cannot constitute a union or collaborative work in order to solve common problems. Thus, he believes that currently, one does not expect from Muslims an effective contribution to the world peace.[316] There are several ossified problems in the Muslim world and the existences of these problems make it easy for some evil powers to manipulate the vulnerable. Additionally, the ongoing problems of poverty, the lack of education for the poor, the states' inability to be one with their citizens, a deficient understanding of the notion of the social state, a lack of democratic governments which give priority to the rights and freedoms of their citizens, various types of internal and external frustrations and, most importantly, the neglect of the spiritual and ethical life of the people have led to a deterioration of the general condition of the Muslim world.[317] Besides these factors, some experts say that uneducated youths might be brainwashed or even controlled by drugs to carry out terrorist attacks. All these explanations show clearly that war waged against the terrorist organizations by police or military forces will not be sufficient to stop them. No amount of wealth, military muscle or technological superiority could erect an effective shield against the actions of desperate terrorists. Gülen has stated that to fight against the ideology of the terrorists we need the arguments of the intellectuals. He also notes that one cannot establish order on the basis of rude power; military measures can only result in disorder and injustice.[318] It is also generally acknowledged that an order achieved by mere force and rude power cannot last long. Gülen expresses his dissatisfaction with the explanation that the reason behind these terrorist activities is religion, and points out that when religion is held to be the source of violence, the actual major factors and powers, goes unnoticed.[319] Because no human was born as a terrorist and the process of terrorism has a historical background, the root cause of terrorism is enormous.

---

[316] Gülen, 'In True Islam Terror Does not Exist,' *An Islamic Perspective: Terror and Suicide Attacks*, 2–3.

[317] Gülen, *İnsanın Özündeki Sevgi*, 202.

[318] Ibid.

[319] Ibid., 202.

Anti-dote of terrorism: education and dialogue

We will consider now Fethullah Gülen's approach to the problem of over-coming the global calamity of terror. It is important to note that, in contrast too many observers, Gülen, acknowledges certain negative developments yet thinks that the world situation is not deteriorating and there will be no clash of civilizations. According to Gülen, those who are looking forward to a catastrophic future for the world and a clash of civilizations, are evil individuals or groups who are unable to impose their world view on the people and hope that global antagonisms will ensure the continuation of their power in the world.[320] Nonetheless, the global political situation does not look hopeful, and we should not be complacent. Gülen argues that the true clash in today's world is not 'between civilizations' but within each civilization, culture and religion. That is a clash between the forces of ignorant, fundamentalist or extremist and those of mainstream, moderate or true believing communities. Gülen emphasizes that education must play a central role in helping to resolve the world's problems. His experience has taught him that the key problem of our modern civilization is education.[321] Today, many schools and other educational institutions established on his advice and initiative, both within Turkey and outside Turkey, are making significant progress to achieve this aim.

Besides education, another important activity initiated by Gülen in the cause of world peace is 'dialogue meetings.' As Ergene pointed out, these meetings are an extension of Gülen's global educational activities which serve to educate people. Although he has been severely criticized by some ultra-nationalists, hardcore secularists and religious radicals, he bravely argues that these dialogue meetings are primarily concerned with religion and are thus a religious duty.[322] Gülen constantly insists on the religious nature of these meetings, being the primary Islamic sources that encourage Muslims to engage in dialogue with adherents of other

---

[320] Aydüz, 2005:237.

[321] M. Enes Ergene, *Geleneğin Modern Çağa Tanıklığı*, 47. Similar to Said Nursi, believing Islam to be the middle way, Gülen placed great emphasis on the importance of moderation and keeping away from want and excess saying 'too much or too little of anything is not good. Moderation is the middle way.' (Said Nursi, *The Flashes*, 43).

[322] www.herkul.org.

faiths. Thus, Gülen says that dialogue is not his invention or innovation, but a revival of one of the most neglected aspects of Islam. His constancy in this regard is very sincere: he states that even if the sensitive political balance of the world changes a thousand times, he would never quit the dialogue meetings; the Islamic sources do allow him only to do so.[323] For Gülen, dialogue and tolerance mean accepting every person irrespective of their status and learning to live together.[324] He is concerned to show that the rights of religion, life, travel, trade, property, free speech and so on are guaranteed by the Prophetic tradition, the best examples are being the document of Medina and the farewell speech of Prophet Muhammad. Although there are ten years between these two events, Gülen says, there is no difference between them in their approaches to the rights of non-Muslims (Jews, Christians) and even of unbelievers. For Gülen this indicates clearly the religious imperative to continue in dialogues. Gülen also accepts that due to a lack of dialogue, some mistakes have been made by Muslims in the history of Islam, but Gülen argues that the history of Islam is also full of good examples of dialogue.

The key word in Gülen's dialogue meetings is love, and this love derives from his understanding of Islam and Sufism practiced in Anatolia. Those who seek to profit from chaos, violence and terror will doubtless fail to understand the conception of love in Gülen's philosophy, and will consequently fail to understand Gülen's worldview. Philosophically speaking, Gülen considers love to be the essence of creation: according to Gülen, love is the most essential element, the brightest light, and the greatest power in every creature in the world. If one is grounded in love, every kind of difficulty in the world can be overcome.[325] Thus, Gülen introduces love as an unquestionable condition for being human. Without love, it is almost impossible to create an atmosphere conducive to dialogue and tolerance. Gülen's love is not an empty conceptualization; it is directly related to his religion, whose commandments he sensitively tries to

---

[323] Ibid.

[324] Ibid.

[325] Gülen, *İnsanın Özündeki Sevgi*, 17; Said Nursi says 'the thing which is most worthy of love is love, and that most deserving of enmity is enmity. It is love and loving—that render people's social life secure and that lead to happiness which are most worthy of love and being loved. Enmity and hostility are ugly and damaging...' (Nursi, *The Damascus Sermon*, 49–50).

put into practice. Gülen says that religion commands love and peace; love makes people truly human and the spirits of the true will rise to Heaven.[326] Clearly, then, love lights the fuse of dialogue and global tolerance; it paves the way to global peace. For Gülen, man can only communicate actively with all humans and other creatures through love, which leads him to help others.[327] Unlike ideologies based on social Darwinism, which suggest that only the powerful are fit to live and the weak should not survive, Gülen, as a Muslim scholar, holds that love derived from Islam has a great capacity to embrace every person in the world irrespective of their beliefs. Relying on his own conviction and tradition, and on the global transmitters of love such as Abu Hanifa (d. 150/767), Ahmad Yasawi (1093–1166), Mawlana Jalaluddin Rumi, Imam Ghazali, and Imam Rabbani (1564–1624), Gülen describes love and tolerance as 'the roses and flowers of our hill'.[328] But this love must be expressed in its practical and living dimension, and so Gülen has inspired the organization of many meetings, in which different people with different religious and cultural backgrounds, come together to discuss the common problems of humanity. The participants of these meetings have initiated various projects and offered many solutions to ameliorate the chaotic situation in our world. Most importantly, these meetings show the people that dialogue is the real remedy for terror, chaos, and intolerance. Gülen, as a sincere believer in the importance of dialogue, has asked his close friends not to name this unfinished process of dialogue (emphasizes that this process is a long way from completion). This also shows his optimistic view of the future.

Conclusion

We have tried to show that Islam and terror are radically opposed even though some manipulative, uneducated or misguided individuals commit terrorist crimes in the name of religion. We have also drawn attention to the mistaken association of *jihad* with war. We then pointed out that Islam considers killing innocent people in the name of religion to be the greatest sin, and has never legitimized suicide. We also focused on Gülen's emphasis on the importance of dialogue in our world. Despite the

---

[326] Gülen, *İnsanın Özündeki Sevgi*, 17.
[327] Ibid., 47.
[328] Ibid., 78.

ravages of terrorist activities and many wars, Gülen's strong and sincere call for dialogue increases our hope that peace may be achieved. Love is situated at the very heart of his understanding of dialogue, and this love is mainly nurtured by faith in Islam and his mystical understanding of religion. Ali, the cousin of the Prophet, declared that he saw Muslims as his brothers in faith and non-Muslims as his brothers in humanity; Gülen agrees. This love necessitates dialogue not only with human beings but also with all of God's creation. When humanity reaches such a level of dialogue, then God's will on earth is achieved. According to Gülen, this is the very purpose of our existence on earth. Clearly, Gülen's discourse provides a welcome antidote to the militancy of much of what passes as Islamic discourse in today's world.

Part Two

Spirituality, Ethics, and Knowledge

Gülen as a Spiritual Leader in a Global Islamic Context[329]

Salih Yücel
Monash University, Australia

Introduction

According to *The Economist*, Fethullah Gülen is the most influential Muslim scholar in the world.[330] *Foreign Policy* places Gülen on the list of 'Top 100 Intellectuals in the World.'[331] An advocate of interreligious dialogue and educational opportunity, Gülen is the author of 60 books and has inspired millions. His admirers can be found in more than a hundred countries where they have established hundreds of educational institutions. While intellectuals have named this 'the Gülen Movement,' the advocates call their activities *hizmet*, the Turkish word for 'service.' It can be described as a 'faith-inspired collectivity' with millions of followers and sympathizers who draw on Islamic spirituality and teaching, constituting one of the largest civil movements.[332]

While respected by a significant part of Turkish society for his humanitarian views and activism, his influence has raised the suspicions of secularists, including politicians, intellectuals, and military persons, who see Gülen's growing influence as a threat to the current secular system in Turkey. Radical religious groups also accused Gülen of compromising the

[329] This article first was published in *Journal of Religion and Society*, Vol 12, 2010. I would like to thank the editor of the Journal for his kind permission for the republication of this article.
[330] 'A Farm Boy on the World Stage,' *The Economist*, Jan 21, 2008.
[331] 'Top 100 Intellectuals in the World,' *Foreign Policy*, May/June 2008.
[332] Hakan Yavuz and John L. Esposito, *Turkish Islam and the Secular State: the Gülen Movement*, xiii; İhsan Yılmaz, 'State, Law, Civil Society, and Islam in Contemporary Society,' *The Muslim World*, 385–412.

Muslim faith by interacting with non-Muslims. Amidst such suspicion, it is necessary to understand who Fethullah Gülen is and what he stands for. This article will review the (1) the spiritual lifestyle of Gülen, (2) the major differences between Gülen and other contemporary Islamic scholars, and (3) the critiques of Gülen's spiritual views and movement and Gülen's responses to these critiques.

Who is Fethullah Gülen?

Gülen is a spiritual leader, religious scholar, intellectual, peace activist, author, poet, and mentor whose life is spent in pursuit of the solution for society's spiritual needs.[333] Many of Gülen's ideas are influenced by the works of Said Nursi (1876–1960), who authored several volumes of Qur'anic exegesis known as *Risale-i Nur Külliyatı* or 'The Epistles of Light.' Other major figures of influence were Alvarlı Muhammed Lütfi, a Sufi sheikh, Mehmet Akif, the national poet, Necip Fazıl, a Turkish Muslim intellectual and poet and Muhammed Hamdi Yazır (1878–1942), a contemporary commentator of the Qur'an.[334] Özdalga argues that mainstream Sunni Islam, the Naqshbandi Sufi tradition and the Nurculuk, Nur Movement have shaped the thought of Fethullah Gülen.[335]

Gülen's education and training was comprehensive. Muhammed Lütfi guided him in matters of spirituality, Gnostic knowledge, and religious practice. Meanwhile, Gülen was also learning Arabic from Sadi Efendi, and proper Qur'anic recitation from al-Qari Haji Sidqi Efendi. By the age of seven, he had memorized the entire Qur'an. During the 1950s, he also studied the theories of modern social and physical sciences. Later, Gülen studied hadith methodology and memorized many hadith from various authentic hadith collections. In addition, he studied rhetoric, philosophy, Islamic history, theology, jurisprudence.[336] While gaining a deep comprehension of the main principles of modern science, he also studied the works

---

[333] İhsan Yılmaz, 'Changing Turkish-Muslim Discourses on Modernity, West, and Dialogue' presented at *Congress of the International Association of Middle East Studies*, Freie Universitat, 5–7 October, (Berlin, 2000) 1–14.

[334] Wanda Kraus, 'Civility in Islamic Activism' in *Muslim World in Transition,* conference proceedings, 165.

[335] Elizabeth Özdalga, 'Worldly Asceticism in Islamic Casting: Fethullah Gülen's Inspired Piety and Activism,' *Critique*, 91.

[336] Latif Erdoğan, *Küçük Dünyam*, 14.

of classical and modern philosophers such as Aristotle, Marcus, Descartes, Kant, Camus, and Sartre.[337] Suat Yıldırım, who has been a very close friend of Gülen for a long time, says 'He would spend a portion of his time daily in Edirne's library, where he would read old history books. He had and still has an ascetic life; he would eat little, sleep only a few hours, and spent a great part of his day in worship.'

One of the turning points in his life was meeting with one of Said Nursi's disciples who guided him to read *Risale-i Nur*. Gülen was inspired by the deep spiritual life of Nursi and golden rules of serving humanity and then he would apply them as principles of *hizmet*, serving to the community. His greatest goal and achievement was to educate the younger generation in both secular and religious sciences, in order to solve their problems of ignorance, and prevent them from spiritual diseases'.[338] Yıldırım added that Gülen has been strongly committed to his goals as one of the major purpose of his life. İsmail Büyükçelebi, one of the close companions of Gülen for almost forty years, observed: 'I have been with Gülen since middle school. He used to preach at İzmir and teach my peers and me at Kestane Pazarı Qur'anic boarding school. He would not only teach us, but also mentored us. He himself would live in a closet-sized room next the school building. He lived a very simple life and spent most of his salary providing for the poor students. He would spend his efforts in worship and education and avoid meaningless or fruitless activities and politics.

Gülen would not only speak at mosques, but he would also speak at coffee houses, universities, and other institutions. Unlike other preachers, Gülen would focus on science and religion, social problems and intellectualism. His inspirational speeches and intellectual approach attracted many university students, middle class business community and congregations in the mosques. He used his influence to encourage individuals to open dormitories, college preparation courses, open schools, start media and publishing companies, and build community centers'.[339] In March 1972, soon after a military coup, Gülen was arrested and detained for four months. It was later revealed that the military had imprisoned specific religious figures alongside many communists and leftists to demonstrate to the public that military leaders were not only against communism.

---

[337] Ünal and Williams, *Advocate of Dialogue: Fethullah Gülen*, 16.
[338] S. Yücel, personal communication, April 4, 2006.
[339] S. Yücel, personal communication, August 5, 2007.

After Gülen was released, he continued preaching until the second military coup in 1980, at which time he retired. Those who loved him and his teachings started the Hizmet Movement (as liberals call it), named 'Fethullahçılar' (Fethullah's followers) by Turkish leftists, and 'Nurcu' (the Light Movement) by traditionalists and conservatives. Gülen never approved of this Movement using his name and viewed it as a sign of disrespect to those who contributed to the Movement.

Despite pressure from his mother and close friends, Gülen never married. When asked about marriage, he answered as Said Nursi answered, 'The suffering of the Islamic community is more than enough. I have not found time to think of myself.'[340]

Observing Gülen's Spiritual Practices

Gülen would divide his day into the following activities: an hour before *imsak* (dawn), he would get up, perform the *Tahajjud* Prayer, read the Qur'an, supplicate in the way of Prophet Muhammad, peace and blessings be upon him, and make *awrad* or *adhkar*, which includes reciting the Names of God. After every obligatory prayer, he would make supplication for those who requested that he pray for them. Then, he would perform the *Fajr* (Morning) Prayer in congregation. After the Prayer, he would again make *awrad* and *dhikr* for fifteen to twenty minutes, followed by recitation of the end of Surah al-Hashr. He would converse with visitors for few minutes before his teaching session would begin. He would ask his students to read from Said Nursi's *Risale-i-Nur* (the Epistles of Light) collection and expound on the specific reading.

The study period would last approximately an hour. Following that, he would breakfast with those around him. After breakfast, he would return to his room to rest until mid-day. I asked those around him what does he do during his free time. I was told that Gülen spent his time taking a short nap, performing *ishraq* supererogatory prayer, reading different books, writing essays about portions of his books or poetry, and contemplating the activities of his Movement. About two hours before the *Zuhr* (Midday) Prayer, he teaches *tafsir*, commentary of Qur'an, hadiths, *fiqh*, jurisprudence, *aqidah*, theology and history of Islam to a selected student group who graduated from divinity schools. The study circle is

---

[340] Gülen, *Fasıldan Fasıla*, 140.

similar to traditionalists' way, which students would sit on the ground but with using modern technology such as computers and projector. Gülen's schedule is based on the Daily Prayers, which is always performed in congregation on the time.

Around noon, he would leave his room and watch the news for fifteen to twenty minutes. He would converse with those around him for half an hour. He would prepare for the *Zuhr* (Noon) Prayer, and pray in congregation. After performing the *Zuhr* Prayer, Gülen would make *awrad* and *dhikr* for at least twenty minutes. While having lunch with others, he would answer questions from his audience about religion, history, philosophy, sociology, psychology, economics, and education. I noticed that he would hesitate to respond to political questions. Sometimes, he would ask those around him about their family or profession, and, occasionally, make comments. He would give special attention to the elderly and young children.

After conversation, he would return to his room to read books or prepare his future own publications; at times, he would invite individuals to discuss their requests further with him. He would then pray the *Asr* (Afternoon) Prayer in congregation and make *awrad* and *dhikr,* invocation of God's Names. There would be another short question and answer session, lasting about half an hour. He would then walk on the treadmill in his room for forty minutes. While on the treadmill, he would make *dhikr.* After the congregational *Maghrib* (Dusk) Prayer, he might or might not eat with others. After the congregational *Isha* (Night) Prayer, he would return to his room and continue his usual activities of reading, writing, supplicating, and *dhikr* until 11:00 P.M. Sometimes, he would speak privately with visitors after the *Isha* Prayer.

In his religious study circles, Gülen would focus more on the love of God, His attributes, the wisdom of the pillars of Islam, faith, and the *Sunnah*, practices and sayings, of Prophet Muhammad, peace and blessings be upon him. In addition, Gülen would explain the details of inner purification, education, and criteria and core principles for the *hizmet* serving the community. Key concepts of Sufism, such as love, *taqwa* (piety), *qalb* (heart), *tawba* (repentance) *zuhd* (asceticism,) *muraqaba* (self-supervision), *ikhlas* (sincerity), *istiqama* (straightforwardness), *ibadah* (worship), *tawakkul* (reliance upon God), *tawadu* (humility), *shukr* (thankfulness), *sabr* (patience), *ihsan* (perfect goodness), and *ma'rifa* (gnosis-knowledge of God) are studied within the group. These deeply spiritual talks could be intensely emotional and there were many times when Gülen would weep, causing others to weep with him. His tears were powerful and had a huge impact on his audience.

Gülen leads a life of seclusion. He has three illnesses: hypertension, diabetes, and heart disease. Because of this, he has dietary restrictions and is under a doctor's supervision all day. In the last twelve years, he has left his relative's residence, located in a small town in Pennsylvania, only to go to the hospital. In an interview with a reporter from Turkey, Gülen said that in the last five years, (now ten years) he had only stepped out onto his balcony a few times. If the weather was nice, he would sometimes go out to the trellis and have a cup of coffee or tea there.[341]

Gülen's decade of seclusion is not like that of a mystic in the mountains. He follows the paths of Imam Ghazali, Mawlana Jalaluddin Rumi, and Said Nursi who used their withdrawal as an opportunity to be intellectually productive and spiritually proactive. Gülen chooses to place his full time, focus, and capacity on his inner life through increased worship and scholarship. Other factors, such as a large number of visitors and Gülen's health, necessitate seclusion. His withdrawal from worldly affairs, however, is not withdrawal from the world. He discourages complete withdrawal from the world, that he views as *dar-i hizmet*, or the country of service to humanity.[342] He continues to pen books and articles, and provides requested guidance and consultation for his visitors, keeping in mind the current spiritual, socio-political and economic conditions.

Gülen's View of Sufism

The basic sources of Gülen's Sufism are the Qur'an, Prophetic tradition, and various Sufi texts; in particular, Said Nursi's seminal work. Gülen defines Sufism in the following manner: 'Sufism is the path followed by an individual who, having been able to free himself or herself from human vices and weaknesses in order to acquire angelic qualities and conduct pleasing to God, lives in accordance with the requirements of

---

[341] Mehmet Gündem, 'Fethullah Gülen Röportajı,' *Milliyet*, January 27, 2005.

[342] Emre Demir, *The emergence a neo-communitarian movement in the Turkish diaspora in Europe: the strategies of settlement and competition of Hizmet Movement in France and Germany*, 226.

God's knowledge and love, and in the resulting spiritual delight that ensues.[343'] In his definition, Gülen focuses on a path by which a person can overcome his weaknesses without the help of a guide. In my talks with Gülen, he stated that 'Sufism is a spiritual journey from one's self to God, by the feet of the heart.' In his book, *Key Concepts in the Practice of Sufism*, he wrote:

Sufism is based on observing even the most 'trivial' rules of the *sha-ria*, Islamic law, in order to penetrate their inner meaning and initiate or travel on the path that never separates the outer observance of the *shar-ia* from its inner dimension, and therefore, observes all of the require-ments of both the outer and the inner dimension of Islam.[344] On Gülen's official website, he explains the spiritual journey 'That spiritual journey has different stations to reach *haqiqa* (the truth). A person will continue on this path until death. Persistence and effort are necessary to reach each station. During this journey, every time an individual rises to a higher sta-tion, he/she must be even more humble.'[345] Gülen quotes the verse: 'The servants of the All-Merciful are those who walk on the earth in modesty, and if the impudent offend them, they continue their way, saying, 'peace'.' (Qur'an: 25:63).[346]

Silsila, the mystical chain that reaches to Prophet Muhammad, peace and blessings be upon him, is a principle of Sufism. In Sufism, in order for a person to mature (*al-insan al-kamil*) and feel Divine Presence, he or she must imitate a spiritual master. In order for this transformation to take place, 'there must be a traditional link with the origin or a spiritual chain.'[347] However, Gülen has argued, 'A person can be a Sufi without a master or by becoming a member of a Sufi order.' Gülen gives the example of Al-Ghazali: 'Although he was a great Jurist and a great Sufi, he did not belong

---

[343] Gülen, *Key Concepts in the Practice of Sufism*, xiv.

[344] Ibid., xiv.

[345] Loye Ashton Defending Religious Diversity and Tolerance in America Today: Lessons from Fethullah Gülen' the paper was presented at international conference entitled *Islam in the Contemporary World: The Fethullah Hizmet Movement in Thought and Practice* at Rice University, Houston, 12 November, 2005 accessed January 7, 2009.

[346] S. Yücel, personal communication.

[347] Zeki Sarıtoprak, 'Fethullah Gülen: A Sufi in His Own Way,' in *Turkish Islam and the Secular State: the Gülen Movement* (eds. Yavuz, M. H. Yavuz and John L. Esposito), 114.

to any Sufi order.'[348] Like al-Hujwiri (d. 1073)[349], a great Sufi master, Gülen says that the first step or key concept of Sufism is *tawba,* repentance. In order to achieve maturity, a person must purify himself or herself of all sins. After that, like many other Sufis, Gülen expresses a desire to gain the knowledge of *sharia*. He states: 'Sharia and Sufism are like two departments of a university, each seeking to teach their students the two dimensions of Islam so that the students can practice them in their lives. These two departments are not in opposition; rather they complement each other. One teaches how to pray, how to fast, and how to give charity, while the other concentrates on what these actions really mean.'[350] Although Gülen never proclaimed himself a sheikh or Sufi leader, the methodology he uses is similar to the methods used by individuals travelling along the Sufi path. Many great Sufis were trained in the *tekke*, the Sufi lodges, by serving others, cleaning latrines, and cooking.[351] During my visit, I observed Gülen's students doing the same acts as Sufi students.

Like great Sufi leaders in the past, Gülen often critiques his *nafs* (carnal soul) like Qushayri, weeps like al-Bistami (804–874), has tolerance towards others like Rumi, abandons the world by heart like Naqshi, and asks his followers to serve their community till death, like Al-Hujwiri (d. 1077) and Nursi. Gülen's criteria for accepting students are unlike those of the Sufi practice. He expects that his students will demonstrate a curiosity to learn, a desire to serve people, a degree of patience, and will practice basic Islamic principles. In order to join the study circle, a person must also know advanced Arabic; but this is not essential for being one of his followers. He does not practice a master-student relationship with his students. Yet he does ask his followers to live an ascetic lifestyle, *zuhd*, by fasting twice a week, eating less, sleeping fewer hours, praying supererogatory prayers, reading Qur'an, making *dua*, supplication, following a rigorous course of study, and making special *dhikr*, invocation of the names of God.

Gülen also places emphasis on the heart, *qalb*. By this term, he does not mean the physical organ, but the spiritual one: 'The heart that is the

---

[348] Sarıtoprak, 'Fethullah Gülen,' 115.

[349] Al-Hujwiri, Abd al-Hassan, a great Sufi and author of famous *Kashf al-Mahjub*.

[350] Gülen, *Key Concepts in the Practice of Sufism*, xx.

[351] Annemaria Schimmel, *Mystical Dimensions of Islam*, 101.

place of faith and the mirror of God'[352] He quotes from the *hadiths* of Prophet Muhammad, peace and blessings be upon him: 'God does not look at your appearance, but he looks at your heart' (*Sahih Muslim*). 'There is a part in the body that when it becomes good, the whole body becomes good, and when it becomes bad, the whole body becomes bad. That part is the heart' (*Sahih al-Bukhari*). As found in other Sufi teachings, it is said that if a person's heart is not clean, that person cannot live an ascetic lifestyle. He quotes from one of the great Sufis, Ibrahim Haqqi: 'The heart is the home of God; purify it from whatever is other than Him, so that the All-Merciful may descend into His palace at night.'[353] Gülen further states, 'A heart full of love of God cannot harbor enmity or hatred towards others.'[354]

While Gülen is far from establishing a Sufi order, his aim is to revive and combine the activism of Prophet Muhammad and his companions, the asceticism of the first generation Sufis, and the Sufi terminological knowledge and consciousness of the later Sufi scholars. At a time when the gap between Sufis and their major critics (Salafis) increase, Gülen's main goal is to re-establish Sufism (spiritual life of Islam) on the basis of the Qur'an and Sunna.

Characteristics of the Hizmet Movement

a. Gülen's works create a marriage between religion and science, tradition and modernity, by combining spirituality with intellectual training, reason with revelation, and mind with heart.[355] Gülen wanted to take the traditional form of Muslim educational discourse as practiced in the *madrasah*, traditional Islamic school and take it to the university format.[356] The principles of the Movement attempt not to recreate a golden past, but to revitalize modernity with traditional values. Gülen's aim is to educate a generation bred on spiritual wisdom, engaged in intellectual pursuits,

---

[352] Gülen, *Key Concepts in the Practice of Sufism*, 69.
[353] Ibid,, 22.
[354] Gülen, *İnsanın Özündeki Sevgi*, 36.
[355] Yavuz and Esposito, 2003:20.
[356] Atay, 'Reviving the Suffa Tradition,' in *Muslim World in Transition: Contributions of the Hizmet Movement* (eds. İhsan Yılmaz et al.), 459–472.

and committed to serve the whole of humanity. For Gülen, 'serving people is serving God.'[357] People means in this context is all human beings.

While other Muslim scholars have aimed to open more *madrasahs*, Gülen has inspired and encouraged his followers to open modern schools and universities, with focus on the sciences and languages. As a result, in Turkey and around the world, his followers have established many educational projects such as child-care centers, college preparation courses, and dormitories for students as well as hundreds of schools and colleges. There are two main priorities in the educational sector in the Gülen Movement: to instruct and lead students to be successful in secular subjects, and ensure that students' moral character reached high standards. While these moral values are based in both Islamic and humanitarian values, there are no major conflicts with modern values. In these institutions, the curriculum is secular, but the majority of teachers are chosen for their noble character. The moral aspects of education are conveyed through teachers' behavior, rather than proselytizing. Due to the unique combination of secular education and an emphasis on moral values, these institutions are thriving and gaining prestige.

The French newspaper *Le Monde Diplomatique* described the achievements of schools established by Gülen's followers in Germany, claiming that the schools could be taken as examples by other German schools for ethnic communities.[358] *New York Times* wrote about Gülen's followers' schools as a gentler vision of Islam and an alternative approach to education that could help reduce radicalism.[359] That these schools can gain approval with the conservative people of Pakistan by offering a different perspective from the fundamentalist *madrasahs* speaks volumes.

b. Another issue in relation to Hizmet activities is the finance. It is important to note that followers of the Gülen Movement contribute anywhere between 3–50% of their income to the Movement's activities in the sectors of education, media, and community gatherings. Among these are people who contribute beyond that amount, following the examples

---

[357] Aslandoğan 2007: 672, Y. Alp Aslandoğan, 'Present and Potential Impact of the Spiritual Tradition of Islam on Contemporary Muslims: From Ghazali to Gülen,' London, Leeds Metropolitan University International Conference Proceedings, 672.

[358] Wendy Kristianesen, 'New Faces of Islam,' July 1997.

[359] Sabrina Tavernise, 'Turkish Schools Offer Pakistan a Gentler Vision of Islam,' *New York Times*, May 4, 2008.

set by Prophet Muhammad and his Companions. In the Movement circles, this is called *himmet.*[360] The followers convene annually for *himmet* during Ramadan, review local, national, or international projects of the Movement, and pledge chosen amounts to sponsor those good works. A second *himmet* gathering is held solely for scholarship funds. Most importantly, Gülen leads this funding through example. According to İsmail Büyükçelebi, from the over 60 best-selling books Gülen has written, Gülen has donated almost 90% of his earnings from book sales to scholarship funds for these institutions established by his followers or for humanitarian aid. Gülen himself focus on generosity and so often encourages his followers to be more generous like companions of the Prophet.

c. Gülen strongly opposes and condemns any form of violence and terrorism. To him, 'A Muslim cannot be a terrorist and a terrorist cannot be a true Muslim because Islam forbids the killing of civilians, children, elders, women, and religious figures, even if your cause is justifiable.'[361] Gülen's influence can be seen in the fact that none of his followers or supporters has committed acts of terror or condoned terrorism in any form, despite oppression and provocation from opposite groups.

d. When extremists, whether they are left wing, right wing, religious or secularist, in Turkey generate conflict, Gülen acts to decrease tensions by expressing his respect for every law-abiding or kind-hearted person, regardless of religious and political views, and their nonviolent ideas. For example, when the issue of banning the wearing of a headscarf in educational institutions and public sectors created tension, Gülen encouraged opposing sides to come to a mutual agreement by insisting that the headscarf should not be a cause of conflict and division and advising people to seek their rights within the boundaries of the law. He also asks that this chronic problem not be exploited for political purposes; rather, it should be considered a human rights issue and solved accordingly. Gülen warns

---

[360] For further details of the movement's funding, see H.R. Ebaugh and D. Koç, 'Funding Gülen-Inspired Good Works: Demonstrating and Generating Commitment to the Movement,' London, Leeds Metropolitan University Internatioanl Conference Proceedings, 2007, 539–551. Thomas Michel, 'Fighting Poverty with Kimse Yok Mu,' Washington DC, Georgetown University Conference Proceedings, 523–533. M.N.Kirk, 'Seeds of Peace: Solidarity, Aid, and Education Shared by the Hizmet Movement in Southeastern Turkey,' Washington DC, Georgetown University Conference Proceedings, 407–434.

[361] Gülen, *Essays, Perspectives, Opinions*, 95.

that protests and any action taken to the streets will not help this cause. Protests only raise tension, especially in Turkey where democracy is still in its developing stages.

e. Being open to all faiths and traditions through dialogue is another characteristic that sets Gülen apart from some spiritual leaders. Since 1991, despite criticism from some religious, political, and media figures, Gülen initiated and participated in interfaith dialogue with Jewish rabbis as well as Greek Orthodox, Armenian, and Assyrian patriarchs, and he has encouraged his followers to do the same. In Turkey at that time, it was taboo for religious leaders to openly dialogue with these religious leaders and minority groups. He met with Pope John Paul II in 1998 at the Vatican. Once inspired by Gülen's acts of building bridges towards other faiths, Gülen's followers established interfaith and intercultural organizations throughout the world, with the U.S being home to 42 of these organizations.[362]

f. Unlike some religious leaders, Gülen has never opposed Turkey's entrance into the European Union (EU). He believes that Turkey's membership in the EU will contribute to world peace and help to prevent a 'clash of civilizations'. He perceives the West as a rival to compete with, not as an enemy to confront. He suggested that Turkey needs to increase its economic powers by incorporating Western economic and political systems.[363] Gülen's views regarding EU membership has influenced mainstream Turkish Muslims' views on that matter. According to European Union survey in July 2007, more than 54% of Turks are in favor of an EU membership.[364]

g. Since Gülen is a well-respected and admired spiritual leader, political parties seek his support, especially during elections. A majority of religious leaders and spiritual leaders directly or indirectly support political groups. Gülen, however, is an exception. He has never supported a specific party. However, he has praised the beneficial acts of political leaders or parties.

h. Gülen's important distinction as a leader is that he tries to maintain peaceful relations with the state or government, the military, media, and political, religious, and social groups. Sociologist Berna Turam, who

---

[362] Now it is over a hundred.

[363] Yavuz and Esposito, 2003:xxxii.

[364] *Hürriyet*, July 11, 2007.

studied the Hizmet Movement for ten years, mentions the principle of Gülen's followers, 'We are not going to fight, and we do not want conflict,' citing it as a reason for the Movement's success.[365] Gülen encourages his followers to respect and accept the differing opinions and beliefs of organizations and individuals. He said, 'Differences are a beautiful part of human nature and developed communities.'[366]

Gülen and His Movement in a Global Islamic Context

Gülen is a major figure in defining the contemporary global Islamic experience. He is a spiritual leader, philosopher, poet, and a thinker, not solely a preacher. His interpretation of Islam has attracted many religious leaders, intellectuals, and politicians in Turkey.[367] Although he is not as well-known as some Muslim leaders or intellectuals in the West, his community is one of the most influential, revivalist Islamic groups in modern Turkey.[368] His influence is not limited to religion. Indeed, he has had an impact on diverse fields including education, the media, business, and the financial sector.

By establishing moral, educational, secular, and humanitarian institutions in Turkey and in other parts of the world, Gülen exemplifies how Islam and modernity can coexist. These institutions have attracted Muslim and non-Muslim, as well as secular and liberal religious groups. The chief characteristic of Gülen's followers is that they do not seek to subvert modern secular states; rather, they encourage Muslims to use the opportunities offered.[369] Gülen sees science and faith as not only compatible but also complementary. He, therefore, encourages scientific research and technological advancement for the good of all humanity.[370] His spiritual Movement is a combination of modernity and traditional values and has contributed to a 'vernacularization of modernity,' redefining moder-

---

[365] Ruşen Çakır *'Gülen Cemaatin Sırları,'* Interview with Berna Turam, *Vatan Gazetesi*, 21 October, 2007.

[366] S. Yücel, personal communication.

[367] Ertuğrul Özkök, *Hürriyet*, March 17, 1993.

[368] Elizabeth Özdalga, 'Following in the Footsteps of Fethullah Gülen,' in *Turkish Islam and the Secular State: The Gülen Movement*, (eds. M. Hakan Yavuz and Esposito, John L.), 85.

[369] Gülen Inspires Muslims Worldwide; *Forbes*, Jan 21, 2008.

[370] Gülen, *Prophet Muhammad: The Infinite Light*, 160.

nity in Islamic terms. Gülen's ideas and actions introduce the possibility of being both modern and Muslim at the same time.[371]

In the last two decades, a new idea has emerged among some intellectuals in Turkey. John Voll observes that these intellectuals are neither fundamentalist nor secularist. For this group, Islam includes secularism and religion, two faces of the same coin.[372] If we have a world of increasing integration of the secular and religious, in a way parallel to the process of 'glocalization' (globalization and localization), the processes are creating a significant frame that is useful to recognize the picture of Fethullah Gülen in the arenas of religion, faith, and life at the beginning of twenty-first century.[373]

To him, modernity and the *sirat al-mustaqim*, the path followed by mainstream Muslims, are not two rivals, but the middle way of interpreting Islam, providing a balance between materialism and spirituality. Many scholars have commented on Gülen's moderate point of view. According to anthropologist Nilüfer Göle, Gülen shakes the dichotomist perception of modernity and Islam. He tries to end the Western monopoly of modernity, and aims to add an Islamic set of meanings to it. Göle emphasized that Gülen works to domesticate excessive rationalism with Sufism and love, and to reconcile individualism and humbleness.[374]

Gülen and Interfaith Dialogue

Gülen has emerged as one of the most persuasive and influential voices in the Muslim community calling for dialogue as a step toward peace. Indeed, he offers 'a way to live out Islamic values amidst the complex demands of modern societies and to engage in ongoing dialogue and cooperation with people of other religions.'[375] In his message at the Parliament

---

[371] Yavuz and Esposito, 2003:7.

[372] John Voll, 'Fethullah Gülen: Transcending Modernity in the New Islamic Discourse,' in *Turkish Islam and the Secular State: The Gülen Movement*, (eds. M. Hakan Yavuz and Esposito, John L.), 243.

[373] Voll, *Fethullah Gülen*, 244.

[374] Ahmet T. Kuru, 'Fethullah Gülen's Search for a Middle Way: Between Modernity and Muslim Tradition,' in *Turkish Islam and the Secular State: The Gülen Movement*, (eds. M. Hakan Yavuz and Esposito, John L.), 117.

[375] Douglas Pratt, 'Gülen's Prospects for Interreligious Dialogue, *Today's Zaman*, November 1, 2007.

of World's Religion Gülen wrote that dialogue with adherents of other religious traditions is an integral part of an Islamic ethic that has been long neglected.[376] Gülen believes that dialogue is among the duties of Muslims on earth in order to make the world a more peaceful place.[377] Michel states that Gülen promotes a cooperation of civilizations through dialogue, mutual understanding, and gathering around shared values.[378] Gülen's response to the clash of civilizations thesis consists of three parts encapsulated in the words: tolerance, interfaith, dialogue, and compassionate love.[379]

Criticisms

Most of Gülen's critics include radical politico-religious groups, some secularists, and *ulusalcılar*, ultra-nationalists. Though few in numbers, liberal and social democrats occasionally criticize Gülen as well. Radical religious groups claim that he compromises religion. Some secularists believe that Gülen intends to secretly gain control of the Turkish state. Nationalists view Gülen not as a patriot, but rather an as engineer behind the schemes of superpowers. In the following sections, we will examine these claims.

Criticisms of politico-religious groups

Politico-religious groups criticize Gülen on three fronts: (1) Gülen's not being against Turkey's EU membership, (2) Gülen's denunciation of Muslim suicide bombers, and (3) Gülen's interfaith activities as compromising Islam. Necmettin Erbakan, a leading religious-political figure since 1969 in Turkey, criticizes Gülen for not supporting his political party. Erbakan's perspectives were published and supported by a media group including Channel 5 TV, and the *Milli Gazete* and *Vakit* newspapers. After meeting with Pope John Paul II in February 1998, Gülen was harshly criticized by a group of Islamists who viewed this meeting as humiliating for going to the extent of travelling to the Vatican and meeting with the Pope.

---

[376] Gülen, 1999, 'The Necessity of Interfaith Dialogue,' www.fethullahGülen.org/about-fethullah-Gülen/messages/972–the-necessity-of-interfaith-dialogue-a-muslim-approach.html accessed January 6, 2009.

[377] Gülen, *Hoşgörü ve Diyalog İklimi* (eds. Selçuk Camcı and Kudret Ünal), 17.

[378] Thomas Michel, in *Towards a Global Civilization of Love and Tolerance*, i-iv.

[379] Richard Penaskovic, 'Fethullah Gülen's Response to the 'Clash of Civilizations' Thesis,' *Today's Zaman*, October 30, 2007.

Furthermore, Gülen was not a chosen representative of Islam or Turkey to engage in such dialogue.[380]

Gülen responded to critics by stating that humility was an attribute of Muslims. Hard-line secularists rebuked him, contending that authorization from the Ministry of Religious Affairs and the Turkish government was necessary.[381] He has also been criticized by radical Muslims for talking less about an 'Islamic State' than he does about a fly. Referring to this criticism, Ali Ünal, one of Gülen's associates, says, 'Yes, the Qur'an speaks of a fly, spider, and ant as evidences of His existence by their very creation, and names its chapters after them. Yet, it does not speak of an Islamic state.'[382]

Gülen was accused of being pro-American for not condemning America's biased Middle East policy. They also criticize him for condemning suicide bombings and not openly condemning Israeli occupation and infringement of human rights. Haydar Baş, a leader of a small religious community, and politician heading the Independent Turkey Party (BTP), a small party which attracted 0.51% votes of the election in 2007, insinuated that Gülen and his followers are 'bad representatives' of Islam who 'cater' to Jews and Christians.[383] Radical religious groups who are strongly anti-secular and some Sufi leaders claim that Gülen does not really oppose the secular state with his ideas and actions. This means that he is compromising religion with the secular and anti-religious groups. Some radical groups even accuse him of blasphemy. They view his interfaith activities as compromising instead of promoting religion.

Some Sufi leaders find fault with Gülen because he is not part of the *silsila* (a spiritual chain of a Sufi order), and, therefore, he cannot be a Sufi leader. It is traditionally known that *silsila* is one of the most important pillars of Sufism, according to the great Sufi leaders.[384] In response to this criticism, Gülen clearly stated through media groups that he is not

---

[380] Şevket Eygi, 'Papalıkla Gizli Anlaşma,' *Milli Gazete*, May 26, 2000.

[381] Necip Hablemitoğlu, '28 Şubat Kararları Sürecine Bir Katkı: Organize Suçlar ve Fethullahçılar,' *Yeni Hayat*, 52 (1999) 3.

[382] Şevket Eygi, *Milli Gazete*, May 26, 2000.

[383] Loye Ashton and Tamer Balcı, Tamer, 'A Contextual Analysis of the Supporters and Critics of the Gülen/Hizmet Movement,' Washington DC, Georgetown University conference proceedings, 105.

[384] Sayed Hossain Nasr, 1999:17.

the leader of a Sufi order, nor is he trying to form a Sufi order. As for not supporting religious parties, such as the Welfare Party (RP), and later on, the Saadet Party (SP), he states that in all parties, there are people who practice or respect their religion, and that partisanship would undermine Islam, especially in the politicized climate of Turkey. Gülen says: 'Religion is the relationship between people and their Creator. The feeling of religion lives in the heart's depths and on the inner world's emerald hills. If you turn it into a display of forms, you will kill it. Politicizing religion will harm religion before it harms a government's life.'[385] As a result of his open arm political views, he and his Movement gained followers and support from a range of political, social, and religious groups.

As for not strongly opposing the secular state or regime, Gülen says that he follows Said Nursi's approach. According to Nursi, since we are living in the modern age, a modern method of persuasion should be used to convince people.[386] Rebelling against the secular regime would cause the death of innocent people, especially Muslims. Nursi asserts that the worst state is better than the lack of any state because the lack of government brings about anarchy.

After the establishment of the Fethullah Gülen Chair in the Study of Islam and Muslim-Catholic Relations at the Australian Catholic University in Melbourne in 2007, Paul Stenhouse, editor of *Annals Australia*, suggested in the *Quadrant Magazine* that Gülen was using the chair and inter-religious dialogue as Trojan horse to achieve his goal of Islamic supremacy. Monash University professor Greg Barton, who has also made a special study of Gülen, dismissed Father Stenhouse's objections, saying that the article was poorly written and 'not particularly well-argued.' He argued against Stenhouse's emphasis on militant behavior of Sufi Muslims in his article, saying that 'For the most part, Sufis are accommodationists rather than confrontational.'[387]

In the face of these severe criticisms, Gülen continues to promote interreligious and intercultural dialogue, asserting that 'Civilized people solve their problems through dialogue'[388]

---

[385] Ünal and Williams, *Advocate of Dialogue,* 36.
[386] Şükran Vahide, *Bediüzzaman Said Nursi,* 101.
[387] Jill Rowbotham, 'Catholic Hits Islamic Chair,' *The Australian,* January 16, 2008.
[388] Gülen, 'The Necessity of Dialogue,' www.fgulen.org, accessed January 20, 2008.

Criticisms of Ulusalcılar (Ultranationalists)

Like some politico-religious groups, the *ulusalcılar* accuse Gülen of unpatriotic and disloyal to Turkey due to his views regarding Turkey's application for EU membership and lack of support towards national parties, such as the Nationalist Movement Party (MHP). Moreover, Gülen does not give his Turkish identity priority in his public and private speeches, sermons, and books, and his openness towards minorities in Turkey is met by skepticism by ultranationalists.

There were also claims from both politico-religious groups and *ulusalcılar* that the Hizmet Movement was receiving funding from foreign agencies, such as the CIA, Saudi Arabia, Mossad, and the Vatican and that Gülen was the mastermind behind a project designed by the US to destroy the Kemalist ideology of nationalism and independence of Turkey.[389] Just as some nationalists praise Gülen for his promotion of education, others criticize his followers for the use of English as an academic language, even though most of the Movement's schools incorporate a Turkish as a second language (TSL) program and hire Turkish-speaking teachers. In response to these views, Gülen says that globalization has made the world into a village. Turkey is either a part of the global village or an isolated country like the communist nations. Therefore, acquiring the language of the global village is essential. As for the political claims, Gülen states that a specific party cannot claim to be the sole representative of a nation and religiousness and that there are patriots and religious individuals in every party.[390] As for his tolerance and dialogue with minorities, Gülen says that these minorities are citizens of Turkey and that the majority needs to respect the rights of minorities.

In terms of funding the educational institutions, Gülen states that the financial source is generosity of the people of Turkey and not any abroad sources. Fuller delves into the topic of funding for the Hizmet Movement's schools and other projects, pointing out the extensive network formed through the hundreds of schools of the Movement, and states that 'funding comes from within the community, and wealthy

---

[389] L.E. Webb, 'Fethullah Gülen: Is there more to him than meets the eye?,' 46–49.
[390] Ünal and Williams, *Advocate of Dialogue*, 36.

businessman for whom building a school has become a modern pious equivalent of building a mosque.'[391]

Criticisms of Leftists

Those who are most critical and noticeable of Gülen's actions are those of the far left-wing, a mix of ex-communists, Maoists, atheists. The strength of this group comes from their active presence in the field of print and broadcast media and advertising. Representing this group in the mainstream media is the *Cumhuriyet* newspaper (right-wing groups in Turkey call it the Turkish *Pravda*). Hikmet Çetinkaya, who has compiled and published his newspaper columns in a book, has been criticizing Gülen since the 1970s.

Radical leftists claim that Gülen is a leader of a religious cult, something forbidden in Turkey since the establishment of the Turkish Republic. They accuse Gülen of secretly trying to control the state and abolish the secular regime and establish a theocracy instead. To achieve his goal, Gülen establishes schools, dormitories, college preparation courses, and other educational institutions all over the world and gets positive coverage in the Turkish media. In addition, he is secretly encouraging his followers to penetrate the military, the judicial system, law enforcement, and the business world. Secularists claim that by opening schools in Russia, Central Asia, the Caucasus, and the Balkans, Gülen is attempting to build a 'Green Belt' around secular Turkey.[392] On numerous occasions, Gülen has publicly asked his closest friends to be nonpartisans, and not to join the government or any parties. In his last interview with Mehmet Gündem for the secular newspaper *Milliyet*, Gülen advised his followers: 'As for the Movement; neither now, nor in the future should our friends have any ambition for government; they should not be engaged in politics, even if all the power and pomp of the world is laid at their feet; my friends who love me and heed my advice should not show a moment's hesitation to push all this away with the back of their hand.'[393]

---

[391] Graham Fuller, *The New Turkish Republic: Turkey as a Pivotal State in the Muslim World*, 57.

[392] Thomas Michel, 'Fethullah Gülen as Educator,' in *Turkish Islam and the Secular State: The Gülen Movement*, (eds. M. Hakan Yavuz and Esposito, John L.), 78.

[393] Mehmet Gündem, *Milliyet*, January 29, 2005.

In 2000, Gülen was sued by state prosecutors for establishing an illegal organization whose objective was to overthrow the secular government and replace it with one based on religious law. The case was finally dismissed in 2006, and further appeals were dismissed by the General Council of the Supreme Court of Appeals on January 24, 2008.[394] Furthermore, they maintain that America wants to establish a soft Islamic regime in Turkey through the Gülen Movement. In response to these accusations, Gülen notes that the schools established by his followers employ the program and the curriculum of the Turkish Ministry of Education. He notes further that the schools are inspected continually, not only by the ministry, but also by intelligence agencies in foreign countries where the schools have been established.[395] From time to time, officials in all sectors of the state, government, law enforcement, and possibly the military, have been known to praise the schools and the perspectives of Gülen. Despite these accusations, former Prime Minister and leader of the Democratic Left Party (DSP) Bülent Ecevit rejected the leftist claims and defended Gülen, his Movement, and his educational institutions, openly in public. Gülen further states that the educational institutions, media groups, businesses, and financial organizations do not belong to him as it is claimed; rather those who respect his ideas and philosophy have established them.

Conclusion

In the last three decades, especially after the collapse of the Soviet Union, religion and religious and spiritual leaders have been the focus of a great deal of public scrutiny. Gülen and his followers are among the most discussed and debated because they are becoming stronger and more influential in Turkey and abroad. According to Yavuz, this gradual strengthening will continue.[396] Despite the criticism and attempts by the opposition to reduce Gülen's influence and his followers' activities, many supports and appreciate the activities of Gülen and his followers by marrying secular educational institutions with religious ethics, Gülen has developed a model of being modern and religious at the same time.[397]

---

[394] Ashton and Balcı, 2008:113.
[395] Michel, 'Fethullah Gülen as Educator,' 69.
[396] Yavuz and Esposito, 2003:3
[397] Ibid., 20.

According to the principles of Sufism, Gülen has not formed a Sufi order. Although the spiritual network has many of the characteristics of a Sufi orders, Sufism for Gülen is not a way of rejecting the world; rather, it is a way of empowering the believer with spiritual tools and good character to help him or her shape and control the world.[398] From spiritual point of view, Gülen is a Sufi but he is unlike other Sufi leaders. As Zeki Sarıtoprak states 'He is a Sufi in his own way'[399] Gülen's way is rooted in traditional Islam with Sufi interpretation in combination with modernity and contemporary intellectualism, which includes Western philosophy that is compatible with Islamic thought. Anthropologists are still asking two important questions: How is Gülen going to use his power and influence in the future, and what kind of transformation will happen after his death? Although there are various predictions, and often his critics express their fears, only time will give us the right answers. Gülen may follow the destiny of al-Ghazali, Rumi or Ibn Khaldun (1332–1406), three of Islam's greatest and influential scholars or spiritual leaders, who had also been criticized in their respective times, but are now well recognized and praised for their ideas, philosophy and works.

---

[398] Ibid., 34.
[399] Sarıtoprak, 'Fethullah Gülen,' 169.

Istighna and *Ithar*: Two Forgotten Principles of *Da'wah* from the Perspective of the Hizmet Movement

Salih Yücel
Monash University, Australia

Introduction

The world is in need of Islam and Islam is in need of representation (*tamthil/temsil* in Turkish). People's ears are full but their eyes are hungry for role models[400] in all areas of life including *da'wah*. *Istighna* and *ithar* are two important but forgotten principles of *da'wah*. *Da'wah* is a form of worship undertaken for the sake of Allah alone, and its reward is to be expected in the Hereafter.[401] To expect any form of reward in this world can harm sincerity and open the path to lesser *shirk*. Verily Allah does not accept people holding any partners to Him in all deeds, including *da'wah*. While the word *da'wah* means 'to call' or 'to invite,' the best form of *da'wah* is living by the religion and values that one espouses. *Da'wah* through action comes before *da'wah* through words. As Khurshid Ahmad said, '*Da'wah* is presented primarily through conveying the message, preaching you may call it, and by practicing it and as such presenting before the world its living example.'[402] Muhammad Sami' Allah defines *da'i* as the ideal person,[403] while Nayeefa Chowdhury defines a *da'i*

---

[400] Gülen, *Prizma-6*, 64.

[401] Nursi, *The Flashes* (trans. Şükran Vahide), 218.

[402] Khurshid Ahmad, 'Christian Mission and Islamic Da'wa,' *Proceedings of the Chambesy Dialogue Consultation*, 44.

[403] Malik, 'Islamic Mission and Call: The Case of the International Islamic University, Islamabad,' in *Islam and Christian-Muslim Relations*, 31–45.

as a role model.[404] Whether ideal or a role model, the *da'i*'s profile must include the practice of *istighna* and *ithar*.

As two pillars of *da'wah*, *istighna* and *ithar* are components of Prophetic character, as well as significant practices of the companions of all Prophets, saints (*awliya*) and great leaders in Islamic history. Well-known examples include Umar ibn Abd al-Aziz (682–720), Tariq ibn Ziyad (689–720), Salah al-Din Ayyubi, Imam al-Ghazali, Abd al-Qadir Jilani, Mawlana Jalaluddin Rumi,[405] as well as Ottoman rulers from the founder Osman Ghazi (1258–1324) to Suleyman the Magnificent (1594–1566).[406] All of these leaders had a simple life, gave away or shared what they received as gifts or spoils of war, and did not leave any inheritance.[407]

These pillars set *da'wah* apart from proselytization. Without these two pillars, *da'wah* can be perceived as an act of self-interest. Indeed in the West, *da'wah* has been perceived as the equivalent of missionary work.[408] Such perceptions harm *da'wah* because of the reputation of missionaries, whose activities were often followed by colonization. Julian Pettifer and Richard Bradley refer to missionaries as 'the pioneers of imperialism'.[409] A famous quote by Archbishop Desmond Tutu sums it up in the following way: 'When the missionaries came to Africa, they had the Bible and we had the land. They said 'let us close our eyes and pray.' When we opened them, we had the Bible, and they had the land.'[410] Even if this is not applicable to all missionary activities, it nevertheless represents a considerable majority of it. To perceive *da'wah* as missionary

[404] Nayeefa Chowdhury, 'Presenting Islam: The Role of Australia-Based Muslim Student Associations,' in *Journal of Muslim Minority Affairs*, 205–224.

[405] For detailed information see Ebu'l-Hasan En-Nedvi, *İslam Önderleri Tarihi*, I, 453, www.darulkitap.com/oku/tarih/islamonderleri/indexaan.htm (retrieved on January 8, 2011).

[406] Gülen, *Prizma-1*, 81.

[407] Ibid.

[408] For detailed information look at: Thomas W. Arnold, *The Preaching of Islam: A History of the Propagation of the Muslim Faith*; Egdunas Racius , *The Multiple Nature of the Islamic Da'wa*, 1–8; David A. Kerr, 'Islamic Da'wa and Christian Mission: Towards A Comparative Analysis,' in *International Review of Mission*, 150–171; Mark N. Swanson, 'On the Teaching of Islam at Luther Seminary,' in *Teaching Theology & Religion*, 172–175; Jane Ellingwood, 'The Programme for Christian-Muslim Relations in Africa (PROCMURA): An Evolutionary Perspective,' in *The Muslim World*, 72–94.

[409] Julian Pettifer, Richard Bradley, *The Missionaries*.

[410] Steven Gish, *Desmond Tutu: A Biography*, 101.

work devalues it. Moreover, some Muslims also defined it as missionary work and misused the word. As it has been dragged far from its original meaning, that word can not be used to describe the activities of the Hizmet Movement. Gulen's understanding and application of *da'wah* is not like that of reactionary Muslim groups who established *da'wah* centres for proselytizing.

It is important to note that while some missionaries gained power and land, their success in that area was also due to the practical contribution they made to the communities they were preaching to. Their establishment of educational institutions and hospitals and provision of humanitarian aid factor into their accomplishments. Yusuf Ali and Abu Sadat Nurullah point out such contributions when mentioning the success of missionaries in Bangladesh over the last 80 years.[411] This is one factor that is lacking in many faith based works today.

In this article, I will explore the concept of *istighna* and *ithar* in the Qur'an and Sunnah and explain why these two pillars are necessary for success in faith based activities. I will also focus on practical solutions by giving examples from the Hizmet Movement, also known in the West as the Gülen Movement.[412]

The notions of *istighna* and *ithar*

Istighna

Istighna is to serve the cause of Islam by all means without any expectations for reward, whether material, social, or otherwise. This means sacrificing one's resources, including time, money, abilities, and networks for serving humanity. In return, a Muslim is to desire Allah's pleasure alone. Wanting financial return and hoping for a political, religious, spiritual or

---

[411] Yusuf Ali-Abu Sadat Nurullah, 'Challenges of Islamic Da'wah in Bangladesh: The Christian Missions and Their Evangelization,' *Journal of the International Islamic University*, 87–108.

[412] Gülen himself never had the personal wealth to be able to sponsor projects. Gülen was so poor that for a number of years he lived in a corner of a local mosque with barely enough space to lie down. In addition to never having had any personal wealth, he prayed for his relatives to remain poor so as not to raise any suspicion of him gaining from his influence. He is the author of more than 65 books. For more information see his official website: fgulen.com.

social position is contrary to *istighna*. Desiring respect for the acts done, or receiving a special title such as *efendi, ustad, alim,* master, or *pir* will weaken the sincerity in serving religion. Even expecting not to fall into difficulties, experience loss and suffering, or receive criticism is against the principles of *istighna*.[413] The best role models in *da'wah,* such as the Prophets and their companions, dealt with danger, sorrow, exile, imprisonment, persecution, torture, and death. Yet in spite of this, they continued to invite others to Islam because their sole purpose was to earn Allah's pleasure. They did not seek to perpetuate a pious image of themselves or to gain a higher worldly status.

Istighna in the Qur'an

There are 12 verses which state that the Prophets refrained from asking for rewards from those to whom they made *da'wah*. Ayahs 10:72, 11:29 and 26:109 refer to Prophet Noah; 11:51 and 26:127 refer to Prophet Hud; 26:145 refers to Salih; 26:164 refers to Prophet Lot; 26:180 refers to Prophet Shuayb; 36:20 refers to two unnamed Prophets or disciples of Prophet Jesus; 6: 90, 34:47 and 12:104 refer to Prophet Muhammad saying 'I do not ask any reward for it'. Prominent Qur'anic exegetes unanimously draw from these verses that reward or return must not be sought or expected when making *tabligh*. According to Tabari (838–923)[414] and Ibn Kathir (1301–1373)[415], *tabligh* is a duty, so a benefit must not be sought. Zamakhshari elaborates on this, saying that the Prophets sought neither personal gain, nor any elevated social status or position, and never desired anything else that would place them above others.[416] From this he concludes that Muslims must follow their examples. Fakhr al-Din al-Razi (1149–1209) goes further, asserting that a person should not even desire a reward by the heart.[417] Qushayri (986–1074) adds that when making *da'wah*, refraining from asking for anything is the *sunnah* of the Prophets and a major principle of all (Companions and) saints.[418]

[413] Gülen, İrsad Ekseni, 67.
[414] al-Tabari, Jami al-Bayan.
[415] Ibn Kathir, Tafsir al-Qur'an al-Karim.
[416] Zamakhshari, Al-Kashaaf.
[417] Fahraddin Razi, Tafsir al-Kabir.
[418] al-Qushayri, Lata'if al-Isharat bi Tafsir al-Qur'an.

The Qur'an and the Sunnah encourage believers to give. Even though they were poor, the Companions were hesitant and did not ask for charity (2:273). In his commentary of the verses mentioned above, Nursi states that if *da'wah*, which he calls *khidhmati imaniyya wa Qur'aniyya* (service to the faith and the Qur'an), is undertaken with the aim of material advantages, it will slowly destroy sincerity and lead to detrimental results.[419] Moreover, he states that this world is the realm of wisdom and the realm of service; it is not the realm of reward and recompense. The wage for deeds and acts of service done here is given in the Intermediate Realm and the Hereafter. Since the reality is this, the results of actions pertaining to the Hereafter should not be sought in this world. If they are given, they should be received not gratefully, but regretfully.[420]

Nursi believed that sincerity is a condition for success in service to the faith, and *istighna* is necessary for sincerity. Nursi lived by his principles. Outside of a few instances, he did not accept gifts, even though he knew it was Sunnah. The accepting of gifts in the Sunnah refers to the exchanging of gifts by two parties. His reasons reflect his *istighna*:

The First: The people of misguidance accuse religious scholars of making their learning a means of subsistence... It is necessary to show this to be false by action.

The Second: Muslim scholars are charged with following the Prophets in disseminating the truth. In the All-Wise Qur'an, those who do this say, 'My reward is only due from Allah' (10:72)[421].

The Third: ...one should give in Allah's name and take in Allah's name. Whereas mostly either the one giving is heedless and gives in his own name and implicitly puts the other under an obligation, or the one who receives is heedless; he leaves the thanks and praise due to the True Provider to apparent causes and is in error.

---

[419] Nursi, *The Flashes*, 218.
[420] Nursi, *The Letters* (trans. Şükran Vahide), 528–529.
[421] Translation of Qur'anic verses are taken the website: www.usc.edu/schools/college/crcc/engagement/resources/texts/muslim/quran.

The Fourth: Reliance on God, contentment, and frugality are such a treasury and wealth that they can be exchanged for nothing.

The Fifth: ... Accepting the people's gifts necessitates considering their feelings and accepting them at times I do not want to... I find it more agreeable to eat a small piece of dry bread and wear clothes patched in a hundred places, and be saved from artificiality and sycophancy.

The Sixth: And the most important reason for self-sufficiency is what Ibn Hajar (1373–1448)... says, 'If you are not righteous it is forbidden to accept something intended for the righteous.'[422]

Istighna in the Sunnah

Prophet Muhammad (pbuh) lived by the principle of *istighna*. Despite remaining hungry for days, he would not ask others for food and other needs.[423] He would sleep on a thin straw mat. Omar ibn al-Khattab saw that it left marks of the Prophet's back and cried, 'When the kings of the Persians and Romans live in palaces, can't you at least have a bed?' The Prophet replied, 'O Omar! Would not you desire that this world be theirs and the next world be ours?'[424] His life of poverty was not due to a lack of support. However, when he would receive a gift or charity, he would give it away to the poor and needy. One night during the final days of his life, he could not sleep. He asked his wife Aisha if there was money in the house. She replied that someone who owed them money brought seven dinars not long ago. The Prophet requested that it be given out

---

[422] Nursi, *The Letters*, 32–33.

[423] All hadiths from six authentic books in this article are taken from the website: www.usc.edu/schools/college/crcc/engagement/resources/texts/muslim/hadith/. Hadith narrated by Aisha, that she said to Urwa, 'O, the son of my sister! We used to see three crescents in two months, and no fire used to be made in the houses of Allah's Messenger (i.e. nothing used to be cooked).' 'Urwa said, 'What used to sustain you?' 'Aisha said, 'The two black things i.e. dates and water, except that Allah's Apostle had neighbors from the Ansar who had some she-camels, and they used to give the Prophet some milk from their house, and he used to make us drink it' (*Sahih al-Bukhari*).

[424] Ibn Hanbal, cited in Fetullah Gülen, *The Messenger of God: Muhammad*, 37.

right away, which Aisha did.[425] He said, 'The upper (giving) hand is better than the lower (receiving) hand'.[426]

Abu Said al-Khudri narrated that some Madinan people asked for (something) from Allah's Messenger and he gave to them. They again asked him for (something) and he again gave to them. And then they asked him and he gave to them again till all that he had was finished. And then he said 'If I had anything, I would not keep it away from you. (Remember) Whoever abstains from asking others, Allah will make him contented, and whoever tries to make himself self-sufficient, Allah will make self-sufficient. And whoever remains patient, Allah will make patient. Nobody can be given a better and greater blessing than patience'.[427]

One final example is from his household. Fatima, his beloved daughter, was suffering fatigue and severe blisters from carrying water from the well and had calloused hands. Upon her husband's request, she asked her father for a servant. The Prophet explained that he could not meet her needs when his companions were still in need themselves. He recommended something better: remembrance of Allah.[428]

Ithar

Ithar refers to the act of giving preference to others over oneself. It is defined by moralists as seeking benefit for the community before thinking about one's own needs. Sufis express this concept using the term tafani. Said Nursi defines this as 'annihilation in the [Muslim] brother'. This means that a person forgets the feelings of his own carnal soul and lives as part of a collective personality, a jama'ah, and ultimately, the Ummah. In that way, each person is like a bodily organ working together and not harming one another. Just as the hand does not harm the eye,

---

[425] Ibn Sa'd, Tabaqat, II, 237–238; Ahmad b. Hanbal, Musnad, VI, 104. Cited in Asım Köksal, İslam Tarihi, www.darulkitap.com/oku/tarih/islamtarihi/islamtarihiasim/indexana.htm, (retrieved on December 24, 2010).

[426] www.usc.edu/schools/college/crcc/engagement/resources/texts/muslim/hadith/ bukhari/076.sbt.html#008.076.448 (retrieved on December 24, 2010).

[427] Sahih al-Bukhari.

[428] www.usc.edu/schools/college/crcc/engagement/resources/texts/ muslim/hadith/muslim/035.smt.html#035.6580 (retrieved on December 27, 2010).

but protects and cleans it, the believers protect and support each other.[429] Other Sufis define *ithar* as preferring the lives and happiness of others over one's own. A person who conducts *da'wah* strives for the well-being and comfort of the community.[430] The opposite of *ithar* is *shuhh* which gives birth to miserliness and self-interest. These distance a person from Allah, the community, and ultimately, Paradise. According to Fethullah Gülen, there are degrees of *ithar* depending on the level and quality of the representation of Islam:

- To look after others while neglecting oneself, such as feeding others while remaining hungry. Observing the rights of all humans and being careful not to tread on any person's rights. This raises a person to a state of perfection.
- Despite everything, to use all bounties, including time, money, health, and personal abilities, only to earn Allah's pleasure, and then to keep these acts to oneself, or even forget the acts so as to remain humble. This degree is above the first.
- The third degree is the highest level of devotion to the community. Gülen points to the sacrifice of Prophet Muhammad during the Ascension. The Prophet had entered paradise and came close to the Divine Presence, but returned to the world to save his *ummah* from Hell and to take his *ummah* to Paradise. This state is a type of annihilation of one's self.[431]

Ithar in the Qur'an and Sunnah

As was mentioned above, *ithar* was an atribute of the *ashab* (the Companions). The Qur'an mentioned this as follows: 'And those who made their abode in the city and in the faith before them love those who have fled to them, and do not find in their hearts a need of what they are given, and prefer (them) before themselves though poverty may afflict them, and whoever is preserved from the niggardliness of his soul, these are the successful ones' (59:9). Tabari commented on this verse referring to the

---

[429] Nursi, *The Flashes*, 216–217. A hadith states: 'The example of the believers in their affection and compassion and benevolence is like the body; if one part of it becomes ill the whole body comes to its aid with fever and sleeplessness' (Bukhari and Muslim).
[430] Gülen, *Sızıntı*, 16–192, 1995, 1–2.
[431] Ibid., 3.

Ansar who shared everything they owned with the Muhajirin (immigrants), preferring their Makkan brothers' well-being over themselves.[432] Qurtubi referred to the incident of Abu Talha and his guest. A poor man came to the mosque in Madina and told the Prophet that he had not eaten for three days. Prophet Muhammad (pbuh) asked his wives one by one if there was anything to offer this man at home. They stated they had nothing. Then the Prophet asked his companions. Abu Talha took up the offer and invited the man to his house. Abu Talha's wife whispered that there was only enough food for one person. Abu Talha told his wife to turn out the light and bring the food. In the darkness, Abu Talha and his wife made it seem like they were eating while the guest ate until the food was finished. For early morning prayer the next day, the Prophet asked, 'What did you do that Allah praised you?' Then he recited the verse above.[433]

During the Battle of Yarmuk, Harith ibn Hisham, Ikrimah ibn Abu Jahl, and Ayyash ibn Abu Rabi'ah were severely wounded and were lying on the ground. Harith asked for water. One of the soldiers brought water. Harith noticed that Ikrimah was looking at him because he was in need of water. Harith said, 'Give the water to Ikrimah'. The soldier took the water to Ikrimah, who noticed Ayyash asking for water, and said, 'Give the water to Ayyash.' The soldier went to Ayyash, but he had already passed away. The soldier returned to Ikrimah, who had also passed. He finally went to Harith who had passed away too.[434] Just like the Prophet, many companions and great leaders in Islamic history would receive many gifts, spoils of war, as well as an income, but they would prefer others over themselves and give these things to others straight away, keeping either a small amount for their needs or none at all. There are numerous examples from the Prophet and the Companions' lives, but due to the limitations of this article, they will not be further explored.

Nursi refers to this level of *ithar* as the peak and views it as a precondition for sincerity. He does not limit the giving of only material items, but continues saying, 'choose your brothers' souls to your own soul in honor, rank, acclaim, in the things your soul enjoys like material bene-

[432] al-Tabari, *Jami al-Bayan*.
[433] al- Qurtubi, *Al-Jamiu li-Ahkam al-Qur'an*.
[434] Ali al-Muttaqi al-Hindi, *Kanzu'l-Ummal*, V, 310; Hakim, *Mustadrak*, III, 242, cited in Muhammed Yusuf Kandehlevi, *Hayatu's-Sahabe*, 1–313.

fits. Even in the most innocent, harmless benefits like informing a needy believer about one of the subtle, fine truths of belief. If possible, encourage one of your companions who do not want to, inform him, so that your soul does not become conceited. If you have a desire like 'Let me tell him this pleasant matter so I will gain the reward,' it surely is not a sin and there is no harm in it, but the meaning of sincerity between you could be damaged.'[435]

It may seem contradictory that, on one hand, there is a lot of emphasis on *istighna* and *ithar*, and on the other hand, financial sources are necessary for ongoing faith-related projects. If people who work for such projects do not seek worldly or financial gain, it raises the question of how they will sustain a living, especially if they devote themselves to it full time. Muslims in different communities and groups have addressed this issue in various ways. I will focus on one of the more successful global movements, the Hizmet Movement, also known in the West as the Gülen Movement. The full-time devotees to community projects receive a salary, but are expected to work overtime or volunteer. This can be anywhere from 5–40 hours a week, depending on the person, and include weekends and holidays. This altruism increases the trust of the community towards the employees in the Movement, which in turn increases the power of the employees to influence others.[436]

The Hizmet Movement as a role model

The Hizmet Movement has established over 2000 schools[437], more than 3,000 tutoring centers and student dormitories in over 150 countries, and over a dozen universities. They are developing the largest Islamic banking institution in Turkey (Bank Asya). Other institutions include TUSKON (Confederation of Businessmen and Industrialists of Turkey) with 53,000 members.[438] They have branched into mass media with the Turkish *Zaman* Newspaper, now published daily in Turkey, Europe, the USA and weekly in eight other countries with a readership of over one

[435] Nursi, *The Flashes*, 216.
[436] Salih Yücel, 'Spiritual Role Models in Gülen's Educational Philosophy,' *Tawarikh, International Journal for Historical Studies,* 65–76.
[437] Cüneyt Özdemir, 5N 1K Programı, 'Gülen Cemaatinin Para Kaynağı Ne?' Interview with Helen Rose Ebaugh, *CNN Turk,* cited in *Milliyet,* 13.01.2011.
[438] Elif Çakır, *Star,* 21.7. 2013.

million in distribution. They have set up five television channels: Samanyolu TV, STV Haber (news), Mehtap TV, all broadcasting in Turkey, and Ebru TV in the US. The Movement also owns Cihan News Agency (CHA) and numerous radio stations. Alongside all of these are several publishing companies which publish in more than 40 languages. There are also humanitarian aid organizations (Kimse Yok Mu), interfaith and intercultural associations, and other civil organizations. While the numbers are not known, this Movement is estimated to employ tens of thousands and grants scholarships to hundreds of thousands of students.

Three reasons for the financial stability of the Movement are the annual *himmet* (fund-raising), the large numbers of volunteers, and the self-sustaining character of its institutions. *Himmet*[439] is the name used for the fund-raising gatherings of the local community. It is translated as spiritual 'aspiration' or 'resolve'.[440] The theological aspect of *himmet*, according to Gülen, includes the more practical religious virtues and duties of beneficence such as *infaq* (charity), *sadaqa* (voluntary almsgiving), and *zakat* (obligatory almsgiving).[441] It is often done during Ramadan, but the foundations are laid throughout the year, during which those in charge reach out to people and business owners, build relationships and emphasise the importance of giving and sacrifice for the well-being of the community. The organizers of these meetings present the past achievements and future goals or projects of the community, and appeal to the spiritual sentiments of the participants to collect funds. The

---

[439] For further information on the *himmet*, refer to Helen R. Ebaugh, *The Hizmet Movement: A Sociological Analysis of a Civic Movement Rooted in Moderate Islam*; Helen Rose Ebaugh and Doğan Koç. 'Funding Gülen-Inspired Good Works: Demonstrating and Generating Commitment to the Movement,' *Muslim World in Transition: Contributions of The Hizmet Movement Conference Proceedings, 2007*, 545–547; Orhan Özgüç, 'Islamic Himmah and Christian Charity: An Attempt at Inter-Faith Dialogue,' in proceedings of the conference, *Islam in the Age of Global Challenges: Alternative Perspectives of the Hizmet Movement*, Georgetown University, 2008, 561–582, available at en.fgulen.com/conference-papers/gulen-conference-in-washington-dc/3102–islamic-himmah-and-christian-charity-an-attempt-at-inter-faith-dialogue (retrieved on January 2,2011); Selçuk Uygur, 'Islamic Puritanism as a Source of Economic Development: Contributions of the Hizmet Movement,' 2007, 176–97.

[440] Özgüç, 2008:561–582.

[441] Ibid.

participants are those within the Movement and the Movement's supporters. Everyone present at the *himmet*, from local affluent business owners to scholarship students, pledge to make donations for the cause. Donations range from 3–50% of an individual's annual income.[442] The collected funds are used for local projects.

Support of *Hizmet* ventures is sustained by generous giving by businessmen associated with the Movement who understand it to be their 'calling' to work hard and produce wealth that can be used for the work of the Movement. These businessmen, whose numbers rank in the thousands, typically donate 10 to 70 percent of their annual income.[443] They belong to local *sohbet* communities with whom they meet on a weekly basis for encouragement, fellowship, devotional studies and philanthropic planning (*istishara*), led by senior members serving as trustees (*mutawalli*), and in their personal commitment (*himmet*) they enjoy remarkable social capital and a sense of purpose.[444] Most importantly, Gülen leads this funding through example. According to İsmail Büyükçelebi, one of Gülen's closest companions for almost forty years, from among the over 65 best-selling books Gülen has written, Gülen has donated almost 90% of his earnings from book sales to scholarship funds for the institutions established by his followers or for humanitarian aid. Gülen himself focuses on generosity, and thereby often encourages his followers to be more generous like companions of the Prophet. Gülen himself lives a very simple life and possesses no more than his books and clothes. Those who are close to him and hold significant responsibility in the Movement follow in his footsteps. They do not own homes or earn more than what they can live on.[445]

The second factor which contributes to financial stability is the great number of people who volunteer for the Movement. The spirit of volunteerism is strong within the Movement, as it is preferred not to receive anything in return. Volunteer hours can range from 4–30 hours per week. People volunteer using their skills (such as construction, mentoring, tutoring) or take part in unskilled work for the projects. The third factor is the

---

[442] Ibid.

[443] Uygur, 2007.

[444] Greg Barton, 'Islam, Dialogue and the Hizmet Movement in Australia,' 114–143.

[445] Salih Yücel, 'Fethullah Gülen: A Spiritual Leader in a Global Islamic Context,' in *Journal of Religion and Society*.

self-sustaining model of these projects. Projects are designed to become economically independent within a few years. For example, a school is first established with community funds. Teachers and volunteers put forth great efforts, mostly overtime, during the first few years to set a high standard of quality education and attain academic excellence with few resources. With academic success, the school can attract more students, including those from affluent backgrounds, and increase tuition. In time, the school makes a profit and expands it services with more campuses and academic opportunities.

The fact that Gülen-inspired projects are always locally based and embedded in local circles of supporters locates authority and decision-making within a structure of horizontal relationships, rather than in a vertical, bureaucratic hierarchy. Being responsible for projects, not only financially but in terms of planning, decision making and accountability, is also a powerful force in involving people in the Movement. From an interview by Helen R. Ebaugh with twelve businessmen within the Movement, one 48 year old businessman in İstanbul said, 'People in the Hizmet Movement turn their ideas into projects, [and] they tell how they accomplished their success. People trust them, if they ask for a project, they expect it from the Creator, not from creatures, and that's why I believe they reach success. If anybody from the Movement comes to my city and asks for help, I try my best to help them and I encourage my friends around me to do the same.'[446]

The transparency of the Movement's income has been controversial, particularly the funding of Gülen-inspired schools, and since the 1970s has continued to be viewed with suspicion and misunderstanding.[447] Gülen opponents, including fanatical secularists, the ultra nationalists, some leftists and even some religious groups claim that the Hizmet Movement receives funding from foreign agencies, such as the CIA, Saudi Arabia, Mossad, and the Vatican, and that Fethullah Gülen was the mas-

---

[446] Ebaugh and Koç, 2007.

[447] Çemen Polat, on the function of Gülen-inspired educational initiatives as business enterprises in the philanthropic fashion, 'The significance of education for the future: The Gülen model of education,' in *International Conference Proceedings*, The State Islamic University, Jakarta, available online www.fethullahgulenchair.com/index. php?option=com_content&view=article&id=666:dr-cemen-polat&catid =75:conference-papers&Itemid=255.

termind behind a project designed by the U.S. to destroy the Kemalist ideology of nationalism and independence of Turkey.[448] In terms of funding educational institutions, Gülen rejects such claims and states that the Movement's financial resources stem from the generosity of the people of Turkey. He says: 'These schools are the fruits of the Anatolian people's hearts that show altruism, which they showed in the Independence War, in a different manner today but the source is their hearts.'[449] Graham Fuller delves into the topic of funding for the Hizmet Movement's schools and other projects, pointing out the extensive network formed through the hundreds of schools of the Movement, and states that 'funding comes from within the community, and wealthy businessman for whom building a school has become a modern pious equivalent of building a mosque.' [450]

Conclusion

A *da'i* is a person who has a passion for sustaining others' happiness even if he or she suffers in the process and works so that others are in peace and security in all aspects. By applying the principles of *istighna* and *ithar*, the *da'i* seeks Allah's pleasure alone. If this is not the case, some Muslims and non-Muslims will interpret the *da'wah* efforts as acts of self-interest. In today's world, the philosophy of serving one's own interests is widespread. This is a key difference between Islamic civilization and contemporary materialistic civilization. According to Nursi, the aim of materialistic philosophy is 'benefit,' whereas the aim of Islam is 'virtue and God's pleasure'. [451]

This aim is further understood with the emphasis placed by the Qur'an and Sunnah on the virtue of giving, especially its preference over receiving and preferring oneself. This giving is not limited to material terms alone, but extends to all aspects of life. A Muslim must give his or her time, energy, knowledge, skills, and other things for the well-being of the local community, *Ummah*, and humanity. *Istighna* and *ithar* are so important that all great Muslim leaders and their close associates saw it

---

[448] Webb, 'Fethullah Gülen: Is There More to Him Than Meets the Eye?' 46–49.

[449] Gülen, 'Değirmenin Suyu,' www.herkul.org/bamteli/index.php?article_id=1646.

[450] Graham Fuller, *The New Turkish Republic: Turkey as a Pivotal State in the Muslim World*, 57.

[451] Nursi, *The Words* (trans. by Şükran Vahide), 421.

as being imperative to practice those principles. Historically, whenever the leader of the Muslims and those who made da'wah followed these principles, they effectively influenced others, conquered people's minds and hearts, and attained success in their endeavors. Great civilizations began with community-minded leaders and people who followed some or all aspects of *istighna* and *ithar*.

Da'wah can only be successful if it follows these principles adapted to the modern world. While the Muslim world is unsuccessful in this regard, it cannot be said that it is strong in regards to giving and managing funds and volunteers. However, with the current atmosphere of revivalism in many Muslim countries, there is good progress that gives hope. Movements and *jama'ats* can learn from each other's experiences. Having studied the Hizmet Movement, other movements can benefit from the Hizmet Movement's model because it has grown exponentially and attracted many supporters. It has adapted Islamic principles, including *istighna* and *ithar* in *da'wah*, to the contemporary world. Gülen began in the 1970s teaching a single Qur'an course with around 30 students. Now the Movement has expanded enormously to include thousands of institutions and organizations with millions of followers, students, volunteers, and supporters. One of the leading factors for its success is the *istighna* and *ithar* practiced by Gülen and leaders in the Movement throughout the world. When *dai's* do not apply *istighna* and *ithar* principles, then self-interest and pride may take hold and blur their priorities. This, in turn, will lead to internal conflicts, disunity in the *jama'at* or community, and the recession of Allah's favour of them from the Qur'anic (8:46) perspective.

A Muslim Perspective on the Ethical Dimension of Life in Relation to Its Beginnings and End: With Special References to the Writings of Fethullah Gülen[452]

İsmail Albayrak
Australian Catholic University/Sakarya University

Introduction

This article discusses certain topics relating to the sacred nature of life as viewed from a Muslim perspective. Among these, abortion and euthanasia, which have been made subjects of lively and intense debate by both religious and secular groups, will be given priority. Our discussion draws attention to some of the differences found within Muslim approaches: while in the West these topics are considered in the framework of bioethics, in Islamic traditions their context is that of, modern medicine, jurisprudence and morality together. Although some theological differences separate the two traditions, it is hoped that this article will help Muslim scholars actively engage with other religious communities in the area of biomedical ethics, and work collectively and coherently for a common goal, helping create awareness within the wider community of their care and sensitivity with respect to issues of life and death. Limitations of space prevent a thorough examination of the voluminous literature produced by scholars of both religions on the

---

[452] This article published in *Journal of Islamic Quarterly,* 57/2 (2013) 85–116. I would like to thank the editor of the Journal for his kind permission for the republication of this article.

many aspects of this complex area. Therefore this article concentrates on the relevant works of Fethullah Gülen, a contemporary Turkish Muslim scholar.

The Concepts of Life and Death in Islam

I would like to begin with a quotation from Bediüzzaman Said Nursi's epistle *Risale-i Nur*. Nursi says 'The greatest Divine gift, bounty, kindness or favour is not making His servant perceive or feel His benevolence.'[453] In my view, of all the countless gifts of God, life is the most unique and the most precious, which we do not value greatly during our daily activities. Its preciousness and importance seem obvious; but theologically speaking, its significance is that 'life' is, first and foremost, one of the most prominent personal attributes of God, *al-Hayy* (Ever-Living) and *al-Muhyi* (Giver of life). The attribute of life has a priority and superiority over other Attributes of God because those other attributes such as His Power, Knowledge and Will cannot be imagined without the existence of life.[454] The Qur'an frequently draws our attention to this fact with these words *allahu la ilaha illa huwa al-hayy al-qayyum* 'Allah, there is no deity but He,—the Living, the Self-subsisting, Eternal.' (2:255) or *wa-tawakkal ala al-hayy alladhi la-yamut* 'And put thy trust in Him Who lives and dies not'. Thus a Muslim considers life as the most important aim of the universe, its greatest result, its most brilliant light, its subtlest leaven, its distilled essence, its most perfect fruit and the source of its perfections.[455]

To stress the importance of life, Nursi makes striking comparisons between the gigantic and inanimate and the tiny and animate. He asks us to contemplate on the following metaphor: a lifeless object, even if it is a great mountain, is an orphan, a stranger, and alone. Its only relation is with the place in which it is situated, and with the things which encounter it. Whatever else there is in the cosmos, it does not exist for the mountain. The mountain has neither life through which it might be related to life, nor consciousness by which it might be concerned. Nursi contrasts

---

[453] In another place, Nursi says: "Yes, an important Divine bounty is not making the person who has given up his egotism perceive the bounty so that he does not become proud and conceited" (Bediüzzaman Said Nursi, *Şualar*, 317).

[454] Nursi says "body (or existence) without life is the same as non-existence, *'adam.*" See Nursi, *Lemaat* (Simplified by Abdullah Aymaz), 42.

[455] Bediüzzaman Said Nursi, *Lem'alar*, 506–507.

the mountain with a tiny living creature, a bee. Its life establishes such a connection with the universe that it is as though the insect concludes a trading agreement with it, specifically with the flowers and plants of the earth. It can say 'The earth is my garden; it is my trading house.' Thus, through the unconscious instinctive senses which impel and stimulate the bee, in addition to the well-known five external senses and inner senses of animate beings, the bee has a feeling for, and a familiarity and reciprocal relationship with, most of the species in the world, and they are at its disposal.[456]

Since life is the comprehensive attribute of God, Islam places great stress on the value of life. Briefly, the bodies of all creatures including human beings are God's creation, but after fashioning the human body from clay, God breathed His own spirit into the body to distinguish humanity from other created beings (15:29, 32:9, and 38:72). This Divine spirit transforms an inanimate human body into a living being having a spirit or soul. Muslim scholars make it very clear that the body (the material aspect of a human being) exists and fully functions together with its spirit, *ruh*; therefore the human body is an important instrument that serves the development of a person's spiritual being. Hence the spirit is neither part of the body nor completely independent of it. Gülen describes the connection between body and spirit in the context of the human being's relation to two realms, namely the seen and unseen worlds. To put it another way: he states that the material aspect of human beings intimately connects them to the other living things around them whereas the spiritual side places them within the Angelic community.[457] Nevertheless, because a Muslim acknowledges the hand of God in all creation, animate or inanimate, His role as the sole life-giver to His best creation makes the human body and soul a complete trust (*amanah*) of the Divine. The proper attitude of human beings towards this trust is a very well-established notion

---

[456] Bediüzzaman Said Nursi, *Sözler*, 679–680.

[457] There is also a metaphorical dimension of life which both Nursi and Gülen point to in their writings. The Qur'an explains this metaphor with its own words: 'Can he who was dead, to whom We gave life, and a light whereby he can walk amongst men, be like him who is in the depths of darkness, from which he can never come out? Thus to those without faith their own deeds seem pleasing' (6:122). In the light of this verse, Nursi and Gülen hold the view that a person can be alive physically, but dead spiritually or emotionally; similarly, a person can be intellectually brilliant but amoral, so their life should be regarded as of little significance.

in Islam: the human being is only a caretaker or steward; the real owner is God. As caretakers, we have to be very sensitive and aware in regard to protecting both our physical and spiritual life. The notion that we own our life and are free to do with it whatever we please is an alien concept in Islam.[458] This sensibility is rooted in the Islamic notion of the sanctity (*hurmah*) and dignity (*karamah*) of the human body, a cornerstone of Islamic legal-moral thinking.[459] In short, Islamic theology tends to see human dignity as residing in the believer's relationship to God, a position which is quite different to the modern secular approach to the definition of human dignity.

Understanding the very essence of human life depends on the recognition of the interaction between the ephemeral physical substance and an eternal spiritual entity that departs.[460] Contemplating this relationship brings the notion of death to the fore. Besides being the Ever-Living and Giver of life, God also has the attribute of taking life, *al-mumit*, or causing death.[461] Several verses in the Qur'an (80:16–23) touch on God's intimate involvement with His creations at the beginning of life and emphasize His interaction with them at every moment up to the end of time; from life to death and resurrection. Here it is important to note that the determination of lifespan is one of God's essential qualities.[462] In Islamic theology, there are various stages of the human soul's existence, which Nursi calls an 'exile' or 'journey'. Each successive stage is longer than the previous one. This long journey passes from the world of spirits (*'alam al-arwah*) through the world (life in the womb, then from birth until death) and then the grave (the intermediate realm, *barzakh*) to the resurrection, a new life in the hereafter.[463]

---

[458] Abdulaziz Sachedina, *Islamic Biomedical Ethics*, 2009, 167–168.

[459] Birgit Krawietz, 'Brain Death and Islamic Traditions: Shifting Borders of Life,' *Islamic Ethics of Life: Abortion, War and Euthanasia*, (ed. Jonathan E. Brockopp), 2003, 194.

[460] Sachedina, 2009:150.

[461] "God gives life and he makes it die," "a person dies when it is written." "Then He shall gather you to the resurrection." (3:156, 3:185, 29:57, 39:42)

[462] A number of Qur'anic verses clearly state that God determines a fixed span of life for every person (Jonathan E. Brockopp, 'The 'Good Death' in Islamic Theology and Law,' in *Islamic Ethics of Life: Abortion, War and Euthanasia*, (ed. Jonathan E. Brockopp), 189.

[463] Nursi, *Sözler*, 36; Krawietz, 2003:199.

The Qur'an's representation of various death themes directs the attention of humanity to the purpose of death, which is always seen as being intimately interconnected with creation and resurrection.[464] Because of this, the Qur'an criticizes unbelieving Arabs who say 'There is nothing but our present life; we die and we live and nothing but time destroys us,' referring to their opinions as mere conjecture and ignorance (45:23). Life is the key to death; it is a preparation for the return to God, while death is the gate or the entrance to eternal life. In this sense, death is never seen as extinction in Islam; rather, it is viewed as an altered state of being.[465] Nursi summarizes this point very well in the interpretation of the verse (67:2) 'Who creates death and life that He may try you, which of you is the best in conduct.' He says: 'This verse makes it understood that, like life, death too is created, and it too is a bounty.' Those who see death as dissolution, non-existence, decay, the extinction of life and the annihilator of pleasures might ask how death could be created and also serve as a bounty. To answer this question, Nursi states:

Death is a discharge from the duties of life, it is a rest, a change of residence, a change of existence; it is an invitation to an eternal life, a beginning, the introduction to an immortal life. Just as life comes into the world through a creation and a determining, so too departure from the world is through a creation and determining, through a wise and purposeful direction. As the death of the seed is the start of the life of the shoot, since it is like life itself, this death is as created and well ordered as life is. Similarly, as a seed sown in the ground becomes a tree in the world of the air, so too a man who is laid in the earth will surely produce the shoots of an everlasting life in the hereafter.[466]

To summarize: since life is the most important bounty and fruit of the universe, and its purpose is creation, then certainly that elevated reality is not restricted to this fleeting, brief, deficient, painful worldly life. The aim and result of worldly life is eternal life in the hereafter; it is life in the realm of bliss, the very stones, trees, and earth of which are alive.[467] The eternity of the spirit is clear evidence of life after resurrection.

---

[464] Sachedina, 2009:146.
[465] Ibid.
[466] Nursi, *Mektubat,* 348–349.
[467] Nursi, *Lem'alar,* 518–519.

Legal-Moral Dilemma

Islamic thought regards ethics as concerning first and foremost the assessment or evaluation of a certain act. This differs from many other philosophical systems where ethics is essentially seen in regard to the constitution of an act. Because of the centrality of law in Islam, Muslim societies and cultures are perhaps best understood through it; I would argue that regarding the moral-ethical issues facing Islamic societies, it is difficult to reach any decision without a full knowledge of Islamic juris-prudence. In other words, law and morality cannot be treated as sepa-rate entities in Islam, where ethics constitute the very foundation of law (*sharia*) and every question of law is also a matter of ethics. Hence many questions today revolve around the topics of abortion, stem cell research, cloning, genetic modification, *in vitro* fertilization, surrogate motherhood, any form of transplantation, environmental protection and even inter-faith relations. For Muslims these are not essentially theological issues but fundamental questions of religious law.[468] When Gülen places great emphasis on dialogue, and declares 'Interfaith dialogue is a must,'[469] many people think that he is merely expressing his goodwill and heartfelt wishes. In fact, his words are clear juristic statements whereby he insists on the reli-gious nature of dialogue meetings, because the basic Islamic sources advise Muslims to engage in dialogue with representatives of other faiths.

Nonetheless, the centrality of law does not mean that Islamic gover-nance is a theocratic system. Muslim societies can be best described as nomocratic (ruled by law) in nature; in other words, in mainstream Sunni Islam there is no well-established religious hierarchy, organized church or ordained clergy with the authority to determine the validity of any reli-gious practice[470] (Shi'ites are somewhat different in this regard). The ques-tion thus arises, who is qualified to speak on behalf of Islam and Muslims? Furthermore, what are the major sources of Islamic jurisprudence? Final-ly, how do the jurists derive legal and ethical norms from the Muslim sourc-es and what ensures the validity of their legal-ethical decisions?

---

[468] Umar F. Abd-Allah, 'Theological Dimension of Islamic Law,' *The Cambridge Companion to Classical Islamic Theology*, (ed. Tim Winter), 2008, 237.
[469] en.fgulen.com/press-room/news/737–gulen-interfaith-dialogue-is-a-must
[470] Abd-Allah, 2008:237.

In general, Sunni jurists are required to provide solutions to every new problem that emerges within society. This juristic law took casuistic form, thus it is not subject to a universally constraining code enforced by a sovereign. Although it embraces the notion of legal majority, it is unusual for jurists to speak with one voice on particular issues. This pluralism allows Islamic law to recognize the validity of different interpretations in the same revealed system. The coexistence of four Sunni schools and the Ja'farite (Shi'ite) school is clear evidence of this pluralism.

Although Islam gives authority first to the jurists, then to the medical doctors, the rapidly changing aspect of biomedical cases makes intelligent ethical decisions difficult unless one first understands the medical procedures themselves. Because of the complex nature of these issues, many Muslim scholars today think that sound legal and ethical reasoning on such matters poses challenges that go beyond the capacity of any individual jurist. Yet, pioneering views can be found in Gülen's work. Since the early 1970s Gülen has argued continuously that the ideal solution would be to create a committee whose membership comprised jurists, medical doctors and scientists under the auspices of a High Religious Presidency to formulate their decision as a collective body.[471] For Gülen, the judgment of an individual jurist has never led to more than a certain probability (*zann ghalib*); however, the committee's collective decision would have the status of a binding opinion. Interestingly enough, in the last two decades we have witnessed great efforts to bring prominent Muslim scholars and physicians together to find convincing solutions to these issues. In relation to our second question, it is safe to say that Mus-

---

[471] Ahmet Kurucan, *Gülen's response to legal questions in 1970s,* 13. Kurucan checked all of Gülen's answers to questions from the 1970s to the present and selected legal responses and legal interpretations. (He is still working on the project.) Gülen comments: "If one day a committee is formed within the Religious Affairs Directorate, and it looks at these matters in detail, both from a medical and a religious point of view, then there will be no other views as to the statements made by individuals on these matters.' Elsewhere Gülen states: 'Twenty or thirty scientists or experts come together and make some statements on matters where Muslims are indecisive. They will say that is that and settle it once and for all'; and 'My only wish in the future is that I hope there will be a perfect committee set up and that they will resolve the matters in which we are indecisive. So that we can say this is the fatwa on this matter. All of the statements we make today are sporadic and are nothing more than personal opinion." (Kurucan, 13, 89).

lims have very well-established categories of sources. The primary sources of Islamic law in descending order of importance are as follows:

- the Qur'an
- the Sunnah of the Prophet (Prophetic tradition)
- *ijma'* (the consensus of jurists by acceptance of the community)
- *qiyas* (the analogical reasoning or exhaustive effort of scholars to find Divine intent in new cases or situations in the light of the norms of the Qur'an and Sunnah)

A number of other pragmatic instruments of jurisprudence have been developed by jurists, such as *istihsan* (juristic preference or equitable discretion), *maṣlaha mursala* (general necessity, law for common good, public interest, or general welfare of humanity), *sadd dhara'i* (preclusion), *'urf* (customary conventions of the people so long as these do not contradict revealed teachings).

It is important to note here that the Qur'an is an unalterable text which is not a simple book of law; it contains only a few hundred verses giving believers clear directives on ethics, rituals and law. As a rule, Muslim jurists considered strictly ritual matters to be beyond the purview of reason; non-ritualistic matters by contrast were seen as accessible to reason, and such matters constitute the greater part of the law. To put it another way, there are many issues concerning which the Qur'an does not make a definite or final statement or judgment. In addition, the Qur'an is not concerned to set forth theories of ethics, but it clearly prescribes moral standards by means of commands, recommendations, permissions, discouragements and prohibitions. Thus every category of act whether classified as incumbent (*farḍ* or *wajib*), recommended (*mandub*), permitted (*mubah*), disapproved (*makruh*) and forbidden (*haram*) in Islam, has been founded upon explicit or implicit rules in the Qur'an or Prophetic traditions. This system clearly shows the richness of the Islamic ethical system, because the value of every human action is morally prescribed.[472]

---

[472] These five standards can be further classified into three categories based on their degree of goodness or badness: the good things to be done are categorized under two levels: obligatory (*wajib*) and recommended (*mandub*). The bad things to be avoided are also categorizes under two levels: prohibition (*haram*) and discouragement/dislike (*makruh*). The third category is given a neutral level, which is the permissible (*mubah*). (Ibrahim Shogar, 'Ethical Discourse in the Qur'an: An Analytical Study of the Term *huda* in Izutsu's Conceptualization,' in *Japanese*

In order to ensure the validity of juridical decisions in the absence of clear Qur'anic or Prophetic textual evidence, Muslim jurists strive to develop general principles and stratagems based on various rational and ethically sound opinions. These principles mainly place equal stress on the importance of the individual and care for the welfare of the community.[473] Some of the most frequently mentioned principles are as follows:

- Efforts to promote the general good; removal of obstructions to that good.
- Necessity overrides prohibition, or necessity makes the unlawful permissible so long as it does not lead to any detriment.
- Efforts either to secure a benefit or prevent harm.
- The greater evil should be warded off by the lesser evil, or the lesser of two plausible.
- No harm, no harassment.
- Judgment of the action depends on the actor's intention.
- Removal of harm/evil is has a priority over attracting the benefits.
- Custom determines the course of action.

These principles allow jurists to utilize them as an authoritative basis for deducing a fresh and universal legal-moral ruling. Gülen frequently uses these principles as reference sources and they form the basis of his detailed juristic explanations. For example, he addresses the issue of blood transfusions, noting that the Qur'an and Prophetic traditions contain no direct rulings and that no discussion on this matter were held during the time of the companions and also by following generations, although in classical works the buying and selling of blood are prohibited on the basis of the practice being unclean and having no benefit. In addition, Gülen points out that since the formative period of Islam there has been a very well-established view among jurists that it is prohibited to use any organ of the human body. Nevertheless, Gülen argues that today blood transfusion constitutes a new phenomenon and problem. People know very well that the practice can be beneficial and even life-saving, therefore it is now permissible. Jurists, Gülen included, have reached this conclusion

Contribution to Islamic Studies: The Legacy of Toshihiko Izutsu Interpreted (ed. Anis Malik Thoha), 198–199).

[473] Donna Lee Bowen, 'Contemporary Muslim Ethics of Abortion,' in *Islamic Ethics of Life: Abortion, War and Euthanasia*, 2003, 61.

by reference to the second of the principles outlined above: necessity makes the unlawful permissible so long as it does not lead to any detriment. Gülen uses this principle frequently. It is also important to note that it is possible to justify the permission of blood transfusions by referencing the Qur'an, which regards saving human life as a fundamental human duty. Gülen argues that to save the life of a sick person blood should be given, with the conditions that during the process of transfusion only the necessary amount of blood should be transfused and there should be no monetary transaction between the donor and receiver.[474] Thus it is clear that modification of legal judgments will not be denounced in Islam so long as they reflect changing times, places and circumstances. In short, change concerning *maṣlaha* (wellbeing of the wider society) necessitates that rulings be changed.

Nevertheless, the new rules derived from the principles mentioned above should be in harmony and correlation with the *maqaṣid al-shariʿa* or *maqaṣid al-khamsa* (objectives, ends or ultimate goals of Islam), namely preservation of religion, life, intellect/reason, children/lineage and property. Briefly, Islam covers all human actions, whether towards other persons or towards God (Islamic law divides legal obligations into two categories, the rights of God and the rights of humanity); the realization of these ultimate goals is the main purpose of the right of God in this world. Having discussed the ethical foundation of Islamic jurisprudence in the light of Gülen's understanding, we will now consider two important ethical issues connected with the value of human life, namely abortion and euthanasia.

---

[474] Kurucan, 89–90. Gülen also gives another example in relation to the notion of necessity: 'There need to be studies carried out on the body so that autopsies, organ transplants and medicine in general can advance so that young doctors can develop. ...In all these cases there should be as many as are necessary. For instance, if needs are fulfilled by five students working on one body, it would not be permissible for each of them to work on a separate body, otherwise there would be no difference between these students and *nabbash* (grave robbers) who severely damage the bodies of the dead. This is because necessity makes that which is illegal acceptable, but only in as much as the amount needed.' (Kurucan, 31). Elsewhere, Gülen states that if it is possible to learn by using artificial materials, that method should be preferred. (Kurucan, 367). Nevertheless, these are his views pronounced forty years ago, there is some possibility that he might change his view in today's world.

Abortion

First of all, it is safe to say that there is no absolutist view in Islam regarding abortion; Muslims never argue either that all abortion is unjust killing or that abortion is always permissible.[475] Though Muslim scholars never promote abortion, the existence of different perspectives allows them to recognize abortion as a necessary practice up until a certain stage of pregnancy under certain conditions. But today, many consider that the great number of abortions has become a serious problem; the statistics indicate that abortion is now a very common practice, despite the fact that in almost all religious traditions abortion is regarded as an illegal act with no exceptions. Şahin Aksoy notes that it is very difficult to discuss the moral acceptability of something which has become so widely practiced throughout the world. At least 50.000.000 abortions are carried out annually worldwide.[476]

Before discussing Gülen's analysis, it is necessary to attend to important questions such as: What is abortion? Is abortion allowed in Islam and if it is allowed what kind of abortions are allowed? Who makes the decision? Abortion is normally defined as the artificial termination of pregnancy. When such a termination occurs naturally it is called a miscarriage.[477]

---

[475] For a similar stand see the article on the Jewish approach to the notion of abortion (Gordon D. Newby, 'House Health Care Bill Discriminates Against Religious Freedom,' *www.religiondispatches.org/archive/2034/house_health_care_bill_discriminates_against_religious_freedom* (December 14, 2011).

[476] Şahin Aksoy, 'Prenatal Diagnosis: Watching Unborn Babies,' (1998), www.fountainmagazine.com/article.php?ARTICLEID=608; Şahin Aksoy, 'Abortion: Mercy or Murder,' (1997), www.fountainmagazine.com/article.php?ARTICLEID=250. It is noted that every year worldwide, 35 women out of 1000 who conceive a child have an induced abortion. Some Muslim countries such as Turkey, Tunisia and Iran have legalized social abortion (abortion for reasons other than the health of the mother) during the first trimester of pregnancy. The rates of abortion in 1996 were 20% in Turkey and 7.8 % in Tunisia. Although Iran belongs to the Shiite school of thought and abortion is prohibited before 120 days, they revised the ruling and have allowed abortion with the permission of two doctors. It should be noted that the abortion rates in Iran are quite high. (See Brown, 2007:53–54, 59).

[477] Alan Brown, 'Christianity,' in *Ethical Issues in Six Religious Traditions* (eds. Peggy Morgan-Clive A. Lawton), 248. Abortion is the intentional expulsion of the fetus from the womb, whereas miscarriage is any untimely delivery brought about unintentionally to cause the death of the fetus before its due term for natural birth (Aksoy,

Although in Arabic many words are used to describe different types of abortion, jurists generally use the word *ijhaḍ*, which denotes a miscarried fetus discharged from the womb before completing the nine-month period of gestation.[478] Jurists are mainly concerned with accidental loss, or miscarriage deliberately inflicted by the wrongful act of a mother, father or a third person because there are incidents narrated in many authentic hadith collections that tell how the Prophet dealt with wrongfully caused miscarriages. Generally, whether or not there is intent, Islamic law punishes those who are responsible for the death of a fetus by imposing a fine of blood money.[479] It is also important to note that because

1997; Brown, 2007:61). The Arabic word for fetus (*janin*) means 'concealed' (derived from *janna*; plurals *ajinna* and *ajunn*). As it is hidden in the mother's womb until it is born, it has no independent claim to a life. When a mother gives birth, *janin* becomes *walad* (Müsfir b. Ali b. Muhammed Kahtani, 'İslam Hukukuna Göre Anne Rahminde Sakat Olan Çocukların Kürtaj Yoluyla Düşürülemesinin Hükmü,' *C.Ü İlahiyat Fakültesi Dergisi*, (tr. Abdullah Kahraman), 2008, 442, 455; Sachedina, 2009:129).

[478] Besides *ijhaḍ* (strictly, abortion before the ensoulment, first trimester), there are also *isqaṭ* (elimination: miscarriage between the fourth and seventh months), *ṭarh* (expulsion), *ilqa* (caused to throw: before 7 months), *imlaṣ* (cause to slip). For instance, when the camel gives birth before its due time, the Arabs say *ajhadat al-naqatu ijhaḍan* (Kahtani, 2008:457; Sachedina, 2009:129).

[479] According to one report, two women (co-wives) were fighting, and suddenly one of them struck the other, who was pregnant, with a tent pole, killing both the woman and her unborn baby. The Prophet made the relatives of the perpetrator responsible for the payment of blood money (*diyah*) on the deceased woman's behalf, and fixed a slave or a female slave as the indemnity, payment known as *ghurra* (Ahmad b. Hanbal, *Musnad*, www.al-islam.com, XXXVII.92 (hadith no: 17436). There are various other traditions which deal with this issue. In one report narrated by Abu Hurayrah, two women from the tribe of Hudhayl had a fight in which one of them threw a stone at the other's belly and caused her to have a miscarriage. See Bukhari, *Sahih*, www.al-islam.com, XXI.220 (hadith no: 6399); Muslim, *Sahih*, www.al-islam.com, IX.40 (hadith no: 3185). Both fines seem to have been imposed on the kin of the offender. One of her male relatives objected: 'How can we pay blood money for someone who neither ate nor drank, nor made any noise...'. There is another anecdote from the time of the second caliph, 'Umar b. Khattab: 'A woman massaged (*masahat*) the belly of another woman, and she miscarried. The case was presented to the second caliph and he ordered the practitioner rather than the pregnant woman to pay. In another incident, a pregnant woman took medicine (*sharibat al-dawa*) and miscarried. Ibrahim al-Nakhai says 'She must free a slave and pay a ghurra to the father'. (Some Shafi'ite and

the Qur'an and hadiths provide textual evidence in support of the gradual transformation of the fetus from biological being to human being, the debates about ensoulment play a crucial role in the discussion of abortion. Although some Muslim scholars maintain that ensoulment occurs at the time of conception,[480] the majority disagrees and approaches the issue from various perspectives.

Hanbalite scholars agree with Nakhai and say *kaffarah* (expiation) is obligatory, whereas Hanafites and Malikites hold it to be an optional act of devotion (*taqarrub*) since the fetus is not unqualified as a human life.) The fetus is qualified to have certain rights as a human in some respect to others in matters such as liberating a slave, inheritance, leaving behind a last will, etc. The fetus has some material and immaterial rights. Material rights relate to *mirath* (inheritance), *wasiyyah* (bequest), *shuf'ah* (pre-emptive rights), *hibah* (donation), and *waqf* (endowment). The value of the *ghurra* is conveniently set at one twentieth of the full blood money; 50 dinar or 500 dirham in the Hanafite school. The *ghurra* belongs to the fetus and is inherited by its kin. The *ghurra* in some ways resembles blood money for the death of a human being, while in others it parallels the compensation paid for the loss of body parts such as fingers and teeth. According to Ibn Hazm, a fetus receives its soul 120 days after conception. After ensoulment, the fetus is alive; before ensoulment, it is not a separate life at all, but is part of its mother. Within the 120 days before ensoulment the' *ghurra* goes exclusively to the woman herself. The minority view held by Hanafites states that it goes to the father. If a woman aborts with her husband's permission, no *ghurra* is due. If a woman aborts without permission of her husband, she must pay *ghurra* and consequently loses her right of inheritance from the fetus. But it is important to note that the fetus (*janin*) should be *mustabin al-khilqah,* i.e. his or her organs are visible. Where the abortion is in question, some modern Muslims say that the judge can punish the person who causes the miscarriage with imprisonment from 6 months to 2 years. If the fetus is a twin, two *ghurras* are paid. There are some historical anecdotes that during the late Ottoman period, two Jewish nurses used to give their pregnant patients some kind of medicine to abort their fetus, and because of this they were deported from İstanbul to Thessalonica. (For details see Therisa Rogers, 'The Islamic Ethics of Abortion in the Traditional Islamic Sources,' *The Muslim World,* 127; Marion Holmes Katz, 'The Problems of Abortion in Classical Sunni *fiqh,*' in *Islamic Ethics of Life: Abortion, War and Euthanasia*, 2003, 28–31; Belkıs Konan, 'Osmanlı Devleti'nde Çocuk Düşürme Suçu,' *Ankara Üniversitesi Hukuk Fakültesi Dergisi,* 327; Mustafa Öztürk, 'Osmanlı Döneminde Iskat-ı Ceninin Yeri ve Hükmü,' *Fırat Üniversitesi Dergisi,* 202).

[480] For instance, Ghazali says '...destruction of the fetus has different degrees. The first degree of existence is when the semen falls into the womb, mixes with the woman's semen and becomes ready to receive life. Spoiling this is an offense. When it becomes a clump and a blood clot the offense is more serious (*kanat al-jinayah*

We will now discuss in some detail how Gülen addresses the issue of abortion. Gülen begins by saying that many bio-ethical questions relating to life and death are not dealt with by the Qur'an and Sunnah directly. There were no such problems during the *takawwun* (formative) and *tadawwun* (compilation of the early juristic works and collections) periods of Islam.[481] Like many Muslim jurists, Gülen begins his argument by stating that the Qur'anic prohibition of killing children is analogous to the prohibition of abortion (6:137, 151, 17:3, 60:31).[482] However, classical scholars[483] do not generally understand that these verses refer directly to intentional abortion. The verses mainly deal with life's sanctity and dignity. Nevertheless, it is important to note that the Qur'an associates

---

afhash). When the spirit is breathed into the fetus and the form is completed (*istawat al-khilqa*), the offense becomes even more serious. The utmost degree of seriousness in the offense is after the child is born alive (Ghazali, *Ihya Ulum al-Din*, www.alwarraq.com, I.402). There is a similar view in the Maliki school (and shared by some Shafi'ites, Ibadites and Imamiyya) that the fetus is ensouled at the moment of conception. The notions of *bi al-quwwah* (potential human beings) and *bi al-fi'l* (actual human beings) play a significant role in the identification of the stages of development of the fetus. (See Bowen, 2003:56–57; Vardit Rispler-Chaim, 'The Right Not to Be Born: Abortion of the Disadvantaged Fetus in Contemporary Fatwas,' *Islamic Ethics of Life: Abortion, War and Euthanasia*, (ed) Jonathan E. Brockopp, Columbia: The University of South Carolina Press 2003, 88). Ibn Qayyim al-Jawdhiyyah says that the fetus before ensoulment is fed like a plant but after that it starts feeling, moving and feeding wilfully (Ibn Qayyim al-Jawdhiyyah, *al-Tibyan fi Aqsam al-Qur'an*, Beirut: Dar al-Ma'rifah 1983, 351). Gülen also refers to this potentiality from time to time in his remarks on abortion.

[481] Kurucan, 89.

[482] 'Do not kill your children for fear of poverty; We provide sustenance for you and for them (6:151); The Qur'an condemns the pre-Islamic practice of female infanticide 'when the infant girl, buried alive, is asked for what crime she was slain'.

[483] Ibn Taymiyya is among the few exceptions who apply the Qur'anic prohibition on killing children to the case of abortion. The attempt to induce the abortion of a pregnant slave's fetus (*isqat al-haml*) is considered unlawful (*haram*) by the consensus of Muslims. It is a category of *wåd* (Katz, 2003:26). In a very significant hadith, Ibn Mas'ud says: 'I asked God's messenger which sin is the gravest with Allah? He replied: That you associate a partner with Allah, while it is He who has created you. Ibn Mas'ud says: I said to him 'Verily it is indeed grave.' Ibn Mas'ud says: I asked him what the next gravest sin was. He replied: That you kill your child out of fear that he shall join you in food; and finally fornication with the wife of one's neighbor.' (Bukhari, *Sahih*, www.al-islam.com, XIII.394; Muslim, *Sahih*, www.al-islam.com, I.238).

infanticide (in verse 6:137) with polytheism. According to Gülen, the Qur'an's instruction not to kill children out of fear of loss of *rizq* (sustenance) shows that infanticide is clear evidence both of the failure of the people's trust in God's power to provide and of the misguided nature of their life.[484] Gülen then proceeds to use one of the Qur'an's most fundamental passages in relation to the stages of the development of the fetus, Chapter 23:12–14:[485]

> Indeed, We created a human out of the essence of clay; then We placed him as [a drop of] sperm (*nutfa:* germ-cell, an embryonic lump) in a place of rest; then We made the sperm into a clot of blood (*'alaqah*); then of that clot We made a lump; then We made out of that lump bones and clothed the bones with flesh (*mudgha*); then We brought this into being as another creature. So blessed be Allah, the best to create![486]

Gülen also draws attention to the Prophetic tradition.[487] There are two important reports: one places the time of ensoulment at the end of day

---

[484] Kurucan, 255.

[485] For similar verses in the Qur'an see 3:6; 16:4; 22:5; 23:13–14; 32:8–9; 39:6; 40:67; 53:45–6; 71:14; 75:37–39; 77:2; 86:6; 96:1–2.

[486] Rispler-Chaim notes the distinction made by contemporary medical dictionaries between embryo (from two to five weeks after fertilization to the end of the seventh or eighth week) and fetus (from seven to eight weeks after fertilization until birth). (See Vardit Rispler-Chaim, 'Between Islamic Law and Science: Contemporary Muftis and Muslim Ethicists on Embryo and Stem Cells Research,' *Comparative Islamic Studies,* 2/1 (2006), 41). Many Muslim scholars, however, follow the division of 'Ali b. Abi Ṭalib, who says 'If the fetus does not go through seven stages, the *'azl* (*coitus interruptus*) cannot be considered the same as killing the daughters alive (*wâd*). These stages are as follows: i. wet clay, ii. drop of sperm, iii. sperm into clot of blood, iv. lump, v. bone, vi. flesh and finally vii. another or new creature, *khalqan akhar* (Ibn Rajab al-Ḥanbali, *Jami' al-'Ulum wa al-Ḥikam,* Mu'assasat al-Risala 1413, I.156).

[487] The Prophet of God told us, and he is the one who speaks the truth and whose truthfulness is confirmed, each of you is gathered in his mother's womb for forty days; then (he is) a clot of blood for the same period; then he is a lump of flesh for the same period. Then God sends an angel who is commanded regarding four things; his occupation, his livelihood, his span of life, and his felicity or damnation (in the afterlife). Then the spirit is breathed into it...(Bukhari, *Sahih,* dhikr al-malâikah, X. 485; Muslim, *Sahih,* VIII.100, qawluhu ta'ala walaqad sabaqat kalimatuna; From 'Abd Allah b. Mas'ud, the Prophet said: 'When the drop of semen

120 and the other specifies the end of day 40, 42 or 45.[488] On the basis of these sources, Gülen says that Muslim scholars unanimously hold the view that abortion after ensoulment is forbidden, irrespective of the method of abortion, whether *ta'qim* or *ijhad*. Regarding the period before ensoulment, Gülen notes that with the exception of the Hanafite jurists, scholars of the four Sunni schools and the Shi'ite Ja'farite school either prohibit or disapprove the abortion without any valid reason. Hanafite jurists, however, argue that it is permissible to perform abortion until the fetus takes on the first signs of human form, *al-takhalluq*.[489] Gülen refers to al-Marghinani's (593/1197) Ottoman commentator, Kamal b. al-Humam (861/1457), who does not consider abortion before ensoulment as an offense/*jinayah*. Thus it appears that the time of ensoulment is crucial in this debate. In contrast to the great majority of scholars, who hold the view that ensoulment takes place 120 days after conception, Gülen identifies the time of ensoulment as the beginning of week seven after conception.[490] Although there are many theological and scientific reasons for this argument, we emphasize here that Gülen reads these hadiths in the light of both the Qur'an and modern medicine. Does Gülen rely on a particular hadith? He makes it clear that he is following the hadith cited by

---

has spent forty-two days (in the womb), God sends an angel to it and (the angel) forms it and creates its hearing, sight, skin, flesh and bones. (See the chapter *kayfiyyat khalq al-adamiyyi fi batni ummihi* in Muslim, *Sahih,* www.al-islam.com, (Kitab al-qadar, 13). Anas b. Malik: God's messenger said: 'Allah has appointed an angel as caretaker of the womb, and he would say 'my Lord, it is now a drop of semen, my Lord, it is now a clot of blood, my Lord, it has now become a lump of flesh, and when Allah decides to give a final shape, the angel says: My Lord, would it be male or female or would he be an evil or a good person? What about his livelihood and his age? And it is all written as he is in the womb of his mother; Some traditions place ensoulment after the completion of 80 or 90 days (See Bowen, 2003:56).

[488] Kurucan, 255.

[489] Attention should be paid to relationship between two words, namely *al-takhalluq* (formation of the creation) and *al-akhlaq* (ethics and morality). *Al-takhalluq* is a transformational word and is derived from the word *akhlaq* that means the emergence of a discernibly human feature. It is an important factor in Hanafite discussions of abortion: the majority of scholars pays attention to the gradual development of the fetus and determine the personhood on the basis of the presence of soul in the fetus, which is qualified to have certain rights as a human being. Ghazali: When the spirit is breathed into the fetus and the form is completed, *wa-istawat al-khilqa* (Ghazali, *Ihya 'Ulum al-Din,* www.alwarraq.com, I.402).

[490] Kurucan, 255.

Muslim in footnote which indicates that ensoulment takes place after 42 nights.[491] Why does Gülen prefer this hadith to the hadith that places ensoulment at the end of 120 days? Bearing in mind Gülen's expertise on hadith, one possible explanation for this preference is the absence of the 'breathing of the spirit' in some versions of the first hadith. Secondly, in reaching this conclusion Gülen reads these hadiths in the light of the Qur'an and reconsiders them carefully. Thirdly, the heart of the fetus starts beating at the end of week six or the beginning of week seven,[492] and Gülen probably takes this into consideration. In addition, as Faruk Beşer argues, if the hadith is mentioned by both Bukhari and Muslim, as a rule Muslim's wording would be preferred.[493] It may be that Gülen has this in mind, but it should be noted that this option is not very clear from his presentation.

Gülen also sheds light on the precise nature of the permissibility of expelling the fetus before ensoulment. Some Hanafite scholars consider this issue in the context of *mubah* (religiously neutral action) while other scholars hold the view that it is not neutral but requires a compelling justification, *'udhr*. For Gülen, abortion before ensoulment is *makruh* (a disapproved action or a legal category close to forbidden, *haram*). Here Gülen makes a distinction between legal rule and natural law (*shari'ah al-fitri-yya/ayat al-takwiniyya*). He says that abortion before ensoulment is not a crime in legal terms but it is a sin in the sense of natural or creational law. In other words, abortion at this stage is not equal to murder but it is like killing an innocent animal (for example a cat) for no reason and of course killing such a creature is a serious offense but not a crime. Thus his opinion is that certain legally valid human actions are morally questionable.[494] Be that as it may, in my recent conversation with Kurucan, who is

---

[491] Kurucan, 255.

[492] In contrast to the heart, the brain and nervous systems develop at the end of the trimester. Kahtani notes that Ibn Qayyim al-Jawdhiyyah wrote in his *Kitab al-ruh* (The Book of the Spirit) that life begins with ensoulment and has nothing to do with the formation of the brain. (Kahtani, 2008:447–449).

[493] Faruk Beşer, 'Kürtaj ve Ceninin Yaratılış Safhaları,' *farukbeser.com/yazi/kurtaj-ve-ceninin-yaradilis-safhalari-9.htm.*

[494] Aborting a child which is alive is forbidden by the Book (the Qur'an), by tradition and by the consensus of Muslim scholars. Once a child has gained the attributes of a child, attempting to take its life is tantamount to murder; he who does it will become a murderer. If a mother loses a baby on purpose she will become a murderer. She must pay the blood money for this act. (Kurucan, 46).

a very close associate of Gülen, I was told that in the light of modern medicine, Gülen urges Muslim scholars to re-evaluate their findings in the light of these hadiths. In other words, Gülen strongly inclines towards the view that the life of fetus begins with ensoulment.

Despite the existence of a clear Hanafite opinion on this issue, Gülen seems very cautious and holds the view that as the modern medicine suggests, the life of fetus begins with conception and with the exception of saving the life of mother, there is no way for abortion. He states that people can benefit from this tolerant Hanafite view and that Hanafite jurists like Abu Hanifa, Abu Yusuf and Muhammad Shaybani carry the responsibility of stating this opinion; and I (Gülen) believe they will overcome the weight of this responsibility in the hereafter. Nevertheless, Gülen, although a strong Hanafite scholar, does not disregard the view of other juristic schools. While taking account of the opinions of some scholars from other schools who concur with the Hanafite view, Gülen notes that the majority regard abortion carried out without good reason before ensoulment as wrong. He argues that the views of the other three schools of thought should be taken into consideration and concludes that abortion without a legitimate reason before ensoulment and formation should be considered a serious offense, *jinayah*.[495]

As mentioned before, there is no question of abortion being permissible after ensoulment, as abortion at this stage is an act of aggression. Jurists generally mention some conditions for permissible abortion, notably the preservation of the mother's health. If the mother's health is in danger, abortion is considered an obligatory solution. There are also many other instances which are debated by Muslim scholars, such as pregnancies resulting from extra-marital relations, from rape[496] or from incestuous relations, pregnancies at too young or too old an age, and abortion of a disabled or abnormal[497] fetus. These issues are among the major chal-

---

[495] Kurucan, 155.

[496] In the last three decades, these issues have been discussed in great detail among Muslim jurists, who generally hold the view that either the child should be given for adoption or, as in the case of Muslim women who were raped during the Bosnian war, abortion in such circumstances is allowed.

[497] Although Gülen refers the decision of necessity and the result of the prenatal test to the committee, he says 'It can now be determined through the genes in the very early stages of the fetus whether or not the child will be born handicapped.' In addition, couple of times in his private conversation Gülen has said that a fetus

lenges facing scholars today. Although permission is sometimes given to a woman whose pregnancy is the result of rape or incest, or who is carrying a severely disabled fetus before ensoulment, it seems that the majority of scholars are still very reluctant to legitimize these kinds of abortions for fear that they may later be obliged to approve other grounds for abortion.[498] There is no general rule; therefore every case must be dealt with individually. Gülen adopts a similar approach. He advocates the delegation of these sorts of decisions to advisory committees, and is therefore mostly silent on the matter of his opinions being used as *fatwa*. Nevertheless he provides large amounts of information on the topics of *coitus interruptus*, sperm banks and organ donations. It will be beneficial to briefly analyze his views on these matters before moving on to the subject of euthanasia.

First of all it should be noted that Gülen discussed these topics as far back as the beginning of the 1970s, at a time when they were unfamiliar among Muslims. In particular in the matters of sperm donation, frozen embryos, surrogate motherhood, *in vitro* fertilisation, and artificial insemination, the community to whom he addressed his views on these topics may well have heard about them for the first time from him. He was asked the question, 'There is a great deal of reference to sperm banks in the Journal on Science and Technology. What is your opinion of this?'[499] and his analytical response is important in terms of our subject. Gülen first considers the matter from a religious-juristic point of view, and then conducts various psycho-sociological analyses. Especially, when discussing matters such as donated sperm, donated ovum, or using the womb of another woman, Gülen focuses mainly on two points. The first is that if the sperm, ovum or vagina belongs to someone else, then one of the five principal objectives of Islam—the protection of progeny—is violated. The

---

who has no 46 chromosomes cannot be considered a proper human. Under these circumstances the majority of jurists do not see anything wrong in having such a child aborted in the first few weeks of pregnancy. That is why these types of matters need to be discussed by an expert Islamic committee rather than from a personal opinion. (From the television interview conducted with Fethullah Gülen by a journalist from Holland (19 Ekim 1995, İstanbul). Global Mufti Qardawi, for instance, does not allow abortion on the grounds of defects after 40 days (Rispler-Chaim, 84).

[498] See Vardit Rispler-Chaim, 84.

[499] Kurucan, 17.

violation of such a very important injunction brings with it a disregard for many ethical and legal institutions such as marriage and various aspects of marriage too. The second point is that such practices go completely against nature as it has been created by God, and a natural outcome of this is the subversion of parentage. Gülen discusses this matter in detail. He argues that a child who originates from the sperm of someone other than the mother's husband may, in the future, be looked upon differently by the mother or her husband, and may not be provided with the same love and care given to the couple's other children. He argues that a man and wife should try to have children in a legitimate way, and regards taking non-rightful routes as an infringement of the laws of nature; he evaluates such an act as an atrocity. Therefore, Gülen views the using of the sperm of a man other than the husband, or the womb or ovaries of a woman other than the wife in order to have children as 'civilized fornication'.[500] Finally, if they are still unable to have children despite their legitimate attempts, or if either the man or the woman is inadequate in this matter, Gülen believes that people should accept that their infertility is natural and the will of God. He advises those who are unable to have children to support financially the education and development of ten children from other families. Gülen calls this way 'a revival'.[501]

Another issue Gülen has frequently been asked to address and a matter that he too has chosen to concentrate on is that of *coitus interruptus*, birth control and family planning. Similarly to his views on sperm and egg donation, Gülen considers this matter from different angles, and in particular adopts the approach taken by Islamic Law. After giving brief information on the nature of *coitus interruptus*, he provides examples from the period of the Prophet, and focuses on the views of the jurists. In short, *coitus interruptus* is defined as taking the necessary measures to prevent conception (the use of birth control pills, or condoms, or the man ejaculating outside the woman). While in Islam it is not permissible for a man or a woman to be completely sterilised, there is an agreement among

---

[500] Kurucan, 17–18

[501] Kurucan, 256. Gülen states that women in particular should not be continuously put through certain treatments like a guinea pig, and they should not be made to think that having a child is absolutely essential. It is interesting that, in contrast to certain Muslim practices in different regions, he also does not recommend that men should take a second wife if their first wife is unable to bear children.

scholars that it is acceptable to practice any of the above so long as it does not cause any harm to the health of the person. The most conspicuous feature of Gülen's approach is the importance he attaches to the views of the majority. Accordingly, in analysing the accounts that hold *coitus interruptus* permissible, he explains in detail the reports narrated by the companions of the Prophet, Abu Sa'id al-Khudri and Jabir. A reading of these accounts in respected books on the hadiths such as *Sahih* of Muslim and *Sunan* of Abu Dawud reveals that some of the companions of the Prophet did not wish to have children from their concubines and asked the Prophet whether it was permissible to use *coitus interruptus*. It is reported that the Prophet told them they could do so if they wished, but that if God has decided that they will have children they will surely have children. Indeed, Gülen notes that the concubine of one of the companions who used the *coitus interruptus* method did become pregnant.[502]

Gülen also cites the prohibitive reports concerning *coitus interruptus*. He focuses especially on the Juzamah[503] hadith, and narrates the words of the Prophet that '*coitus interruptus* is equal to disguised or minor infanticide.'[504] Gülen deals with the matter in the light of the Qur'anic verse which discusses the pagan act of burying infant girls alive, also noting the views of the Imam Abu Ja'far al-Tahawi, who attempts to find the middle route between these two different opinions. According to al-Tahawi, in matters where there were no provisions the Prophet at first accepted the provisions of the People of the Book (the Jews) and forbade *coitus interruptus*. However, when he found out what their approach was he stated that *coitus interruptus* was permissible, thus overruling the previous provision.[505] Gülen is inclined towards the permissibility of *coitus interruptus,* quoting the words of the Prophet to those who wished to use the method: 'He did not forbid us'. Of course this is not the only factor which

---

[502] Kurucan, 14; There are many hadiths on the matter. For relevant hadiths see Bukhari, *Sahih,* bab bay' al-raqiq, VII.476; Muslim, *Sahih,* bab hukm al-'azl and bab jawaz al-ghayla, VII.307 and 323–324; Abu Dawud, *Sunan,* bab ma jaa fi 'al-azl, VI.78.

[503] Can also be read as Judama. Judama binti Wahb al-Asadi.

[504] Gülen further cites the views of Ibn Hazm on the matter. As is well known, Ibn Hazm believes that neither using medicine nor *coitus interruptus* are permissible. (Kurucan, 46). For detailed information see Hüseyin Atay, 'Kur'an ve Hadiste Aile Planlaması,' *Ankara Universitesi İlahiyat Fakültesi Dergisi,* 18 (1970), 17.

[505] Kurucuan, 47

leads Gülen to this view. He believes that while some jurists approach with caution *coitus interruptus* which has been performed out of necessity, it is important that the majority of Hanafite scholars (Gülen refers here to fundamental Hanafite sources such as *Multaqa*, *Durar* and *Ibn 'Abidin*) view it as acceptable. He says that Muslims only possessed the possibility of *coitus interruptus* on this matter, that the *fatwa* on this was not issued by him but by the jurists, and that he had said that it could be done in the light of these *fatwas*.[506]

Gülen's approach to family planning or birth control[507] is similar to that stated above. His opinions on the matter are given cautiously, and he is opposed to a systematic (enforced) method of birth control. However, while not actually recommending it in so many words, he does say that any planning sincerely desired by the family can be carried out through methods such as *coitus interruptus*. Therefore, he sees any long-term planning using medical intervention as harmful to both women and to society as a whole.[508] Finally, even if he does not directly touch upon topics such as cloning humans and producing healthier babies through genetic engineering, an examination of his opinions in general shows that Gülen is very sensitive and cautious in such matters.

Euthanasia

As we previously mentioned, one of the ultimate goals of Islamic law is to protect life. For this reason, Islam not only declares life to be absolutely sanctified but also encourages believers to exert great efforts for its protection. The Qur'an equates saving one person's life with saving the whole human race. By the same token, killing one person is equal to killing the whole of humanity. Thus human beings are not free to do whatever they wish with their body. They should exert the utmost caution and take all the necessary steps to protect their life. From this point of view, not only is suicide prohibited in Islam but also wishing for death is forbidden.[509] Thus, Muslim scholars never recognize the termination of a

---

[506] Kurucan, 47

[507] Regarding this topic, Gülen uses the terms *tahdid al-nasl* and *tanẓim al-nasl*.

[508] Kurucan, 18.

[509] Gülen considers smoking a gradual suicide (tedrici intihar) and regards excessive speed which leads to a fatal car crash as suicide also. (Gülen, *Gurbet Ufukları*, 221–223; *Zaman*, (01.09.2006); Kurucan, 12, 174).

life by any form of active intervention.[510] According to Islam, this kind of action is a punishable crime of deliberate homicide.[511]

Traditional anecdotes and many other materials on committing suicide provide ample evidence against active forms of euthanasia. Gülen also gives detailed explanations and links voluntary euthanasia directly

---

[510] Interestingly, Gülen says 'For a start, the legal systems of the world have said nothing concrete or final word on this matter. So, if we permit it, we would first of all be saying something contrary to global law. That is to say, if we were to say it should be, it could be construed as a contravention of human rights...' (Interview).

[511] Gülen gives detailed information about how Islam respects the lives of both Muslims and non-Muslims and how both have the same inviolability and dignity. Even their dead bodies have this respect, since, according to Gülen, human beings are considered mirrors which manifest the meanings of the attributes and power of God. Gülen uses many reports to indicate that the Prophet and his companions showed their respect for others, referring especially to the example of when they stood up silently out of respect for the body of a Jewish man being carried by members of his community who were passing in front of them. Gülen notes that the jurists state that if one is sitting while a funeral procession is passing by, they should stand up and if the corpse is carried or if the funeral procession is being conducted on foot, then one should not sit down until the corpse is placed on the floor. (Kurucan, 30). After referring to the hadith 'The dead body of a believer is as valuable as it was when alive,' Gülen reminds us of a verse from the Qur'an which states God honored the children of Adam (17:70). Due to this respect, not even a single strand of a human being's hair can be sold. Islam also rejects the practice of cremation, even if the deceased person has requested in their will that their body be cremated; such a will has no validity in Islam. Causing damage to the dead body is considered the same as causing damage to a living person: 'Breaking the bone of one believer who is dead, is like breaking it while he is living (Ahmad b. Ḥanbal, *Musnad,* www.al-islam.com, 49.328). Discussing another anecdote about the respect due to the dead, Gülen writes: If someone were to swallow a diamond belonging to another and then die, only if his heirs wished it could his stomach be opened up and the diamond retrieved. However, you have to be careful when removing the diamond as there will be a wound the size of the diamond. If they do not wish it the diamond cannot be removed. After people are buried their bones cannot be scattered left, right and center; graves cannot be used for any other purpose, due to the respect for the person. (Kurucan, 30, 90, 36–38). Gülen's opinion on autopsy is consistent with his view of the inviolability of the dead body: if it is truly necessary it can be carried out, but if not it should not be. Gülen provides a number of examples about *huquq al-mayyit*, the rights of the dead body. (See different details in Sachedina, 2009:175–177; Krawietz, 2003:198–199).

to suicide in many respects. First of all, the Prophet makes many clear statements which explain that any attempt to commit suicide by throwing oneself from a cliff or a mountain, drinking poison, or using a knife or other weapon will be doomed to eternal punishment.[512]

Furthermore, there are reports of incidents during the time of the Prophet in which the body of a suicide was brought to him; in one case the man had killed himself with an arrowhead and the Prophet did not pray over him.[513] The most frequently mentioned example is that of a mighty warrior who fought for the cause of Islam and performed great feats during one of the battles. When he was injured, he killed himself. The Prophet then described the result of this sinister act, saying that the man would never enter paradise and God had supported His religion with the efforts of a sinful person (in this report the Prophet refers to paradox).[514] Similarly, in the case of the fatally wounded warrior who falls on his own sword to hasten death, God said 'My servant hastened himself to me and so I make paradise unlawful for him.'[515]

Clearly then, any act intended to damage or kill oneself wipes away all the good deeds accumulated by the servant and dooms the person to hell.[516] These anecdotes are important sources for Muslim scholars, including Gülen himself, to refute the claim of killing in the case of unbearably painful suffering, hopeless incurable illness, or any kind of injury and great sufferings. He says 'If a person who has only two minutes left to live were to say 'I can no longer cope with the pain,' and take his own life, then

---

[512] Bukhari, *Sahih,* 18.74; Elsewhere, Gülen argues: 'If a person causes problems for himself due to his own actions of his own free will, or due to his own carelessness, then he will be responsible for that. For instance, if he took a knife and cut himself trying to commit suicide, but did not die and was only wounded, he will be deemed responsible for harming the body which has been loaned to him'. (Gülen, *Fasıldan Fasıla-2,* 319).

[513] Bukhari, *Sahih,* V.129.

[514] Ibid., 20.273.

[515] Ibid., V.152.

[516] According to a report of another incident during the expedition of Khaybar, ʿAmir b. Sinan, a poet companion, while fighting against a Jew with his sword, injured himself unintentionally and consequently died. As a result, the *Ansar* (helpers of the Prophet) thought that all his good deeds would be in vain. However the Prophet clarified that ʿAmir would have two rewards. Clearly, a different intention leads to different results (Ahmad b. Ḥanbal, *Musnad,* 33.274; Bukhari, *Sahih,* 21.95).

according to religion he would be a murderer. So, in this respect, a doctor that helps a patient to die, saying 'He is about to die anyway' is subject to the same provisions.'[517] In addition, Gülen points out that much pain today can be easily relieved by medication or by suitable neurosurgery. In other words, every effort should be exerted to kill the pain not the patient by developing fully adequate pain management. In rare exceptional situations, Gülen says, the pain goes beyond bearable limits (when the painkiller does not relieve or mitigate the pain), and in this situation, according to Gülen, this uncontrolled pain causes the afflicted person to faint naturally (shari'ah al-fitriyyah).[518] More importantly, Gülen, in his interview with a journalist from the Netherlands in 1995, repeats several times that in Islam a legal judgment should be based on a clear and very well defined fact. In this case, Gülen continues, the notion of pain is extremely relative because even the pain of toothache, headache, or the dropping of stones from the kidney or bladder causes some people serious sufferings.[519]

Here it is important to note that like many other scholars Gülen frequently reminds the reader about the importance of efforts to find cures for diseases and sufferings within ethico-religious boundaries. He cites a famous Prophetic tradition: 'God did not send down any disease without creating its cure with the exception of old age (in another report it says 'death'), therefore seek to cure the disease.'[520] Furthermore, the report contains the expression fa-tadawaw (seek together the cure of diseases); this prompts Gülen to make another comment to the effect that the report urges believers to engage in collective efforts to find suitable treatments for every kind of ailment.[521] Muslims believe that any kind of ill-

---

[517] Kurucan, 368.

[518] Gülen commented further on the matter: 'However, if one day the world legal systems and Islamic legal experts can evaluate pain on a computer, and if the sick people are about to die, if these experts begin saying that this pain is unbearable, this pain is making sick person unconscious, or if the experts say something new and different, then it will not be me who has made that judgement, it will be them'. (Interview).

[519] Taken from the Turkish translation of an interview carried out by a Dutch reporter in İstanbul (19 October 1995). I would like to thank Cemal Türk for providing me with the text of this interview.

[520] Muslim, Sahih, XI.210; Abu Dawud, Sunan, X.343, 371; Tirmidhi, Sunan, VII.349, 403.

[521] Gülen, Fikir Atlası, 165–167.

ness or suffering is always to be regarded as either a trial from God to confirm believers' spiritual situation or as expiation for their sins.[522] They are not evil but the realities of life and there is much other wisdom behind them. As the Prophet himself remarked, 'No disease, hurt or sadness befalls a Muslim, even if it were the prick that is received from a thorn, but God expiates some of his sins for that experience.'[523] Thus Gülen says that a believing patient or sufferer should accept with great patience whatever comes from God. The Prophet Job ('Ayyub) is the greatest example of this suffering and patience. Gülen also notes that this earthly deprivation will be rewarded in the hereafter; therefore believers should see a positive role for many diseases and sufferings, accepting that they play an important part in bringing the believer to a higher spiritual and moral station and in developing a stronger sense of trust in God in the face of various calamities. Thus believers should never consider pain and suffering as a legitimate basis for euthanasia.[524]

Nonetheless, we have to admit that the advent of modern medical support intervention together with the notions of brain death, vegetative state, post-coma unresponsiveness and so on both challenge and make more complicated the traditional understanding of death.[525] For Muslims, crucial questions are: what exactly constitutes the state of death? What is the exact location of the human spirit? And What is the precise time when the human spirit departs? Although Muslim scholars admit that the separation of the soul is not open to direct empirical observation, the majority associate the concept of death with the complete cessation of the heart beat.[526] Modern medical experts, however, do not consider the failure of

[522] For details concerning the Prophetic traditions see Bukhari, *Sahih*, V.129, 152, XVIII.74, XX.273; Muslim, *Sahih*, www.al-islam.com, XI.210; Abu Dawud, *Sunan*, www.al-islam.com, X.371; Tirmidhi, *Sunan*, www.al-islam.com, VII.403.

[523] Ahmad b. Ḥanbal, *Musnad*, XX.299.

[524] Interestingly, pain is the primary reason for the request in only about 5% of cases. Instead, it is a refusal to endure the final stages of deterioration, both mental and physical. (Margaret P. Battin, 'Euthanasia: The Way We Do It, the Way They Do It,' in *Ethical Issues in Modern Medicine* (eds. Bonnie Steinbock, John D. Arras, Alex J. London), 503).

[525] The longest survival of brain death exceeded 37 years (*Ethical Issues in Modern Medicine*, 341).

[526] See the detailed discussion in Abdulaziz Sachedina, *Islamic Biomedical Ethics*, 2009, 125–171.

cardiac and respiratory functions to be a valid indicator of death. They even accuse Muslim scholarship of failing to see how the operation of many organs connects life with the functions of the human brain. Thus for them, the brain plays a significant role in determining the very concept of life and is also an important criterion for the establishment of death.[527]

Regarding the question of brain death, it is generally seen by Muslim scholarship as a warning (*nadhir*) but not a complete death.[528] Nevertheless, Muslim scholars, including Gülen himself, do not consider the withdrawal of life-sustaining treatments from irreversibly brain-dead patients as euthanasia, so long as well-informed consultations with physicians (five doctors) and other people involved in the patient's treatment take place.[529] In other words, passive euthanasia or allowing the patient to die by withholding treatment following the professional advice of doctors is not real euthanasia. In this case, the death is regarded as having been caused by the person's pre-existent disease rather than the intentional act of turning the respirator off. Although Gülen does not make a distinction between partial brain impairment and irreversible loss of brain functions, we can understand from his presentation that he takes both into consideration. Therefore, it seems he implies that sometimes delaying

---

[527] Most Muslim scholars consider that when the heart stops, the departure of the soul has occurred. As long as this separation has not taken place, the patient has to be regarded as living. Nevertheless, Muslim scholars have developed a series of notions which are called characteristics of death (*'alamat*) or signs of death (*'amarat*) such as glazing of the eyes, stopping of the breath, relaxation of the feet, bending of the nose, deterioration or decomposition of the body, whitening of the skin, sweating of the forehead, discharge of fluids from the eyes, discharge of sperm, parting or wrinkling of the lips (Sachedina, 2009:146–148, 152). The patient's acceptance of medicine and food are considered a sign of physical life, and many scholars also refer to the continued growing of nails and hair.... (Krawietz, 2003:200). Some jurists pay attention to the blood flow test as a reliable indication of stable life. To base one's validation of death on lack of movement or of pulse is, however, considered somewhat problematic in modern medicine. Clearly, there are some differences between classical Islamic understandings of death and the concepts of modern medicine. Furthermore, there are others who maintain that death occurs only when there is no electrical activity in brain at all (Sachedina, 2009:157–160; *Ethical Issues in Modern Medicine,* 343).

[528] Krawietz, 2003:200.

[529] Gülen provides the example of Turkish businessman İhsan Kalkavan's brother. (Interview).

the irreversible death of the patient through a life-support system can be regarded as serious damage, to the detriment of both patient and relatives.[530] Because of the changing nature of the issue, it is quite difficult to arrive in certain conclusion.

Conclusion

The British historian and thinker, Arnold Toynbee, states that the 'life span of any civilization can be measured by the respect and care that is given to its elderly citizens and those societies which treat the elderly with contempt have the seeds of their own destruction within them'.[531] Today, what is happening in bioethics is, of course, symptomatic of what is happening in society at large for both Muslims and Christians. Unfortunately, our modern world encourages the excessive consumption of entertainment to avoid considering serious existential questions. Intensive individualism, sexual freedom outside marriage, lack of spiritual support, hopelessness, discontentment with life at an early age, and many other issues are accelerating and aggravating these symptoms. In addition, the birth rate in the developed world is decreasing while the elderly population is increasing, and this brings with it a number of serious problems, whereas in the developing world, the population is growing faster than its existing resources. We are living in a paradoxical and chaotic world; one in which our understandings of life, birth, death and dying are losing their moral context. We urgently have to ask ourselves 'what sort of world do we want?'

Islam and, other religions of the world, urge their followers to look after their sick people, render them service and spiritually support them. This is the definition of mercy. Life is precious from its beginning to its end, and even the end of life is precious. The young generations should stop thinking about the elderly in terms of their problems and needs, attention to which may restrict their own freedoms. I think that, despite some theological differences, Muslims and Christians can find a great potential in their religious traditions that might provide a way of wisely

---

[530] Interview.

[531] Shabbir M. H. Alibhai and Michael Gordon, 'A Comparative Analysis of Islamic and Jewish End-of-Life Ethics: A Case-Baed Approach,' *Muslim Medical Ethics: From Theory to Practice,* (eds. Jonathan E. Brockopp - Thomas Eich), 182.

addressing these life-and-death issues. Perhaps that would be a noble task for both communities to begin with.

When we look at Gülen's approach to such crucial issues it can be seen that he is very sensitive in the case of abortion because the increased use of abortion results in multiple problems and increasing social disintegration. For Gülen, abortion damages not only the fetus but also the individual, family, community and social order as a whole. It is very clear that he is aware of the legal situation which paves the way for certain types of abortion; however, he tries to balance this legal understanding with ethical argument in order to discourage people from resorting to abortion whenever they wish. Clearly, Gülen displays both realism and responsiveness to human needs, demonstrating the flexibility that Islam grants to Muslims in dire situations. We observe a similar caution in his approach to euthanasia. There is no active or assisted euthanasia in Islam; nevertheless he insists that medicine and religion must work together to comfort the terminally ill through understanding the process and moment of suffering and death.

Gülen's Approach to Qur'anic Exegesis[532]

İsmail Albayrak
Australian Catholic University/Sakarya University

Introduction

In this article, we will focus on the exegetical works of Fethullah Gülen. Although Gülen has not written yet a complete exegesis on the Qur'an, we will refer to his important exegetical works to address where he stands in relation to diverse modern Muslim scholarship on the Qur'an. This chapter will examine Gülen's re-reading of the Qur'anic text, his approach to the nature and status of the Qur'an as Divine revelation, the notions of abrogation, clear (*muhkam*) and allegorical (*mutashabih*) verses, thematic unity among the chapters and verses of the Qur'an, Qur'anic narratives and the occasion of revelation. The main questions that we will tackle in this context are: what is the difference between Gülen's reading of the Qur'an and that of his counterparts adhering to both classical and modern approaches? Does Gülen offer a new reading differing from others, or does he follow very well established exegetical traditions? How does he deal with modern sciences and ongoing scientific developments in relation to Qur'anic verses? Do Muslims need a new type of hermeneutics in their interpretation of the Qur'an?

Gülen's view of the nature and status of the Qur'an

In order to properly evaluate Gülen's exegetical approach, it is important to look at his general opinions on the nature and status of the Qur'an.

---

[532] This essay published in my edited book entitled *Mastering Knowledge in Modern Times: Fethullah Gülen as an Islamic Scholar*, New York: Blue Dome Press 2011, 1–37.

We primarily focus here on his opinions about the nature of the Qur'an, the notion of revelation, its place in primordial existence, the epistemic value of the Qur'an, its universality, its authority or power in forming Muslim societies, and the role played by the Qur'an in defining the relationship between God and the creation, and as a consequence, the relationship between human beings and the universe.

There are significant similarities between Gülen's approaches to the above-mentioned issues and the approach of classical and modern Muslim scholars. Despite these similarities, the discourse produced by Gülen is quite different from both his contemporary and classical counterparts. Moreover, we come across a variety of additional information in Gülen's accounts. As other scholars, Gülen states that the Qur'an is a unique book that preserves its Divine origin. It comes directly from the everlasting 'Speech' attribute (*kalam*) of God and therefore, the Qur'an is the eternal Word of God. Nonetheless, Gülen notes that God's speech is different from the speech of His creatures, and human beings are not able to comprehend all dimensions of His speech. Following the *Maturidi* school of thought, he provides detailed information about inner speech (*al-kalam al-nafsi*) and outer speech (*al-kalam al-lafzi*). In normal speech we see letters, words, sentences etc. This speech is channeled into letters, words, and sentences and becomes spoken words, the *al-kalam al-lafzi.* There is another type of speech that is not spoken with sound but is spoken as inner speech to oneself; this is called *al-kalam al-nafsi.*[533] Gülen gives many examples of inner speech from the Qur'an such as the Prophet Joseph's speech about his brothers in verse (12:77). 'They said: If he has stolen—well, a brother of his stole before. But Joseph (endured their false accusation in silence and) held it secret in his soul and did not disclose it them. He said (to himself): 'You are indeed in a bad situation (now and say so). God has full knowledge of what you allege.'[534] Gülen believes that whenever the Qur'an is heard, listened to, recited or written down, Muslims understand the inner meanings in the outer words and sentences. For instance, when a Muslim reads the verse *inna alladhina kafaru* (those who disbelieve ...), the expression *inna* is composed of a *hamza* and a *nun*. When we state or write them, we simultaneously see the existence of this *al-kalam al-nafsi* (inner speech) in the *al-kalam al-lafzi* format, and feel the weight

---

[533] Gülen, *Fatiha Üzerine Mülahazalar* [*FÜM*], 22.

[534] See also the verse of (7:205); Gülen, *FÜM*, 22–23.

of the Divine Word.[535] Therefore, Muslims never bore of repeating the Qur'an even if they do not understand the meaning. if they get bored with the literal word and meaning of the Qur'an, they never become tired of its inner meaning. In short, we may not be able to point to this indefinite nature of the inner speech (the meaning), but we always sense it.

According to Gülen, one cannot express pleasure with this inner meaning, whatever is said can only be amazement or astonishment.[536] Gülen's explanation of the nature of the Qur'an is worth examining. Clearly, he considers the inner meaning, which is embedded in the letters and words of the Qur'an, as essential. He also puts great emphasis on the incomprehensible nature of this meaning.[537] With this approach he raises his objection to two schools of thought. On the one hand, he criticizes the *Mu'tazilites* who hold that the speaker is the creator of the word; on the other hand, he rejects the idea of the *Kharijites* who claim that the Word of God is composed of letters and sounds. In conclusion Gülen considers the Qur'an as the most precious eternal diamond of the *lawh al-mahfuz* (Guarded Tablets).[538]

Another important topic relating to the nature of the Qur'an is the notion of *wahy* (revelation). Gülen is very cautious about several issues relating to the Qur'anic revelation such as the way in which the Prophet received the revelation, the difference between revelation and inspiration, the effects of the revelation on him, recording of the revelation etc. Gülen states that the manifestation of revelation in the form of Qur'anic scripture is the most suitable way to convey the message of God. He also adds that this type of revelation corresponds to the level of human understanding.[539] Having followed the classical definition of the term *wahy* (revelation), Gülen points out the richness of the meaning of this term in Arabic. Moreover, he frequently draws attention to the Prophet's reception of the revelation. Although the Qur'an and Prophetic traditions give extensive information about the difficult nature of this process, Gülen argues that because the final Prophet is the only person who has experienced the revelation, he is the one who knows the exact details of this difficult experience. Revelation's unique association with the Prophet makes its

---

[535] Gülen, *FÜM*, 23.
[536] Ibid.
[537] Ibid., 24.
[538] Gülen, 'Kur'an,' *Yeni Ümit*, 3.
[539] Gülen, *Sohbet-i Canan*, 20.

detailed comprehension impossible for others.[540] Nevertheless, Gülen cautiously explains the process of revelation with an example:

> For instance, receptors transfer the signal of the alphabets of Morse into everyday letters and words. Every signal is equal to the specific letter. A person who uses this receptor knows which sign is equal to which letter. In order to make the process of revelation understandable, we can use this comparison. Briefly, (may God forgive my analogy if I am wrong) God puts thousands of the spiritual receptors inside the nature of the Prophet to allow him to receive every Divine signal as a specific word.[541]

In addition, Gülen argues that it is not wise to claim that revelation came to the Prophet as meaning and the Prophet himself put these meanings into the form of letters (words).[542] Furthermore, he adds to the discussion by saying that because of the complete match between the receiver and the received, there is no single anecdote in the Qur'an and traditions recorded of the Prophet asking God to repeat verses while receiving them from Him. In short, denying the Divine origin of the Qur'an and reducing revelation to the limits of human understanding is an alien notion, in Gülen's understanding.[543] On the basis of the verse (42:51) 'It is not fitting for a man that God should speak to him except by inspiration or from behind a veil, or by the sending of a messenger to reveal, with God's permission, what God wills: for He is Most High, Most Wise,' Gülen also argues that all the Prophets before Prophet Muhammad, peace and blessings be upon him, received their messages in a similar way. According to him, the word *wahy* connotes objectivity and this is the main difference between revelation (*wahy*) and inspiration (*ilham*). In other words, inspiration is subjective, open to interpretation, without witnesses, and not binding; whereas revelation is subjective but binding and confirmed by witnesses. Although both revelation and inspiration come from God, the receiver of the inspiration never communicates with the Angel Gabriel.[544]

Because of the strong association of Qur'anic revelation with the speech of God, Gülen constantly asserts that the Qur'an itself is a Divine bless-

---

[540] Ibid., 19–20.
[541] Ibid., 20.
[542] See the discussion of the late Fazlur Rahman, *Islam*, 31.
[543] Gülen, *Sohbet-i Canan*, 19–20.
[544] Gülen, *Kalbin Zümrüt Tepeleri-3*, 110–111.

ing. Like Bediüzzaman Said Nursi, Gülen reiterates that the Qur'an is a book of wisdom, ritual, law, prayer, contemplation, reflection, etc.[545] Because the Qur'an is a Divine manifestation, Gülen considers the Qur'an extremely important within the circular and interdependent relationship of the universe, human beings, and the Qur'an. Gülen points out that the universe is the universe of God (*kainat Allah*), the Qur'an is the Book of God (*kitab Allah*), and a human being is the servant of God (*ibad Allah*). One of the common themes among these three entities is God (*Allah*) who manifested Himself in the Qur'an.[546] The attributes of God can only be known fully through this eternal speech of God. For Gülen, the Qur'an is the brightest and most enduring miracle of the Prophet. Its language and style are beyond any description and any rules of ethics, morality, social relations and law that contain the basis of modern disciplines and sciences. Strictly speaking, Gülen considers the Qur'an to be the shortest spiritual way to God. It is an endless source of solutions to many modern problems. So Gülen holds the view that it is the Book from which one cannot stay away.[547]

Gülen's approach to the Qur'an might be reminiscent of a kind of traditional reading of the Qur'an, but in fact it is not. He simply refers to various dimensions that one can reach via the Qur'an. For a sound and authentic communication, Gülen points out the necessity for a strong connection between the sender and receiver of the message. If there is no harmony between them, there is no relationship.[548] In various places Gülen states that the Qur'an is (spiritually) a very jealous text, if you do not hold it firmly or open yourself to it completely, it is quite difficult to benefit from it.[549] The crux of the matter, according to Gülen, lies in the correct understanding of the Qur'anic status that facilitates a relationship between human beings and God. He never sees the Qur'an as a neutral, theoretical or descriptive book, but a way of life and a prescriptive text that shapes individuals and societies. Gülen expresses dissatisfaction with the kind of analysis that deals with the Qur'an solely on an epistemological basis. He argues that there are various levels of relationship between human

---

[545] Ibid., 47–48.
[546] Ibid., 25.
[547] Gülen, 'Kur'an-ı Kerim ve Meali Üzerine,' *Yeni Ümit*, 4–5.
[548] Gülen, *Fasıldan Fasıla-3*, 155.
[549] Gülen, *FÜM*, 7.

beings and the Qur'an. One of them is the notion of guidance. He believes that the Qur'an is primarily a book of guidance. It is the determiner while the human, as its object, is the determined one. This perception indicates that if we accept the Qur'an as the Word of God, it means that we automatically accept that its messages are contemporary.

This point brings us to another notion, namely the universality of the Qur'an. Although the Qur'an is revealed within a known historical context, it is generally considered both as a historical and an unhistorical oral text. Gülen thinks that if there was no Qur'an, there would be no real and valid judgments for eternity.[550] From this perspective one should not conclude that Gülen thinks that the Qur'an provides a legal rule for every single event or conveys a general law applicable to all local issues. For him, one of the faults of this approach is making the Qur'an solely an ethical book or a judicial book. Gülen's emphasis on the universality of the Qur'an is far removed from this kind of reductionism. For instance, when Gülen comments on the verse (21:30) 'Do not the unbelievers see that the heavens and the earth were joined together (as one unit of creation), before We clove them asunder? We made from water every living thing. Will they not then believe?' He reiterates that the Qur'an uses the expression *kafaru* (who did not believe) not only to describe Bedouins who tried to understand the stars with their naked eyes but also to address modern faithless human beings who close their eyes to the truth.[551]

Gülen's frequent emphasis on the status of the Qur'an goes even further as he says that every Muslim should consider the Qur'an as if it is being revealed to him or her unceasingly. This is the first step for understanding the universality of the Qur'an.[552] Gülen considers memorization a superficial act if the Qur'an does not allow the person who committed it to memory to re-think and re-shape his life.[553] Thus, one should read the Qur'an as if s/he is hearing it from God, the Angel Gabriel and the Messenger of God.[554] As well as stressing the external dynamics of the Qur'anic recitation (competence with the language of the Qur'an, recitation in accordance with the rules of *tajwid* etc.), Gülen regularly emphasizes the necessity of serious engagement with the Qur'an, entering the mysterious world of

---

[550] Ibid., 54.
[551] Ibid., 41–42.
[552] Gülen, *Prizma-3*, 97.
[553] Gülen, *Fasıldan Fasıla-3*, 155.
[554] Gülen, *FÜM*, 14.

the verses, and internalizing their meanings from the bottom of one's heart. He also draws attention to the importance of reciting the Qur'an with immense sensitivity and humility.[555]

Gülen's general approach to exegesis

In this section we are going to analyze Gülen's general attitude towards exegesis. His evaluation of traditional and rational exegesis and the issue of Qur'anic translation will also be discussed. Finally we will focus on the notion of *tanasub* (harmony among the verses and chapters of the Qur'an).

Evaluation of exegesis

Gülen frequently states that being the word of God does not contradict the Qur'an's revelation in Arabic. The Qur'an itself refers to this fact several times. Two broad approaches to exegesis have been adopted by many commentators, namely textual and historical analysis of the Qur'an since the formative period of exegesis. Gülen summarizes his own understanding of exegesis as follows:

Exegesis is produced in order to understand a text. From the Qur'anic perspective, this task is carried out via linguistic and literary analysis together with intertextuality, Prophetic traditions, and exegetical reports. In addition to all these, one also needs the light of the heart and the mind (faith) in his interpretation of the Qur'an. If the exegetes place stress on historical analysis, it is described as traditional (*riwayah*), if priority is given to linguistic analysis, it is called rational exegesis (*dirayah*).[556]

Gülen discusses various exegetes whose works are classified under above stated categories. He mentions, for example, Tabari (d. 310/922), Samarqandi (d. 373/983), Zamakhshari, Razi (d. 606/1209), Baydawi (d. 691/1286), Ibn Kathir (d. 774/1372), Suyuti (d. 911/1505), Alusi (d. 1270/1854) and some Ottoman commentators such as Abu al-Suud (1490–1574), Kamalpashazadah (d. 940/1534), Muhammad Hamdi Yazır (1878–1942) and Konyalı Mehmet Vehbi (1861–1949).[557] While referring to continuous exegetical traditions, he also draws attention to some exegetical schools. Be that as it may, Gülen, as a man of *via media*, always

---

[555] Gülen, *Fasıldan Fasıla-1*, 195.
[556] Gülen, 'Kur'an-ı Kerim ve Meali Üzerine,' 5–6.
[557] Ibid.

keeps the balance between *dirayah* and *riwayah* in his exegesis. In contrast to some modern thinkers who criticize the insistence of the classical exegetical works on many reports, textual analysis and specific references to detailed linguistic information, Gülen unhesitatingly borrows methodologies from this classical heritage. For instance, we come across references in Gülen's Qur'anic interpretation dealing with whether a word has a definite article or not, whether the objects are prioritized or delayed, whether the verb is transitive or intransitive (i.e., the structure of the verb) as well as the meaning of the conjunctions, derivations, and many other linguistic issues. The verb *ihdina* (guide us to the right path) in verse 1:5 is a good example of his methodology. Gülen states that the verb *hidayah* is mentioned in both transitive and intransitive forms. Therefore the meaning of the word changes according to its usage. Briefly, for Gülen there are two types of guidance: with an intermediary and without an intermediary (without any means). Gülen says that despite the presence of every possible intermediary, one cannot obtain guidance, whereas sometimes one can be guided without any assistance. Gülen derives this interpretation from the linguistic nature of the word which is both transitive and intransitive according to its usage.[558]

Gülen is not a simple imitator of past exegeses. He sometimes criticizes these exegetes, offering alternative interpretations.[559] According to Gülen, there are three levels of meaning in the text: *lafzi* (literal meaning), *aqli* (to understand some realities in the text intellectually), and finally *dhawqi* (goes beyond the text so as to understand, experience or to 'taste' the meaning).[560] Elsewhere Gülen explains that the Qur'an addresses people's straightforward understanding, their minds as well as their hearts, and their inner spiritual faculties such as *sirr, khafi,* and *akhfa.*[561] If there is no contradiction in the text in relation to these levels of understanding, this text is a complete text. Gülen argues that since the Qur'anic text is an accurate text, its interpretation should also be carried out properly.[562] At this point it is worth mentioning that unlike many modern thinkers, Gülen lays down an undisputed condition for the correct understanding of the

---

[558] Gülen, *FÜM,* 196–97.
[559] Gülen, *Kuran'dan İdrake Yansıyanlar [KİY]-1,* 47, 93; *KİY-2,* 347.
[560] Gülen, *FÜM,* 97–98.
[561] Gülen, *KİY-1,* 30.
[562] Ibid., 30–31.

Qur'an, namely powerful faith in God. In order to feel every level of Qur'anic meaning, this essential element is a *sine qua non* of the exegetes.[563] Moreover, he also suggests that currently the interpretation of the Qur'an is beyond the skills of individuals and that it requires the collective effort of experts from various sciences.[564]

Translation of the Qur'an

Another important issue regarding the Qur'an in the modern era is the translation of the Qur'an into various vernaculars. Gülen's thinking on the translation of the Qur'an is full of insight. If someone studies Gülen's partial translation of the Qur'an in his written and oral works, one will see the significance of his approach to the subject matter. Bearing in mind the notion of *i'jaz* (inimitability) and *ijaz* (precision), Gülen sees the Qur'an as a unique text. He states that not only the content, but also the style of the Qur'an is a miracle. Using classical arguments Gülen explains that the Qur'an is a miracle from three perspectives: *nazm* (composition), *jazalah* (beauty of diction—purity of speech) and *tanasub* (harmony among the chapters and verses of the Qur'an).[565] On the basis of these notions he considers the Qur'an as the easiest book to read, even though it is absolutely impossible to produce anything similar to Qur'anic text.[566] Thus Gülen believes that it is almost impossible to translate such a multi-dimensional text. Gülen also argues that translation does not do justice to the Qur'anic text because a perfect translation should simultaneously include clarity (*sarahat*) and inference (*dalalah*), summary (*ijmal*) and detailed explanation (*tafsil*), particular (*khusus*) and general (*umum*) meanings, unconditional (*itlaq*) and restricted (*muqayyad*) implications.[567] In fact, it is impossible to achieve everything in a translation.

Gülen's skepticism concerning the translation of the Qur'an is not limited to the above-mentioned arguments. Deficiencies introduced from various perspectives in the translations show that an exact translation of the Qur'an is impossible. Because of this limitation Gülen insists on reading some kind of explanatory translation rather than literal translations.

---

563 Gülen, 'Dar Bir Zaviyeden Düşünce Sistemimiz,' *Yeni Ümit*, 3.

564 Gülen, 'Kur'an-ı Kerim ve İlmi Hakikatler–I,' *Yeni Ümit*, 2.

565 Gülen, Gülen, *FÜM*, 52–53.

566 Gülen, *KİY-1*, 21.

567 Gülen, 'Kur'an-ı Kerim ve Meali Üzerine,' 4.

He also strongly advises that these explanatory translations should be carried out by experts who are familiar with the literary eloquence of the Arabic language. In addition, Gülen explains that every translation should pass through the filters of major Islamic disciplines such as exegesis, Islamic jurisprudence, theology, and Prophetic tradition.[568] Moreover, he suggests that translators benefit from cultural, sociological, psychological, anthropological, and communications research. These sciences can make important contributions to achieving a complementary meaning. Gülen also argues that Muslims who are knowledgeable in Arabic and Islamic sciences should read some explanatory translations but ordinary Muslims should be directed to the exegetical works rather than studying the Qur'an from mere translations. The reason for Gülen's disapproval is quite clear since there are many mistakes in current translations. Gülen draws attention to some dogmatic and literary mistakes in modern Turkish translations.[569] He also criticizes many Turkish translations in terms of their poor language. This is quite a complicated issue, but many Arabic words are already used in Turkish and it is difficult to translate some common Qur'anic terms into pure Turkish.[570] Gülen also expresses his dissatisfaction with the translations of some specific names such as *al-Rahman* and *al-Rahim* as well as other Names of God.[571]

The notion of *tanasub* (harmony)

There is another important issue that comes to fore in modern exegesis, the notion of *tanasub* (harmony among the verses and chapters of the Qur'an). According to classical exegetes, this is the most prestigious science in Qur'anic exegesis although very few commentators have paid it sufficient attention.[572] Bearing in mind that the Qur'an was revealed over a period of twenty-three years, some scholars questioned the existence of the notion of *tanasub* in the Qur'an, while others have praised it as an important exegetical device. However, Western scholars' criticism of Qur'anic text from the point of view of thematic and chronological order

---

[568] Ibid.
[569] Gülen, *KİY-1*, 199.
[570] Gülen, *FÜM*, 173, 196.
[571] Ibid., 90.
[572] Zarkashi, *al-Burhan fi Ulum al-Qur'an*, I, 130–32; Suyuti, *al-Itqan fi Ulum al-Qur'an*, II, 976–77.

in particular, have recently encouraged a great number of modern Muslims to look at this issue in detail. Gülen, like many modern commentators, uses this exegetical device frequently, but not as a reaction to the Western scholars or classical scholars. In his article entitled 'Eternal Music,' Gülen explains why he concentrates on the notion of *tanasub*: 'The Qur'anic verses and chapters are not collected randomly; they are arranged according to Prophetic order, *tawqifi*.'[573] This approach lets Gülen explore the Qur'an to find the strong relationship between the verses and chapters as if they were all revealed at the same time and were concerned with one specific topic.[574] Thus, according to Gülen, reading the Qur'an without referring to the previous and following sections or passages, but concentrating on similar narratives located in different chapters leads the reader to error.[575] While explaining the relationship between the opening chapter and the following chapters of the Qur'an Gülen states that:

> The relationship between Surah Fatiha and other Surahs is very interesting. On the one hand Fatiha stands in the Qur'an like a lonely star in the sky which has no connection with other stars and planets; on the other hand, it looks like a sun which has a strong relationship with the other stars and planets. Stars look like Qur'anic chapters and verses because one of the meanings of the verses of the Qur'an is *najm* (star). Like the stars of the sky which have close but different relationships among them, Qur'anic verses also have very strong, but at the same time different connections with each other.[576]

Gülen focuses on not only the relationship between verses and chapters but also the relationship between words and letters. In addition, he sometimes gives detailed information about the ending of verses that are called *fawasil*.[577] In conclusion, Gülen finds a very interesting affiliation between verses and chapters. The reason for his concentration on the notion of *tanasub* can be associated with his theological understanding of Qur'anic text, and to some extent, his relationship to Muslim exegetical traditions.

---

[573] Gülen, *FÜM*, 20–21.

[574] Ibid., 98.

[575] Gülen, *Fasıldan Fasıla-1*, 185.

[576] Gülen, *FÜM*, 94, 109.

[577] See verses 9:111 and 14:5. Gülen, *KİY-1*, 182.

Issues related to the methodology of exegesis

In this subheading we will focus on some methodological issues related to Gülen's understanding of exegesis. First of all we will deal with the notion of *asbab al-nuzul* (occasions of revelation), and then we will discuss the status of Qur'anic narratives and *israiliyyat* (non-Islamic materials in Qur'anic exegesis) reports. We will also concentrate on very important hermeneutical devices in Muslim exegetical traditions, namely the notion of *naskh* (abrogation), *muhkam* and *mutashabih* (clear and allegorical verses of the Qur'an).

Asbab al-nuzul (occasions of revelation)

For classical exegesis, various reports of the occasion of revelation are very important hermeneutical devices for the interpretation of the Qur'an. Despite the high esteem with which these reports are held by classical scholars, pre-modern Muslim intellectuals have criticized them and argued that they are the main hindrance to understanding the Qur'an. Thus they express skepticism about the origin and authenticity of these reports. These scholars insisted on deriving the historical context of the verse directly from Qur'anic presentation or textual context of the verses, *qarina haliyyah*.[578] Recently, modern Muslim Qur'anic scholarship has rediscovered the importance of these reports. The motives for such an interest stem from different aims. In particular, because of the influence of Western historical criticism, they have developed new approaches in defining the relationship between revelation and the events that occurred during the twenty-three-year period of the revelation. First of all, they generally argue that the Companions of the Prophet never perceived the Qur'an as a book, even though it was written down though not compiled as an ordered text. Furthermore, the dialogue between God and man during the period of revelation was so lively and immediate that people were mostly aware of the occasions of revelation. To put it another way, the Companions did not try to understand the Qur'an on the basis of textual analysis, but followed Qur'anic teachings and put what they had learnt into practice immediately. Modern Muslims asked whether the instructions that are provided in the Qur'an should be followed regardless of

---

[578] Daud Rahbar, 'Sir Sayyid Ahmad Khan's Principles of Exegesis: Translated from his Tahrir fi Usul al-Tafsir I–II,' *The Muslim World*, 1956, 324.

time, place, and circumstances. Because many of these scholars reduced the Qur'an to being only an essential religious and ethical Scripture, they claimed that if the real purpose (or cause/*illah*) of the verse(s) was found, one might be justified in going beyond its literal meaning.[579]

According to Gülen, reports of the occasions of revelation are also important, but he finds the modernists' frequent emphasis on the reports of the occasions of revelation exaggerated, and consequently he tries to limit the role of occasion in understanding the Qur'an. He does not consider the occasion of revelation (*sabab nuzul*) as the occasion of existence (*sabab wujud*).[580] The connection between condition (*sabab*) and revelation (*nuzul*) is not a *sine qua non* relation. According to Gülen, it is inaccurate to argue that if there is no occasion (*sabab*) there will be no revelation (*musabbab*).[581] In fact, due to its considerable theological connotation, instead of using the expression *sabab al-nuzul,* Gülen, prefers to use *sabab al-iqtiran* which means that although God will send the verse(s), because of His Divine wisdom, and His revelation comes down in connection to a particular point in time.[582] Nonetheless, he sees the relationship between occasion and revelation from a hermeneutical point of view; namely, the occasion of revelation is an auxiliary means in the interpretation of Qur'anic verses.[583] Furthermore, Gülen highlights the fact that many verses in the Qur'an were revealed on no specific occasion. This clearly indicates that events (conditions) in seventh-century Arabia did not determine the incidence of revelation; but on the contrary, revelation determined or shaped events. In addition, those verses that came as a direct response to specific questions should not be considered as answers to those specific queries. We can state this issue in the famous technical formula: the specific nature of the *sabab* (occasion) does not hinder the generality of the rule. Gülen frequently uses this rule in his exegesis. He believes in this rule's dynamism and that it conveys the message of the

---

[579] İsmail Albayrak, 'The Historical Status of the Qur'an: Modern Discussion among Turkish Academics,' *Islam and Christian-Muslim Relations*, 457–69.

[580] Ergün Çapan, 'Kur'an'ın Tarihselliği ve Tarihselci Yaklaşım,' *Yeni Ümit*, 38.

[581] Gülen, *KİY-2*, 180–81.

[582] Gülen, *Fasıldan Fasıla-2*, 180–181.

[583] Tahsin Görgün, 'Dil, Kavrayış ve Davranış: Kur'an'ın Vahyedilmesi ve İslam Toplumunun Ortaya Çıkışı Arasındaki Alakanın Tahliline Mukaddime,' *III. Kur'an Haftası: Kur'an Sempozyumu*, 149.

Qur'an in a timeless manner. For instance, regarding the interpretation of the verse 2:114 'And who is more unjust than he who forbids that in places for the worship of God, His name should be celebrated? ...' Gülen comments that:

Considering the occasion of revelation of above verse, it is generally stated that the verse targets those who prevented the Jewish people from reaching the temple in Jerusalem for prayer. However, if adhered to strictly, this interpretation narrows the scope of the verse. Once, Meccan pagans tortured and prohibited Prophet Muhammad, peace and blessings be upon him, from praying at the Ka'ba. Consequently, this verse addresses every tyrant who hinders or impedes believers from praying in their places for worship.[584]

One of the significant aspects of these reports is to demonstrate to believers to what extent the combination of theory and praxis is important in Islam.[585] In addition, Gülen considers these reports as databases for understanding the background of some verses. He explains that, just as with those who first heard the Qur'an, these reports provide later generations of Muslims with the means to grasp the meaning of the verse with vivid understanding of the context of the event.[586] Moreover, he regards the verses which begin with the formula 'if they ask you, say ...' as the most important evidence of the vitality of the occasion of revelation.[587] Gülen points out that even God Himself, who knows everything and every event better than anyone else, refers to the specific occasion of revelation to convey a general message to a mass audience. Gülen conveys these reports in various ways; sometimes he only mentions the report and makes no further comment (e.g., 18:28, 33:5 and 93:4), whereas sometimes he narrates these reports while warning his readers not to limit the meaning of the verses with these reports (e.g., 5:54[588] and 36:20).[589] Gülen adds that

---

[584] Gülen, KİY-1, 66.

[585] Gülen, KİY-2, 182.

[586] Ibid.

[587] Faruk Tuncer, 'Fethullah Gülen's Methodology of Interpreting the Qur'an,' www.fethullahgulen.org/conference-papers/the-fethullah-gulen-movement-ii/2240–fethullah-gulens-methodology-of-interpreting-Qur'an.html, 10.

[588] 5:54. 'You who believe, if any of you go back on your faith, God will soon replace you with people He loves and who love Him....'

[589] 36:20 'And there came from the uttermost part of the city a man running. He cried: 'O my people! Follow those who have been sent!''

if a scholar cannot widen the scope of a verse or interpret it in various ways; he should not be considered a real *faqih* (jurist). His comment on verse 36:20 displays this approach clearly: no matter that the verse in question concerns unbelievers, hypocrites or Jews and Christians, whether its occasion of revelation indicates this or that event, environment or people, we should find a connection between the verse and our own conditions, personality or environment.[590] For Gülen this is the unique way to be continuously addressed by the Qur'an. Finally, he points out some verses that cannot be understood without reference to the occasion of revelation such as verse 87:9.[591] Having used linguistic and historical anecdotes Gülen concludes that the verse says, 'Advise them because your advice will definitely benefit them.' In this case the occasion of revelation is important in capturing the spirit of the Qur'an.

Qur'anic narratives and the notion of *israiliyyat*

Qur'anic narratives constitute more than one third of the Qur'an and therefore, every Muslim has to consider them. In the modern period there are two important issues concerning Qur'anic narratives; historical truthfulness and their interpretation in the light of *israiliyyat* reports. Recently, some contemporary scholars have questioned the historic veracity of these narratives, and conclude that there is no obligation to think that these stories are historical facts. They are presented in the Qur'an as a fiction to provide strength to early Muslims at a distressing and hopeless time.[592] Others use various ways to rationalize their contents rather than denying their historical authenticity.[593] Expressing his dissatisfaction with both approaches, Gülen reveals that he has no doubt about the historical accuracy of Qur'anic narratives. He claims that in order to deny the historical truthfulness of these stories, some people choose an unwise understanding by equating them to metaphors or similes. In fact for Gülen, these stories are very vivid and have been taken directly from the lives of previous individuals and nations. Similarly, Gülen argues that

---

[590] Gülen, *KİY-2*, 331–332.

[591] 87:9 'Therefore give admonition in case the admonition profits (the hearer).'

[592] Said Şimşek, *Günümüz Tefsir Problemleri*, 368–369.

[593] Rahbar, 1956:325–332.

nobody has right to deny their historical accuracy by examining them through the lens of symbolism.[594]

Nonetheless, he gives very important clues regarding the manner in which one should approach to Qur'anic narratives. First of all, he strongly asks the reader to enter the heart of the dialogue and narration of these stories and apply them to their own lives. Thus, he states that if contemporary Muslims perceive the characters in these narratives as significant figures mentioned in Qur'anic narratives, in the same way as Prophets and saints who lived a long time ago, one never gets real benefit from these stories. According to Gülen, Muslims have to bring these accounts into their own daily lives, they have to internalize these figures and most importantly, they have to draw lessons from their stories within the confines of Qur'anic presentations and as far as Qur'anic narrative allows them to do so.[595] Gülen holds the view that the main purpose of these stories is to reveal to believers a small part of the universal rules that will persist until the Day of Judgment.[596] At this stage, according to Gülen, it is important to note that the reader should ask not only about the meaning of the narrative, but also about the effect of that narrative in their life. Gülen's interpretation of the verse (18:94)[597] is very illustrative. This verse talks about how Gog and Magog spoiled the land. Consequently weak people asked Dhu al-Qarnayn to set a barrier between them and Gog and Magog. Gülen says that this barrier may be interpreted as the Great Wall of China or the Iron door in Caucasia. However, when we look at the issue in the light of other verses, it is difficult to identify it as a specific barrier only. It really needs additional serious study. Indeed, we need to look at the people behind the barrier rather than focusing on the barrier itself. As long as society stands firm with powerful and dynamic spiritual and ethical values, it will avoid Gog and Magog's sedition and disruption. Gülen also disputes the possible meaning of the verse and says that the main features of just rulers and the conditions for the continuity of states and similar questions should be considered in this particular narrative. Otherwise, we

---

[594] Gülen, *KİY-2*, 327; Davut Aydüz, 'Fethullah Gülen ve Kur'an'ı İdrake Açtığı Ufuk,' www.yeniumit.com.tr/konular.php?sayi_id=959&yumit=bolum2.

[595] Gülen, *Fasıldan Fasıla-1*, 188, 195; Gülen, *KİY-2*, 332.

[596] Gülen, *KİY-2*, 331.

[597] 18:94 'They said: 'O Dhu'l-Qarnayn! Lo! Gog and Magog are spoiling the land. So may we pay thee tribute on condition that thou set a barrier between us and them?''

only achieve the narration of a story from the depths of the historical record. Indeed, the benefit of this story to the reader would be very limited.[598]

Similarly, after giving a brief account of the Prophet's meeting with *jinns* in the interpretation of the verse 72:1–2,[599] Gülen argues that the Prophet's experience, of living in a complex and intricate physical and metaphysical world, is beyond our understanding. Moreover, it is also beyond the realms of our responsibility to discuss the issue. What is important for us to concentrate on the lessons that we can derive from the knowledge that Prophet Muhammad's message incorporates the group of *jinns*.[600] Concerning the people of Jonah in verse 10:98,[601] Gülen also displays his view about what is significant in the Qur'anic narrative: 'No matter where these people live, whether in Mosul, the village of Nineveh, or any other place, it does not change the result. The crux of the topic here is to re-evaluate God's warning and circumstantial evidence in the verse and to continually guard against any possible danger on this path.'[602]

From time to time Gülen gives detailed analysis of the narrative to shed light on our current situation. To do so, he takes every element such as time, space, characters, and the social, political and geographical conditions of the event into consideration.[603] This analysis allows him to make further comment on various contemporary issues. The Qur'anic verse 36:20 is worth mentioning in this regard, 'Then there came running, from the farthest part of the city, a man, saying 'O my people obey the messengers.'' Basing his view on the exegesis of classical commentaries, Gülen elucidates the expression *aqsa al-madinah* in his work. Briefly, he states that various exegetes interpret this expression in three ways; the remote part of the city, the upper class of the society and finally, influential people. Gülen, without implying his preference, concludes that the man mentioned in the verse came from a remote part of the city where rich and aristocratic people lived as if they distanced themselves from the local way

---

[598] Gülen, *KİY-2*, 240.

[599] 72:1–2.

[600] Gülen, *KİY-2*, 388.

[601] 10:98 'Why was there not a single township (among those we warned), which believed, so its faith should have profited it, except the people of Jonah? When they believed, we removed from them the penalty of ignominy in the life of the present, and permitted them to enjoy (their life) for a while.'

[602] Gülen, *KİY-1*, 194.

[603] Gülen, *Prizma-3*, 96–98.

of life and its belief.[604] He sometimes displays his preferences concerning rival interpretations of the narrative on the basis of a variety of textual and contextual evidence. In the interpretation of verses 11:70–71,[605] Gülen deals with the question of why Sarah (wife of the Prophet Abraham) was standing while her husband's guests were giving him good news. Having mentioned four possibilities, he inclines to the last one, and notes that when she heard she was going to give birth despite being an older woman, she began to menstruate. Following on from this comment Gülen never neglects saying that God knows best.

With regard to the *israiliyyat* reports it is safe to assume that he takes a quite different approach from many modernist Qur'anic readers. Gülen thinks that *israiliyyat* reports are neither completely true nor completely false. Therefore, we sometimes see *israiliyyat* reports in his exegesis. However there are other accounts of *israiliyyat* which he criticizes severely. He does not remain silent when he comes across *israiliyyat* reports concerning Prophetic immunity from sin or any report that distorts a vital Islamic understanding. The criteria for the acceptance of these reports lie behind their conformity to Qur'anic narratives. For instance, in his explanation of Surah an-Naml (Ant), he says that modern thinkers should investigate the wisdom and significance of why this Surah begins with *huruf muqatta'ah* (detached letters) and focus on the latest scientific developments in the study of ants. But if they forget the real purpose of God and start discussing whether it is a red or black ant or other details, the main aims behind the literal meanings of the verses disappear or die gradually.[606] Furthermore, in his exegesis he rigorously criticizes the people who use *israiliyyat* as a tool to satisfy their own desires. While he is dealing with Qarun in verse 28:76,[607] he says that some commentators attempt to find a kinship between Moses and Qarun. Then he argues that the main reason for promoting this relationship is to show that despite Qarun's closeness to Moses, he never benefited from such a great Proph-

---

[604] Gülen, *KİY-2*, 329–330.

[605] 11:71–72 'And when he saw their hands reached not to it, he mistrusted them and conceived a fear of them. They said: 'Fear not! Lo! we are sent unto the folk of Lot. And his wife was standing (there), and she laughed: but We gave her glad tidings of Isaac, and after him, of Jacob.'

[606] Gülen, *Fasıldan Fasıla-1*, 188.

[607] 28:76 'Now Qarun was of Moses's folk, but he oppressed them ....'

et. In fact, there is no single explanation in the Qur'an and Prophetic tradition to justify their connection as relatives.[608]

As stated above, Gülen never provides the opportunity for any dogmatic misunderstanding in his exegetical approaches. His comment on verse 12:24[609] is very important in this context. Gülen argues that some commentators hold the view that the Prophet Joseph is free from every kind of human inclination, desires or lust as if he were not human, while others portray him as a person who suffers the pressure of these desires. Gülen, as an advocate of the middle way, says neither point of view is correct. According to Gülen, Joseph had desires but he controlled them with his Prophetic determination under the guidance of God.[610] At the same time, he rejects all reports and interpretations which deify or ascribe inferior status to the Prophet Joseph.

We rarely come across references to the Scriptures of the People of the Book and *israiliyyat* in his explanation.[611] Gülen's approach reflects his sincerity in preferring the mode of a more sensitive classical exegetical tradition rather than being resistant to these types of reports for political or ideological reasons.[612] Furthermore, exegesis as an Islamic discipline is more flexible than any other basic Islamic science such as Islamic law, theology or Prophetic tradition. Instead of dwelling only on *asl* (origin and authenticity) in exegetical reports, experts from the past to the present focus on *fasl* (moral lessons). So Gülen sees no problem in following in their footsteps.

The notion of *naskh* (abrogation)

The denial of the phenomenon of abrogation in the Qur'an during the nineteenth and twentieth centuries is another important aspect of modern exegesis. When we look at Gülen's exegetical works, we see that he

---

[608] Gülen, *KİY-2*, 302.
[609] 12:24 'She verily desired him, and he would have desired her if it had not been that he saw the argument of his Lord ....'
[610] Gülen, *KİY-1*, 199–200.
[611] There is very good example concerning the Prophet Solomon's employment of jinns in 34:12 (Gülen, *KİY-2*, 324–325).
[612] For instance, Abu Rayya considers Ka'b al-Ahbar a Zionist for the interpolation and insertion of these reports in the exegesis. G. H. A. Juynboll, *The Authenticity of the Tradition Literature: Discussion in Modern Egypt*, 120–38.

does not engage much with important verses related to the notion of *naskh*. It seems that he does not want to focus on such a technical issue in his general works. Nonetheless, in his other works, he deals with the notion of abrogation from different angles. Instead of concentrating on the types of *naskh*, their number in the Qur'an, its relation to the Qur'an and *sunnah*, he prefers to look at the issue from a broader perspective. First of all, Gülen finds the theory of abrogation very meaningful. Thus discussion about whether the *naskh* really exists in the Qur'an is unimportant for Gülen. His only concern is to draw a big picture about the question of what *naskh* really is. In a similar way to Said Nursi,[613] Gülen gives primary importance to verse 13:39 'God erases whatever He wills, and establishes (whatever He wills). With Him is the source of ordinance.' This verse illustrates how Gülen sees the notion of abrogation. For Gülen, abrogation is not a simple hermeneutical device of jurists, but it is an eternal law of God in the realm of human life. Abrogation is the name of every change in our life and universe. It is related to cultures, economies, social life, animate and inanimate creatures, and is also related to their modification, adaptation, and ecological change.[614] Gülen continues as follows:

According to Divine wisdom, God changes, annuls, abrogates what He wills in both His religious commandments (Holy Scriptures) and rules of nature. He sometimes changes societies, and systems, lets some nations perish and others exist. He manifests His names, *jalali* (majesty, wrath and rage) and *jamali* (beauty and blessing) in the universe. Through the manifestation of these names some people become happy, while others become sad. Similarly, He abrogates and changes some rules in His Divine law and brings forth another. Instead of the Prophet Adam's *suhuf* (Divine text or pages) He declares the pages of the Prophet Noah. When the time comes He announces His new revelation to the Prophet Abraham. He takes

---

[613] Gülen uses Nursi's argument here. According to Nursi, there are two significant concepts concerning changeable and unchangeable things. One is *imam-ı mubin* which is related to the realm of the unknown or the unseen, *ghayb*. This is a notebook of Divine destiny which hides the original forms of both past and future. In addition, it is a manifestation of God's attributes of *ilm* (knowledge) and *amr* (commandment). The other is *kitab-ı mübin* which is related to the realm of the seen, *shahadah*. This notebook is the manifestation of God's attributes *qudrah* (power) and *ijad* (invention) which is related to the formation of things in the world; Nursi, *Sözler*, 533.

[614] Gülen, *Kalbin Zümrüt Tepeleri-4*, 104–112.

something out of the old pages and inserts a new one, and then shapes it as a Holy Scripture to be presented to the Prophet Moses. Afterwards, he brings more dimension and depth to the book with Psalms and proclaims them to be from the mouth of the Prophet David. With the Gospel, He brings a spiritual dimension to humanity in addition to the Torah. Finally, through the words of the Prophet Jesus He gives the good tidings of Ahmad who enables the greatest change in human history.[615]

Although Gülen strongly believes that there is no change or abrogation in the fundamentals of faith, there are many changes in its secondary issues or details. To support this idea, he compares the time of the Prophet Adam with childhood (*sabah*/early morning), and the era of Prophet Muhammad, peace and blessings be upon him, with middle age (*asr*/afternoon). He holds the view that this is completely related to the maturity of humanity.[616] Obviously, he tries to say that people at the time of the Prophet Adam are different from the people of Prophet Muhammad's time. Hence, change in some details is inevitable. Thus, Gülen considers the denial of *naskh* (abrogation) as the denial of the history of humanity on earth.

Nonetheless, rather than referring frequently to the notion of abrogation, Gülen is determined to see Qur'anic verses as very active and relevant. He goes on even further and says that there are Qur'anic verses concerning the People of the Book that should be examined seriously by Muslims. Verse 3:188: 'Think not that those who exult in what they have given, and love to be praised for what they have not done. Think not they are in safety from the doom. A painful doom is theirs,' is a very good example of this. Gülen states that there are many important lessons and advice for Muslims to derive from all the verses of the Qur'an, even though they address non-Muslims—unless such verses are abrogated. To support his approach, Gülen uses an important legal methodology, namely *shar'u man qablana shar'un lana* (the laws of previous religions are also law for us). Clearly, he tries to combine the ethical dimension of the verses with their legal enactment on the basis of the notion of abrogation.[617] Thus, instead of denying the content of the verses, he prefers to use every statement of the Qur'an.

---

[615] Ibid.

[616] Gülen, *Asrın Getirdiği Tereddütler-3*, 20–28.

[617] Gülen, *Fasıldan Fasıla-1*, 181–182.

Gülen also uses this hermeneutical device in his rational and traditional explanations to pave way for a new *ijtihad* (analogy). However, in his usage, Gülen's point of view is quite different and unique from both pre-modern scholars who reject *naskh* completely and contemporary scholars who accept it to prove that the Qur'an is simply a historical text and can only be understood in this specific historical context. Gülen is aware of the necessities of modern life and the many changes in society. Equally, he believes that Muslims can achieve advancement in modern life by depending primarily on their own tradition. Progress is not accomplished by freeing oneself from the accumulations of the past, but rather by building upon its foundations and developing its traditions by means of new solutions and discoveries. To sum up, his approach to the notion of *naskh* in his exegetical works is similar to the understanding of exegetes rather than that of jurists. Thus, he is interested in a more general rule of abrogation rather than a specific juristic approach.

The notion of *muhkam* and *mutashabih* (clear and allegorical verses)

Generally Qur'anic exegetes focus on three verses of the Qur'an when they discuss *muhkam* and *mutashabih*; (11:1) 'a Scripture whose verses are perfected, *uhkimat ayatuhu*' indicates that all the verses of the Qur'an are *muhkam*; while (39:23) 'God has sent down the fairest discourse as a Book, co-similar in its oft-repeated, *kitaban mutashabihan mathaniya*,' shows that all the Qur'anic verses are *mutashabih*. Finally there is another type of verse (3:7) that states that some parts of it are *muhkam* and the others are *mutashabih*. The verse runs as follows:

> It is He who sent down upon thee the Book, wherein are verses clear that are the essence of the Book, and others ambiguous. As for those in whose hearts is swerving, they follow the ambiguous part, desiring dissension, and desiring its interpretation; and none knows its interpretation, save only God. And those firmly rooted in knowledge say, 'We believe in it; all is from our Lord'; yet none remembers, but men possessed of minds.

Gülen deals with the notion of both *muhkam* and *mutashabih* from various perspectives. Primarily, he draws attention to the idea that one should not forget that this difficulty or ambiguity in *mutashabih* has nothing to do with God. Gülen, from the beginning to the end, emphasizes on this and he approaches the topic from the reader's viewpoint. Thus, only human beings are bound to *muhkam* and *mutashabih*. God, however, knows everything in all its detail. For those who want to understand the Qur'an, *muhkamat* is very important, as Gülen maintains that these verses allow the reader to distinguish between right and wrong. He implies that there are *thabitat* (eternally valid or firmly fixed things) in the Qur'an that need to be referred to continuously. So Gülen likens the *muhkamat* to a searchlight that helps the reader understand *mutashabihat*.[618] According to Gülen, *mutashabihat* means the verses of the Qur'an that lack clarity. However, absolute ambiguity is not intended. He argues that there are various wisdoms behind the existence of *mutashabihat* in the Qur'an and therefore, it is wrong to see *mutashabihat* as a static term.

Since the Qur'an is a living book, the interaction between it and the reader is very important. The more one immerses oneself in the Qur'an the more one starts finding new insights in it.[619] So *mutashabihat* indicates that there are abundant realities in the Qur'an, many of which are unknown to humankind. Through these verses the Qur'an forces believers to reflect upon and contemplate the Qur'an. Gülen strongly believes that these verses are open to inspire receptive people. He believes that the existence of such verses in the Qur'an is essential evidence for the universality of the Qur'an and Islam. Because there are both very knowledgeable and ordinary believers among the Muslims, the Qur'an addresses both intellectuals and the general population. Thus, the Qur'an is sometimes very precise and sometimes very deep in meaning and can be applied to a wide variety of issues. The understanding of *mutashabihat* is also conditioned by time. In other words, when the exact time comes, the meaning will be understood by those who believe. This precise time, however, is related to the gradually occurring needs of people and events.[620]

Like many of his predecessors, Gülen divides *mutashabihat* into four categories; *khafi* (hidden), *muskhil* (obscure), *mujmal* (concise) and *mutashabih* (unclearness) and then narrows the scope of the absolute *mutashabihat* in the Qur'an. Using the methodology of juristic language,

---

[618] Gülen, 'Kuran-ı Kerim ve Meali Üzerine,' 2.

[619] Ibid., 3.

[620] Zeki Sarıtoprak and Ali Ünal, 'An Interview with Fethullah Gülen,' *The Muslim World*, 447–67.

Gülen suggests that *mutashabihat* should be read in the light of *muhka-mat*. Even his indirect comment on the letter *waw* (whether it is a con-junctive particle—*waw al-atf*—or a letter which shows the beginning of a new sentence—*waw al-'isti'naf*) about verse 3:7 supports this approach. In short, he adheres to the idea that many *mutashabihat* will be clarified through the interpretation of knowledgeable scholars.[621]

Besides the existence of different levels of meanings, there is anoth-er important aspect of the existence of *mutashabihat* in the Qur'an, name-ly the allegorical language of the Qur'an concerning some anthropomor-phic verses. Because it is also related to theology, this is extremely impor-tant in Gülen's approach to the Qur'an. Firstly he says that to remove ambiguity (*majhul*) by means of another ambiguity (*majhul*) is not healthy. The literary skill of the Qur'an is very important in this regard. The Qur'an uses *tashbih* (metaphor) and *tamthil* (similes) to clarify some verses. Concerning God's attributes and names, miracles etc., Gülen says that the Qur'an always employs understandable concepts in its explanation of the unknowable. For instance, for those who do not believe in the virgin birth of Jesus, the Qur'an asks them to look at the way that Adam was created.[622] Despite the Qur'an's emphasis on *mutashabihat*, many could not understand the delicacy of the issue and indulged in various discus-sions. Gülen describes the issue of the interpretation of *mutashabihat* as *mazallat al-aqdam* (slipping of the feet, lapse). Thus, the correct under-standing of *mutahsabihat* leads people to prove the existence of God with-out indulging in anthropomorphic explanations or denying the truth, *ith-bat bi-la tashbih wa tamthil* and *tanzih bi-la ta'til wa inkar.*[623]

Finally, it is important to note that according to Gülen, the existence of *mutashabihat* in the Qur'an is also an obstacle in facing the achieve-ment of an exact translation of the Qur'an. Believing that the Qur'an can-not be translated, he is cautious even to use the term *ma'al* (explanatory translation), because some verses contain *muhkam* and *mutashabih* togeth-er (there is an *ijtima'* of *muhkam* and *mutashabih*) and therefore, the mean-ings cannot be easily identified by any translation.[624]

---

[621] Gülen, 'Kur'an-ı Kerim ve Meali Üzerine,' 4.

[622] Gülen, *Yaratılış Gerçeği ve Evrim*, 103–104.

[623] Gülen, *Kalbin Zümrüt Tepeleri-4*, 179–183.

[624] Gülen, *KİY*, 140.

Exegetical traditions

In this section, Gülen's position will be discussed in relation to various exegetical traditions in Islam. Although we are not going to go into detail, we will present Gülen's usage of mystical, theological, and legal verses in his exegesis.

Mystical interpretation of the Qur'an

Many Muslim thinkers express their dissatisfaction with the mystical interpretation of the Qur'an. One of the disadvantages of this attitude is the loss of the strong traditional connections between *fiqh akbar* (theology), *fiqh zahir* (law) and *fiqh batin* (Sufism). In contrast to many modern Qur'an readers, Gülen offers some mystical explanations in his commentary to reconnect the inner and outer dimension of modern men and women. When we look at Gülen's mystical interpretations, we see that in accordance with his previous approach, he follows a moderate line. Having mentioned the Prophetic report that indicates the different levels of meanings in the Qur'an, Gülen also argues that as with the branches and knots of trees, there are numerous deep meanings in the Qur'an.[625] Gülen believes that after explanation of the literal meaning, it is wrong to ignore the mystical interpretation of the Qur'an, but that this does not contradict the literal meaning. Since he wrote a four-volume mystical work[626] in which he thoroughly covers the Qur'anic text and mystical concepts, we will not re-visit that but will primarily focus on his another book about the mystical interpretation of the Qur'an.[627] At this point, it is important to note that Gülen's mystical exegesis gives priority to quality rather than quantity in terms of the numbers of verses that he has dealt with.

Where his exegetical works are concerned, one of the most interesting issues that Gülen raises is the relationship between the reality of the Ka'ba and the reality of Ahmad (Prophet Muhammad, peace and blessings be upon him). Having analyzed verses (2:144), (5:97), and 6:124) he also gives detailed information about the concept of *nur al-muhammadi* (the Light of Prophet Muhammad) in the interpretation of verses (24:35) and

---

[625] Gülen, 'Kur'an-ı Kerim ve İlmi Hakikatlar-I,' 4.

[626] See Gülen, *Kalbin Zümrüt Tepeleri-1-4.*

[627] We mean the book entitled *Kur'an'dan İdrake Yansıyanlar.*

(48:29). Briefly, there are different dimensions in the Prophethood of Muhammad, peace and blessings be upon him; one dimension is that of being a human, and the other is a spatial dimension. For Gülen, both the Prophet and Ka'ba were created together (as twins) in the 'world of possibility' (*alam al-imkan*).[628] The reason for the Prophet's prayer and wish to direct his face to the Ka'ba lies in this metaphysical relationship. The Prophet wishes to re-unite with his twin (the beloved). On the other hand, the Ka'ba, the heart of the world and the space which connects the world with heaven is waiting to embrace his twin (the Prophet).[629] Gülen explains some mystical wisdom behind the birth of the Prophet in Mecca, near the Ka'ba and the Ka'ba's existence in the birthplace of the Prophet. Furthermore, he uses another mystical terminology, namely *maqam jam* (the place of meeting or the place that brings two into one). In short, the Prophet brings both the physical and spiritual realms together and represents some kind of middle way between two excesses. Gülen gives the Prophet David and Solomon as examples. According to Gülen, God allows David to deal with the physical world and provides everything for his service. Similarly, God also provides unseen creatures to assist Solomon. The reality of Ahmad, according to Gülen, represents the meeting place or space in these two dimensions, namely the unification of the physical and metaphysical realms.[630]

Gülen's approach to mystical interpretation allows him to use some technical terms such as *ma'iyyah* (togetherness with both God and the Prophet), *ubudiyyah, ibadah* and *ubudah* (level of worship), *qurb–bu'd* (closeness to God–remoteness), *rida* (acceptance), *sakinah* (tranquility) and the notion of *tawhid* (the Unity of God) and many other Qur'anic terms. It is also interesting to note that following classical Muslim scholarship, Gülen uses some Arabic letters or dots to derive mystical interpretations from them. This kind of interpretation is rare. We can give an example from the beginning of the *basmala* which starts with the letter *b* (preposition) and the dot under this letter.[631] In addition to his own interpretations, Gülen also quotes from Muslim mystics such as Imam Ghaza-

---

[628] Gülen, *KİY-1*, 72.
[629] Ibid. 148, 160.
[630] Gülen, *KİY-2*, 325–326, 354.
[631] Gülen, *FÜM*, 78–79.

li, Mawlana Jalaluddin Rumi, Ibn Arabi, Imam Rabbani, Ibrahim Haqqi, Mawlana Khalid and Said Nursi. However, Gülen never considers his mystical exegesis as the final interpretation of the verse. Furthermore, he is so careful that he frequently uses some precautionary expressions in his mystical interpretations.

Theological exegesis

One of the important features of modern exegesis is to place Qur'anic commentary ahead of all other disciplines and expect it to fulfill the function of every other Islamic discipline. Thus, Gülen's approach in this regard is worth investigating. It is safe to assume that Gülen has great respect for the traditional division of Islamic disciplines. It is understood that he does not generally use exegesis to discuss theological issues. Instead, he repeatedly redirects his reader to theological literature. Gülen has written a volume which is specifically compiled to deal with theological issues.[632] Nonetheless, from time to time Gülen tackles some theological questions in his exegetical works without going into details. Many of his theological explanations are provided in his work as additional information. Despite the originality of his own discourse, he follows the Sunni framework in his analysis.

Gülen's main focus on theological issues in his exegesis is mostly related to the absence of sin in the natures of the Prophets. The Prophet Jonah's departure from his town without waiting for God's response,[633] and the Prophet Solomon's smiling posture in verse (27:19)[634] are important exam-

---

[632] See Gülen, İnancın Gölgesinde-1-2.

[633] 21:87 'And (mention) Dhu'n-Nun (Jonah), when he went off in anger and deemed that We had no power over him, but he cried out in the darkness, saying: There is no Allah save Thee. Be Thou Glorified! Lo! I have been a wrong-doer'. Gülen approaches to this verse from theological perspective and says that the ordinary believers' action can be considered mistake on the part of *muqarrab* (the closest people to God). Because Jonah did not receive any revelation to leave his hometown, his departure is considered a minor mistake rather than sin. (Gülen, KİY-2, 266–269).

[634] The translation of the verse 27:19 is as follow 'So he (Solomon) smiled, wondering at her (and) word, and said: My Lord! grant me that I should be grateful for Thy favor which Thou hast bestowed on me and on my parents, and that I should do good such as Thou art pleased with, and make me enter, by Thy mercy, into Thy servants, the good ones'. According to Gülen, the Qur'an uses the term *dahk* for

ples. Gülen makes a great effort to analyze sensitively some dogmatic verses of the Qur'an. For instance verses of (4:142)[635] and (3:54)[636] which talk
about God's *khud'a/makr* (cheating!) can be mentioned. Gülen criticizes
some translations and focuses on the implications of these translations.
In brief, he says that no one has the right to imply that God is trying to
cheat people in the same way that people cheat each other. God's aim in
these verses is to convey the meaning that whoever cheats someone,
will have his cheating come back to him; he will fall into his own trap or
God will definitely bring his plot to him.[637] Gülen's discussion of the teaching does not follow a systematic theological pattern in his exegetical works.
Nevertheless, he sometimes gives detailed information about some important issues such as the relationship between the Will of God and the will
of human beings. In the interpretation of verse (2:10)[638] Gülen says that
some exegetes deal with this verse from the perspective of the rule *al-jaza
min jins al-amal* (the punishment of the person in accordance with his
actions). According to Gülen, this explanation is not satisfactory. Gülen elucidates that some people have very bad intentions, and if they have any
opportunity to put their bad intentions into practice, they immediately do
so. This verse shows the vicious circle between their intentions and actions.[639]
Then, he tries to provide a definition for the notion that humanity has a will
based on the understanding of the Mu'tazilites and Jabriyyahs.[640]

Another important issue on which Gülen concentrates in his exegesis is the act of repentance just before death. Gülen points out the quality of the repentance of Pharaoh mentioned in verse (10:90).[641] He explains

---

Solomon's smile and this smile is different from excessive or lauder smile of ordinary people. (Gülen, *KİY-2*, 295).

[635] 4:142 'The hypocrites they think they are surpassing Allah, but he will surpass
them: when they stand up to prayer, they stand without earnestness, to be seen
of men, but little do they hold Allah in remembrance.'

[636] (3:54 'And Unbelievers) plotted and planned, and Allah too planned, and the best
of planners is Allah.'

[637] Gülen, *KİY-1*, 83.

[638] 2:10 'In their hearts is a disease; and God has increased their disease ...'

[639] Gülen, *FÜM*, 184–185.

[640] Gülen, *KİY-1*, 37.

[641] 10:90 'We took the Children of Israel across the sea: Pharaoh and his hosts followed them in insolence and spite. At length, when overwhelmed with the flood,

this verse in the light of another verse (40:85). Having used some inter-textual evidence such as Pharaoh's repentance, 'I believe in the God whom Moses and the Children of Israel believe in,' Gülen concludes that people like Pharaoh are strong materialists and it is very difficult for them to accept faith. Thus they (people like Pharaoh) committed a sin while they were attempting to repent.[642] Apart from these issues, Gülen also debates some theological problems such as whether *jinns* know the unseen future or not,[643] the identification of the holy spirit in (2:87),[644] and the deep theo-logical meaning of the words *rahman* (in relation to *wahidiyyah*) and *rahim* (in relation to *ahadiyyah*).[645] Clearly, Gülen maintains an understanding of classical theology, but also, in the meantime, he addresses modern read-ers through bringing in some new issues and different explanations. It is also important to note that the quantity of theological discussion in his exegetical works is very limited.

Legal exegesis

Although basic Islamic disciplines have very strong connections between each other and complement each other, there are also differences among them as well. The science of jurisprudence has superior status over many other Islamic disciplines. Gülen, however, does not use this discipline in his exegesis to pave the way for his legal opinions. Although the existence of his many legal judgments assigned him the status of a *mujtahid*, he preferred to preserve a distinction between exegesis and jurisprudence. Nevertheless, it does not mean that he has nothing to say about legal issues in his exegesis. It has been observed that he sometimes deals with legal issues but not extensively. His legal exegesis implies that he approach-es the issues from the exegetical point of view rather than juristic evalu-ation. For instance, he has a specific chapter (legal judgments) in his book *FÜM* where he discusses the inner meaning and function of *basmala* from the perspective of various schools of thought. Similarly, we find his legal arguments in the interpretation of the word *shatr* (towards) in the verse

---

he said: 'I believe that there is no god except Him Whom the Children of Israel believe in: I am of those who submit (to Allah).'

[642] Gülen, *KİY-1*, 191–192.
[643] Gülen, *KİY-2*. 327.
[644] Gülen, *KİY-1*. 62–63.
[645] Gülen, *FÜM*, 20, 90–93, 192–193.

(2:144). With regard to that verse, he discusses the direction towards Ka'ba in accordance with traditional commentaries.[646] It is also important to note that Gülen strikes a good balance between law and ethics (morality). His Qur'anic judgment focuses on this balance. In other words, law does not solve every problem unless it is being supported by strong ethical values. Thus, he extends the meaning of the verses beyond their legal limitations. For instance, concerning interpretation of verse (2:115),[647] Gülen argues that believers not only search for the direction of the Ka'ba before they pray but also insists on their not forgetting God at any time in their daily lives.[648]

Modern issues

Under this heading it is possible to discuss various issues in the context of Gülen's exegesis such as his frequent emphasis on social and ethical issues, psychological analysis in his commentaries, and finally various remarks and deductions that conclude his exegesis. However, there is not enough space in this chapter to show the various features of Gülen's exegetical analysis. Thus we are going to focus on one issue only, namely Gülen's scientific exegesis.

Scientific exegesis

An important aspect of Gülen's exegesis is his approach to scientific interpretation. While discussing his method, we will also refer briefly to the notion of the miracle that takes place in his exegesis. It has been observed that in comparison to some of his contemporaries, Gülen displays a moderate attitude towards scientific explanation. According to Gülen, the Qur'an is not a book of science[649] and as a result, he does not see the discussion of scientific details as the primary part of exegesis; instead, he considers it a secondary hermeneutical device that supports the essential meaning of the verses. He states precisely that the Qur'an neither

---

[646] Gülen, KİY-1, 75.

[647] 2:115 'To Allah belong the East and the West: whithersoever ye turn, there is the presence of Allah. For Allah is All-Embracing, All-Knowing.'

[648] Gülen, KİY-2, 284.

[649] Gülen, 'Kur'an-ı Kerim ve İlmi Hakikatlar-I,' 5–6.

rejects scientific interpretation completely, nor gives it sacred status.[650] First and foremost the Qur'an presents itself as a book of guidance, a universal message, and a book of life. So, the meaning of life and the relationship between the Creator and His creatures are more significant than scientific explanation. Therefore, Gülen believes that the Qur'an focuses on the things that have priority in the presence of God. Nevertheless, Gülen does not dismiss scientific interpretations in his exegesis. He holds the view that the Qur'an stems from God's attribute of *kalam* (speech) while the universe and everything in it is derived directly from His attributes of *qudrah* (power) and *iradah* (will), indicating that God creates and forms everything in a perfect manner. Then he concludes that if the word and work of God are the reflections of the above-mentioned attributes, there should be a necessary harmony between them. He further argues that it is an obvious error to perceive a conflict between science and the Qur'an. In Gülen's perspective, it is similar to a man having two eyes that work together and never contradict each other.[651] Thus one should not disregard either of them. Interestingly, he makes a distinction between *ilm* (real science or knowledge) and *bilim* (expressed in Turkish as meaning a more materialistic knowledge). He argues that the former is the common property of Muslims that leads to Absolute Truth (God), while the latter is the product of a sheer positivistic understanding of science. [652]

Thus, the exegete should be very careful in using science in his exegesis. Because whatever advanced level may be achieved by science, no one can fully comprehend both the mystery of the universe and the Qur'an. Although Gülen has complete trust in the scientific truthfulness of the Qur'an, he is still very careful not to read the Qur'an completely in the light of scientific developments. He argues that

> if we do not want to fall into error, we should believe only in facts that cannot be rejected. Therefore, we have to study science according to its own rules, but if we believe in its discoveries we should not think that we have exhausted the Power of God. There might be many things that we do not accept today but will be accepted in the future. The exegete should not

---

[650] Gülen, 'Science and Religion,' *Knowledge and Responsibility: Islamic Perspectives on Science*, 40.

[651] Gülen, 'Science and Religion,' 34; Gülen, *FÜM*, 27; Gülen, 'Kur'an-ı Kerim ve İlmi Hakikatler-I,' 5–6.

[652] Gülen, 'Science and Religion,' 34.

hurry to bring unproven scientific developments together with the eternal words of God. Thus he insists on not narrowing the significance of Qur'anic verses. There will always be unknown things in the scientific realm, *al-mawjud (or al-ma'lum) al-majhul*/unknown known.[653]

He also criticizes some Muslim commentators who try to associate every new scientific discovery with verses from the Qur'an. According to Gülen, such an approach would imply that Muslims have an inferiority complex about science, which would also allow them to put the Qur'an on a secondary level.[654]

Furthermore, when the exegete has difficulty in reconciling a fundamental incompatibility between the Qur'an and what is thought to be a scientific finding, he should not attempt to distort the truth of the Qur'an, but has to reconsider the scientific explanation. In other words, an established scientific discovery cannot be in contradiction with the Qur'an; if it is thought that there is, then the scientific finding in question might need further research. Gülen sheds light on the fact that some passages related to time clearly prove the fallacy of outdated scientific discoveries. Such examples reveal Gülen's confidence in the information contained in the Qur'an.[655] He also strongly believes that a part of the Qur'an will be explored in every scientifically competent age.[656] He supports this explanation with the verse 41:53 *'Soon will We show them Our signs in the (furthest) regions (of the earth), and in their own souls, until it becomes manifest to them that this is the truth. Is it not enough that thy Lord doth witness all things?'* According to Gülen, the expression of *sa-nuri* (We will show) in the form of the future tense demonstrates clearly that the Qur'an speaks to the first addressees of the Prophet by saying, 'you do not know many of Qur'anic verses and signs, We will show them in the future.' Regarding the phrase 'to whom We will show them,' Gülen focuses on the Arabic expression

---

[653] Gülen, *KİY-2*, 346; in his scientific explanation, Gülen always uses the word *fihi nazar* which means that this is not an absolute interpretation, there might be others. (Gülen, 'Kur'an-ı Kerim ve İlmi Hakikatler-II,' *Yeni Ümit*, 2–5).

[654] Gülen, *Asrın Getirdiği Tereddütler-3*, 128–129; Gülen, 'Kur'an-ı Kerim ve İlmi Hakikatler–II,' 2–5).

[655] Gülen, 'Kur'an-ı Kerim ve İlmi Hakikatler–I,' 5–6; in another place, Gülen likens scientific development to people's clothes. When these scientific discoveries become old enough, people throw them away like old dresses (Gülen, 'Science and Religion,' 49).

[656] Gülen, 'Kur'an-ı Kerim ve İlmi Hakikatler–I,' 5–6.

him which means 'them' in this verse. To put it another way, the Qur'an says 'not you' but 'they' who will come in the future will know. Finally, he comments on the expression of *yatabayyana* (it becomes manifest to them) and states that the Qur'an will explain everything as time passes, and each explanation and discovery will be fulfilled through previously explored facts. Humanity's only task is to make a serious effort to search the Qur'an for answers. In this way, the Qur'anic truth will gradually emerge.[657] Thus, Gülen states that the Qur'an addresses not only current time but also the time up until the Day of Judgment.

At this juncture, it is important to find an answer to the question concerning the eligibility of scientific exegesis. According to Gülen, in order to comment on Qur'anic verses from a scientific point of view, one should primarily have a very strong faith in the Qur'an. Moreover, exegetes need to explore the Qur'anic world without becoming weary of the search. One has to keep using a very well-established methodology in interpreting the Qur'an. Finally, Gülen reminds the reader that advanced knowledge of Arabic, and expertise in social, scientific and Islamic sciences are imperative for a proper interpretation. As he mentions, these requirements indicate that scientific exegesis of the Qur'an is beyond the limited understanding of individuals in the modern period. Consequently, Gülen calls for a collective effort to accomplish a scientific exegesis.[658]

When we look at Gülen's own scientific interpretation, it is obvious that he uses various hermeneutical and scientific devices. Although his scientific interpretation of verses is limited in quantity, they are rich in quality. For example, he gives enough details about the creation of everything in pairs[659] and the power of the atom in Surah Saba' (34:3).[660] Gülen draws attention to the linguistic analysis of the word *kull* (every) in verse (51:49). He explains that if the word *kull* becomes a noun phrase attached to the indefinite noun *shay* (thing), it signifies generality. On the basis of

---

[657] Gülen, *KİY-2*, 346; Gülen points out that the Qur'anic expressions *tafakkur, tadhakkur*, and *tadabbur* which means 'contemplation' encourage believers to seek scientific knowledge from the Qur'an (Gülen, 'Science and Religion,' 43–45).

[658] Gülen, 'Science and Religion,' 33.

[659] 51:49 'And all things We have created by pairs, that haply ye may reflect.'

[660] 34:3 'Those who disbelieve say: 'The Hour will never come unto us.' Say: 'Nay, by my Lord, but it is coming unto you surely. (He is) the Knower of the Unseen. Not an atom's weight, or less than that or greater, escapeth Him in the heavens or in the earth, but it is in a clear Record.''

this elucidation, Gülen concludes that everything in the universe is created in a pair. Atoms are not exceptions. Nonetheless, he makes clear for us to understand that people who witness the revelation of the Qur'an but did not know atoms, electrons, protons or neutrons. Today, we know that every creature exists as part of a pair.[661] Gülen is always cautious in his grammatical analysis of the Qur'an in the light of modern science. He reiterates that we can never exhaust the treasures of the Qur'an as measured by today's level of scientific developments. In fact, we do not know what atomic physics will show us in the future. Furthermore, Gülen also comments on the above-mentioned second verse and says that the expression *mithqala dharrah* (atomic weight) refers to the theory of the existence of atomic weight in every element, which has only been discovered very recently.[662] In addition, he focuses on Lorenzi's electron theory, the explosion of neutrons, and the formation of energy after a reaction etc. and finds different scientific hints in various verses of the Qur'an.[663]

There are other verses where Gülen's approach is made from a scientific point of view; these include the expansion of space,[664] the circular shape of the earth,[665] its compressed nature or the earth's polar extremes,[666] the heavens and the earth being at first one piece and their partition, the creation of every living thing from water,[667] the formation of milk in a cow's body,[668] the rotation of the sun in its specific orbit,[669] the separation of the two seas, and so on and so forth.[670] Some of Gülen's scientific interpretations go beyond the limitations of the exegesis. His information about the creation of human beings and the formation of the fetus and its various stages in the womb[671] are good examples of his comprehensive interpretation. Similarly, he gives a lengthy explanation about the phenome-

---

[661] Gülen, *FÜM*, 32.
[662] Ibid., 33–34.
[663] Ibid., 34–35.
[664] 51:47.
[665] 70:30.
[666] 39:5.
[667] 21:30.
[668] 16:66.
[669] 36:38.
[670] 55:19–20.
[671] 22:5; 22:12–14.

non of winds to fertilize clouds and bring rain.[672] But Gülen never disregards the real reason behind all these incidents in his analysis. His strong statement concerning rain is worth mentioning here: 'Whether rain is caused by positive and negative drops, clouds or any other thing; the main point is that the real formation is carried out by God. He is the One who reconciles winds and clouds, negative and positive.'[673] Thus, Gülen intentionally brings God to the attention of the reader on every occasion. After summarizing both classical and modern approaches to the verses, he focuses on the scientific interpretation.

On the other hand, he frequently warns the reader about some deficient scientific interpretations. At this point, it is worth mentioning the association of the *dabbah* (beast) with the AIDS virus in the explanation of verse 27:82.[674] According to Gülen, the verse, in its content, talks about the appearance of the beast when the signs of the Day of Judgment are apparent. He analyzes several words in this verse together with many Prophetic traditions and then concludes that to confirm that the verse is referring to the AIDS virus is to narrow its scope. According to Gülen, these kinds of interpretations are not objective and are generally contrary to the meaning of the verse.[675]

Gülen believes that the truth is not something that the human mind produces. Truth is independent of human production, and is created by God. As the words of God manifest the works of God in the universe, the Qur'an is in complete harmony with nature. Both do not contradict each other.

Having said that, Gülen then confirms the reliability of the miracles mentioned in the Qur'an. Indeed, he offers various logical explanations to strengthen the validity of the miracles. His strongest evidence for the miracles is the Qur'an itself. Thus, he criticizes many scholars who do not accept the miracles mentioned in the Qur'an and in Prophetic tradition. Contrary to those exegetes, Gülen not only accept these miracles but also provides some scientific explanations. The narrative in verse 2 (2:73)[676]

---

[672] 15:22; 24:43.

[673] Gülen, *FÜM*, 39.

[674] 27:82 'And when the Word is fulfilled against them (the unjust), we shall produce from the earth a beast to (face) them: He will speak to them, for that mankind did not believe with assurance in Our signs.'

[675] Gülen, 'Science and Religion,' 48; Gülen, *İnancın Gölgesinde-2*, 133–136.

[676] 2:73 'So We said: 'Strike the (body) with a piece of the (heifer).' Thus God bringeth the dead to life and showeth you His Signs: perchance ye may understand.'

about the identification of the killer is a proper example of Gülen's science-based explanation of the miracles. Gülen reveals various dimensions of the verse as follows. He acknowledges it as a miracle. Gülen also believes that this verse encourages humanity to go further in scientific exploration. He then gives some information about how some brain cells stay alive after death. This verse should be read in the light of modern genetics, biology and autopsy practices. For example, he comments that this verse may shed light on the identification of the unknown killer in the future.[677] Although he is careful about not falling into the trap of rationalization of the miracles, he encourages modern thinkers to pay attention to the miracles attributed to the Prophets in the Qur'an, and to be inspired by them to conduct further scientific research.[678]

Conclusion

What is Gülen's place among Qur'anic exegetes? Some might see him as a stereotypical traditionalist who embellishes his exegesis with some modern discourse. For others, who approach him more sympathetically, he is a progressive Muslim intellectual who has sufficient religious and scientific background to offer changes to the interpretation of various Islamic disciplines. In the light of our analysis, it is safe to assume that Gülen is actually a representative of the Ottoman exegetical school. He is well-acquainted with classical commentaries and established tradition and at the same time he is also familiar with modern science. Because of this strong connection, it is inappropriate to view his exegetical efforts merely from the perspective of intellectualism.

Concerning the methodology of the exegesis, Gülen is representative of *via media*. He uses reports on 'the occasions of revelations' while sometimes criticizing these reports. His approach to the notion of *israiliyyat* follows a similar pattern. When looking at his analysis of the notion of abrogation and *muhkam* and *mutashabih*, we notice his broader understanding of the issues. To sum up, we can situate Gülen somewhere between traditionalist and modernist scholars in his evaluation of these hermeneutical devices. Gülen stays on the middle path while interpreting the nature of the Qur'an, the relationship between scientific developments

---

[677] Gülen, *KİY-1*, 59.
[678] Gülen, 'Science and Religion,' 35; Gülen, *KİY-1*, 50.

and Qur'anic verses etc. He also argues against the wholesale adoption of a scientific, literary or classical approach. Instead, he suggests that Muslim scholars and interpreters of the Qur'an should use an approach that is rooted in Islamic tradition and experience, without neglecting modern developments. With regard to the mystical, theological and legal interpretation of the Qur'an, we see his style as being moderate and following traditional literature, while giving credit to modern interpretations and scientific explorations.

Gülen's quotations of contemporary thinkers, and philosophers and theologians from West and East are worth exploring in a separate work. It is also important to note that Gülen brings the idea of interfaith dialogue to his exegetical endeavor though it is not discussed it here since it is beyond the scope of this article. If his exegesis is considered in the light of interfaith dialogue, it would be an original contribution to the literature of modern Muslim exegesis. Finally, Gülen's analyses have social, psychological, cultural and philosophical dimensions that differentiate his Qur'anic exegesis from that of his many classical counterparts.

Bibliography

Abd-Allah, Umar F., 'Theological Dimension of Islamic Law,' *The Cambridge Companion to Classical Islamic Theology*, (ed) Tim Winter, Cambridge: Cambridge University Press, 2008.

Agai, B., 'The Hizmet Movement's Islamic Ethic of Education,' M. Hakan Yavuz and John L. Esposito (eds). *Turkish Islam and the Secular State: The Hizmet Movement.* New York: Syracuse University Press, 2003.

Ahmad, Khurshid, *Islam and Its Meaning and Message*, Islamic Council of Europe, London, 1976.

_____ 'Christian Mission and Islamic Da'wa'. *Proceedings of the Chambesy Dialogue Consultation,* Leicester: The Islamic Foundation, 1982.

Akasheh, Khaled, 'Nostra Ateate: 40 Years Later,' *L'Osservatore Romano* (Weekly Edition in English), 28 June 2006.

Aktan, Hamza, 'Acts of Terror and Suicide Attacks in the Light of the Qur'an and the Sunna,' *An Islamic Perspective: Terror and Suicide Attacks*, New Jersey: Light, 2004.

Albayrak, İsmail, 'The Historical Status of the Qur'an: Modern Discussion among Turkish Academics,' *Islam and Christian-Muslim Relations*, 17 (2006).

_____ 'The Juxtaposition of Islam and Violence,' *Muslim Citizens of the Globalized World: Contribution of the Hizmet Movement* in (eds.) Robert A. Hunt-Yüksel A. Aslandoğan, Baltimore: Light, 2007, pp. 119–130.

Alexander, Scott C., 'We go way back: The history of Muslim-Catholic relations is one of both confrontation and dialogue.' *U.S. Catholic*, February 2007.

Ali, Yusuf and Abu Sadat Nurullah, 'Challenges of Islamic Da'wah in Bangladesh: The Christian Missions and Their Evangelization,' *IIUC Studies,(Journal of the International Islamic University)* (2007), pp. 87–108.

Arnold, Thomas W., *The Preaching of Islam: A History of the Propagation of the Muslim Faith*, Lahore: Sh. Muhammad Ashraf, reprint of the 1913 edition.

Ashton, Loye, 'Defending Religious Diversity and Tolerance in America Today: Lessons from Fethullah Gülen,' the paper was presented at international conference entitled *Islam in the Contemporary World: The Fethullah Hizmet Movement in Thought and Practice* at Rice University, Houston, 12 November, 2005.

_____ and Tamer Balcı, A Contextual Analysis of the Supporters and Critics of the Gülen/Hizmet Movement, Georgetown University international conference proceedings, *Islam in the Age of Global Challenges: Alternative Perspectives of the Hizmet Movement Conference*, 2008.

Aslandoğan, Yüksel Alp, 'Present and Potential Impact of the Spiritual Tradition of Islam on Contemporary Muslims: From Ghazali to Gülen,' London, Leeds Metropolitan University International Conference Proceedings, 2007.

_____ 'Historical Background of Turkish Democratization and Gülen/Hizmet Movement's Contributions,' (unpublished article), pp. 1–20.

Atay, Hüseyin, 'Kur'an ve Hadiste Aile Planlaması,' *Ankara Üniversitesi İlahiyat Fakültesi Dergisi*, 18 (1970).

Atay, Rıfat, 'Reviving the Suffa Tradition,' in İhsan Yılmaz et al. (eds) *Muslim World in Transition: Contributions of the Hizmet Movement*, London: Leeds Metropolitan University Press, 2007, pp. 459–472.

Aydın, Mahmut, *Dinlerarası Diyalog: Mahiyet, İlkeler ve Tartışmalar*, İstanbul: Pınar, 2008.

Aydüz, Davut, *Tarih Boyunca Dinlerarası Diyalog*, İstanbul: Işık, 2005.

Ayoub, Mahmoud, 'Christian-Muslim Dialogue: Goals and Obstacles,' *The Muslim World*. Hartford: 94, (2004).

Barazangi, Mimat Hafez, M. Zaman Raquibuz and Omar Afzal, *Islamic Identity and the Struggle for Justice*, Gainsville: University of Florida Press, 1996.

Barton, Greg, 'Progressive Islamic Thought, civil society and the Gülen Movement in the national context: parallels with Indonesia,' Proceedings from *Islam in the contemporary world: The Fethullah Gülen Movement in thought and practice*. Rice University, Houston, 2005.

_____ 'Islam, Dialogue and the Hizmet Movement in Australia,' in proceedings of the conference, *Islam in the Age of Global Challenges: Alternative Perspectives of the Hizmet Movement*, Georgetown University, November 14–15, 2008, pp. 114–143.

Battin, Margaret P., 'Euthanasia: The Way We Do It, the Way They Do It,' in *Ethical Issues in Modern Medicine*, (eds) Bonnie Steinbock, John D. Arras, Alex J. London, New York: McGraw-Hill, 2009.

Bayraktar, Mehmet, *Dinlerarası Diyalog ve Başkalaştırılan İslam*, İstanbul: Kelam, 2011.

Beck, Herman L., 'Beyond Living Together in Fragments: Muslims, Religious Diversity and Religious Identity in the Netherlands,' *Journal of Muslim Minority Affairs*, 33 (2013), pp. 111–127.

Boase, Roger, (ed), *Islam and Global Dialogue: Religious Pluralism and Pursuit of Peace*, England: Ashgate, 2005.

Borelli, John, 'Interreligious Dialogue as a Spiritual Practice,' in proceedings of the conference, *Islam in the Age of Global Challenges: Alternative Perspectives of the Hizmet Movement Conference*, Georgetown University, November 14–15, 2008, pp. 114–143.

Bowen, Donna Lee, 'Contemporary Muslim Ethics of Abortion,' in *Islamic Ethics of Life: Abortion, War and Euthanasia*, (ed) Jonathan E. Brockopp, Columbia: University of South Carolina Press, 2003.

Brown, Alan, 'Christianity,' in *Ethical Issues in Six Religious Traditions*, (eds.) Peggy Morgan-Clive A. Lawton, Edinburgh: Edinburgh University Press, 2007.

Brockopp, Jonathan E., 'The "Good Death" in Islamic Theology and Law,' in *Islamic Ethics of Life: Abortion, War and Euthanasia*, (ed) Jonathan E. Brockopp, Columbia: University of South Carolina Press, 2003.

Bukhari, Abu Abd Allah Muhammad b. Ismail, *al-Jami al-Sahih*, İstanbul, 1981.

Bulaç, Ali, 'Jihad,' *An Islamic Perspective: Terror and Suicide Attacks*, New Jersey: Light, 2004.

Camcı, Selçuk and Kudret Ünal, *Hoşgörü ve Diyalog İklimi*, İzmir: Merkur Pub. 1998.

Chowdhury, Nayeefa, 'Presenting Islam: The Role of Australia-Based Muslim Student Associations,' in *Journal of Muslim Minority Affairs*, 26, 2, (2006), pp. 205–224.

Çakır, Elif, *Star*, 21.7.2013.

Çakır, Ruşen, 'Gülen Cemaatinin Sırları' [The Secrets of Gülen's Followers], interview with Berna Turam, *Vatan Gazetesi*, 21.10.2007.

Çapan, Ergün, 'Kur'an'ın Tarihselliği ve Tarihselci Yaklaşım,' *Yeni Ümit*, 15 (2002).

_____ 'Suicide Attacks and Islam,' *An Islamic Perspective: Terror and Suicide Attacks*, New Jersey: Light, 2004.

Çetin, U., 'The Educational Philosophy of Gülen in Thought and Practice,' Robert A. Hunt and Yüksel Aslandoğan (eds). *Muslim Citizens of the Globalized World: Contribution of the Hizmet Movement.* New Jersey: Light, 2006.

Demir, Emre, The emergence a neo-communitarian movement in the Turkish diaspora in Europe: the strategies of settlement and competition of Hizmet Movement in France and Germany, London, Leeds Metropolitan University international conference proceedings, 2007.

Ebaugh, Helen R., *The Hizmet Movement: A Sociological Analysis of a Civic Movement Rooted in Moderate Islam*, London: Springer, 2009.

_____ and Koç, Doğan, 'Funding Gülen-Inspired Good Works: Demonstrating and Generating Commitment to the Movement,' *Muslim World in Transition: Contributions of The Hizmet Movement Conference Proceedings*, London, Leeds: Leeds Metropolitan University Press, 2007.

Ellis, Kail O.S.A, 'Vatican II and the Contemporary Islam, ' *New Catholic World*, vol.23, no.1386 (Nov/Dec. 1988), p. 269.

Ellingwood, Jane, 'The Programme for Christian-Muslim Relations in Africa (PROCMURA): An Evolutionary Perspective,' in *The Muslim World Journal*, Volume 98, Issue 1, 2008, pp. 72–94.

Erdoğan, Latif, *Küçük Dünyam*, İzmir: Nil, 1995.

Ergene, M., *Geleneğin Modern Çağa Tanıklığı*, İstanbul: Yeni Akademi, 2005.

Eygi, Şevket, 'Papalıkla Gizli Anlaşma' ['Secret Agreement with Papacy'], *Milli Gazete* [National Gazette], May 26, 2000.

Faruqi, Isma'il R., 'Common Bases between the Two Religions in Regard to Convictions, and Points of Agreement in the Spheres of Life,' *Dialogue Seminar of the Islamic-Christian*, 1976. Tripoli: Popular Office of Foreign Relations, Socialist Peoples Libyan Arab Jamhariya, 1981.

Fazlur Rahman, *Islam*, Chicago: The University of Chicago Press, 1979.

Fuller, Graham, *The New Turkish Republic: Turkey as a Pivotal State in the Muslim World*. Washington DC: Unites States Institute of Peace, 2008.

Gish, Steven, *Desmond Tutu: A Biography*, Greenwood, CT: Greenwood Press, 2004.

Görgün, Tahsin, 'Dil, Kavrayış ve Davranış: Kur'an'ın Vahyedilmesi ve İslam Toplumunun Ortaya Çıkışı Arasındaki Alakanın Tahliline Mukaddime,' *III. Kur'an Haftası: Kur'an Sempozyumu 13–14 Ocak 1997*, Ankara: Fecr, 1998.

Gündem, Mehmet, 'Fethullah Gülen Röportajı,' *Milliyet*, January 27, 2005.

Hablemitoglu, Necip, '28 Şubat Kararları Sürecine Bir Katkı: Organize Suçlar ve Fethullahçılar' *Yeni Hayat* (New Life), 52, (1999).

Haddad, Yvonne and Wadi Haddad, (eds.), *Christian-Muslim Encounters*, Gainesville: University Press of Florida, 1995.

Hanioğlu, M.Ş, 'İslamcılık Üzerine,' *Sabah*, 2.9.2012.

Hendrick, J., 'The Regulated Potential of Kinetic Islam: Antithesis' in *Global Activism. Muslim Citizens of the Globalized World: Contributions of the Hizmet Movement*, Robert A. Hunt and Yüksel A. Aslandoğan (eds). New Jersey: Light, 2006.

Hopkins, Nick, Ronni Michelle Greenwood and Birchall Maisha, 'Minority understanding of the dynamics to intergroup contact encounters: British Muslims' (sometimes ambivalent) experiences of representing their group to others,' *South African Journal of Psychology*, 37/4 (2007), pp. 679–701.

Ibn Qayyim al-Jawdhiyyah, *al-Tibyan fi Aqsam al-Qur'an*, Beirut: Dar al-Ma'rifah 1983.

Ibn Sa'd, *Al-Tabaqat al-Kubra*. n.d.

Idris, Edward Cardinal Cassidy, *Ecumenism and Interreligious Dialogue: Unitatis Redintegratio*, Nostra Aetate, New York: Paulist Press, 2005.

Imam Rabbani, *Mektubat*, trans. by Hüseyin Hilmi Işık, İstanbul: Hakikat, 2001.

Isfehani, Ebu Nuaym, *Hilyetu'l Evliya*, trans. into Turkish by Said Aykut, İstanbul: Şule, 1995.

Juynboll, G. H. A., *The Authenticity of the Tradition Literature: Discussion in Modern Egypt*, Leiden: Brill 1969.

Kahtani, Müsfir b. Ali b. Muhammed, 'İslam Hukukuna Göre Anne Rahminde Sakat Olan Çocukların Kürtaj Yoluyla Düşürülemesinin Hükmü,' *C.Ü İlahiyat Fakültesi Dergisi*, (tr.) Abdullah Kahraman, 12/1 (2008).

Kandehlevi, Muhammed Yusuf, *Hayatu's-Sahabe*, İstanbul: Akçağ, 1982.

Karlığa, Bekir, 'Religion, Terror, War, and the Need for Global Ethics,' *An Islamic Perspective: Terror and Suicide Attacks*, New Jersey: Light, 2004.

_____, *Kültürlerarası Diyalog Sempozyumu*, İstanbul: Erkam, 1998.

Katz, Marion Holmes, 'The Problems of Abortion in Classical Sunni *fiqh*,' in *Islamic Ethics of Life: Abortion, War and Euthanasia*, (ed) Jonathan E. Brockopp, Columbia: University of South Carolina Press, 2003, pp. 28–31.

Kayaoğlu, Turan, 'Preachers of Dialogue: International Relations and Interfaith Theology,' international conference proceedings, *Muslim World in Transition: Contributions of the Hizmet Movement*, Leeds Metropolitan University Press, 2007.

Kaymakcan, Recep, 'Christianity in Turkish religious education,' *Islam and Christian-Muslim Relations*, 10/3 (1999), pp. 279–293.

Kerr, David A., 'Islamic Da'wah and Christian Mission: Towards A Comparative Analysis,' in *International Review of Mission*, Volume 89, Issue 353, pp. 150–171.

Kirk, M.N., 'Seeds of Peace: Solidarity, Aid, and Education Shared by the Hizmet Movement in Southeastern Turkey,' Washington DC, Georgetown University Conference Proceedings, 2008, pp. 407–434.

Koç, Doğan, *Strategic Defamation of Fethullah Gülen - English vs Turkish*, Maryland: University Press of America, 2012 .

Konan, Belkıs, 'Osmanlı Devleti'nde Çocuk Düşürme Suçu,' *Ankara Üniversitesi Hukuk Fakültesi Dergisi*, 57/4 2008.

Köksal, M. Asım, *İslam Tarihi*, İstanbul: 1987.

Kraus, Wanda, 'Civility in Islamic Activism' in Muslim World in Transition' Conference proceedings, London, Leeds University Metropolitan Proceedings, 2007.

Krawietz, Birgit, 'Brain Death and Islamic Traditions: Shifting Borders of Life,' *Islamic Ethics of Life: Abortion, War and Euthanasia*, (ed) Jonathan E. Brockopp, Columbia: The University of South Carolina Press, 2003.

Kristianesen, Wendy, 'New Faces of Islam,' *Le Monde diplomatique*, English language edition, July 1997.

Kuru, Ahmet, Fethullah Gülen's Search for the Middle Way Between Modernity and Muslim Tradition. M. Hakan Yavuz and John L. Esposito (eds). *Turkish Islam and Secular State: The Hizmet Movement,* New York: Syracuse University Press, 2003.

Malik, Jamal, 'Islamic Mission and Call: The Case of the International Islamic University, Islamabad' in *Islam and Christian-Muslim Relations,* 9, 1, 1998, pp.31–45.

Mawdudi, Syed Abul Ala, *Haqiqat-i-Jihad,* Lahore: Taj, 1964.

_____ *The Islamic Way of Life,* Delhi: Markazi Maktabi Islami, 1967.

Mevlana, *Mesnevi,* (tr.) Veled İzbudak, İstanbul: MEB, 1990.

Michàlis S. Michael, 'Framing Interfaith Dialogue in Australia's Multicultural Setting: Mounting an Interfaith and Intercultural Network in Melbourne's Norther Region,' *Religion, State and Society,* 41/1 (2013), pp. 35–63.

Michel, Thomas, 'Fethullah Gülen as Educator,' M. Hakan Yavuz and John L. Esposito (eds). *Turkish Islam and the Secular State: The Hizmet Movement.* New York: Syracuse University Press, 2003.

_____ 'Fighting Poverty with Kimse Yok Mu' Georgetown University international conference proceedings, *Islam in the Age of Global Challenges: Alternative Perspectives of the Hizmet Movement Conference,* 2008.

Mohammadi, A., *Islam Encountering Globalisation.* London: Routlegde Curzon, 2002.

Moscovici, Serge and Elisabeth Lage, 'Studies in social influence III: Majority versus minority influence in a group,' *Europe Journal of Social Psychology,* 6/2, pp. 149–174.

Muslim b. Al-Hajjaj, *al-Jami al-Sahih,* İstanbul, 1982.

Mutlu, İsmail, *Dinlerarası Diyalog Nasıl Başladı, Nasıl Gelişti?,* İstanbul: Mutlu, 2009.

Nasr, Sayed Hossain, *Sufi Essays.* Albany, NY: State University of New York Press, 1999.

Nasr, Seyyed Vali Reza, 'Mawdudi and the Jama'at-i Islami: The Origins, Theory and Practice of Islamic Revivalism,' in *Pioneer of Islamic Revival,* edited by Ali Rahnema, London, Zed Books, 1994, pp. 98–123.

Nursi, Said, *Emirdağ Lahikası-I.* İstanbul: Envar, 1992.

_____ *Şualar.* İstanbul: Envar, 1993.

_____ *Sünühat,* İstanbul: Sözler, 1993.

_____ *Flashes,* Translated by Şükran Vahide, İstanbul: Sözler, 1992.

_____ *The Reasonings: A Key to Understanding the Qur'an's Eloquence,* trans. Huseyin Akarsu, New Jersey: Tughra Books, 2008.

_____ *The Letters,* trans. Şükran Vahide, İstanbul: Sözler, 1995.

_____ *The Damascus Sermon,* İstanbul: Sözler, 1997.

_____ *Sözler,* İzmir: Şahdamar, 2006.

_____ *Şualar,* İstanbul: Envar, 1993.

_____ *Lemaat* (Simplified by Abdullah Aymaz), İstanbul: Şahdamar, 2005.

_____ *Lem'alar,* İstanbul: Işık, 2004.

_____ *Mektubat,* İstanbul: Şahdamar, 2006.

Oruç, Mehmet, *Dinlerarası Diyalog Tuzağı ve Dinde Reform,* İstanbul: Arı, 2004.

Öktem, Niyazi, *Çağımız Hıristiyan Müslüman Diyalog Önderleri,* İstanbul: Selis, 2013.

Özdalga, Elisabeth, Worldly Asceticism in Islamic Casting: Fethullah Gülen's Inspired Piety and Activism. *Critique,* 17, (2000), pp. 83–104.

_____ 'Following in the Footsteps of Fethullah Gülen,' In M. Hakan Yavuz and Esposito, John L. *Turkish Islam and the Secular State: the Gülen Movement,* New York: Syracuse University Press, 2003.

Özdemir, Cüneyt, *5N 1K Programı, Gülen Cemaatinin Para Kaynağı Ne,* Interview with Helen Rose Ebaugh, *CNN Turk,* cited in *Milliyet,* 13.01.2011.

Özdemir, İbrahim, 'Promoting a Culture of Tolerance through Education: with Special Reference to Turkey,' *Teaching for Tolerance in Muslim Majority Societies,* (eds) Recep Kaymakcan and Oddbjørn Leirvik, İstanbul: DEM, 2007, pp. 77–90.

Özkök, Ertuğrul, *Hürriyet,* 17.3.1993.

Öztürk, Mustafa, 'Osmanlı Döneminde Iskat-ı Ceninin Yeri ve Hükmü,' *Fırat Üniversitesi Dergisi,* 1/1, 1987.

Penaskovic, Richart, 'Fethullah Gülen's Response to the 'Clash of Civilizations' Thesis,' *Today's Zaman,* October 30, 2007.

Pettifer, Julian and Richard Bradley, *The Missionaries,* London, BBC, 1990, pp. I–III.

Phan, Peter C. and Jonathan Y. Tan, 'Interreligious Majority-Minority Dynamics,' *Understanding Interreligious Relations,* (eds) by David Cheetham, Douglas Pratt, and David Thomas, Oxford: Oxford Press, 2013.

Pratt, Douglas, 'Gülen's Prospects for Interreligious Dialogue, *Today's Zaman,* November 1, 2007.

Racius, Egdunas, *The Multiple Nature of the Islamic Da'wa,* Helsinki: Valopaino Oy, 2004.

Rahbar, 'Sir Sayyid Ahmad Khan's Principles of Exegesis: Translated from his Tahrir fi Usul al-Tafsir I–II,' *The Muslim World,* 46, (1956).

Rispler-Chaim, Vardit, 'The Right Not to Be Born: Abortion of the Disadvantaged Fetus in Contemporary Fatwas,' *Islamic Ethics of Life: Abortion, War and Euthanasia,* (ed) Jonathan E. Brockopp, Columbia: The University of South Carolina Press, 2003.

_____ 'Between Islamic Law and Science: Contemporary Muftis and Muslim Ethicists on Embryo and Stem Cells Research,' *Comparative Islamic Studies*, 2/1 (2006).

Rogers, Therisa, 'The Islamic Ethics of Abortion in the Traditional Islamic Sources,' *The Muslim World*, 89 (1999).

al-Roubaie, Amer-Shaifiq al-Alvi, 'Globalisation in the Light of Bediüzzaman Said Nursi's Risale-i Nur,' *Globalisation, Ethics and Islam: The Case of Bediüzzaman Said Nursi*, (eds) Ian Markham and İbrahim Özdemir, USA: Ashgate, 2005.

Rowbotham, Jill, 'Catholic Hits Islamic Chair,' *The Australian*, January 16, 2008.

Roy, Oliver, *Globalized Islam.* London: C. Hurs & Co Ltd., 2004.

Sachedina, Abdulaziz, *Islamic Biomedical Ethics*, Oxford: Oxford University Press, 2009.

Sarıtoprak, Zeki, 'Said Nursi's Teachings on the People of the Book: A case study of Islamic social policy in the early twentieth century,' *Islam and Christian-Muslim relations*, 11/3, (2000), pp. 321–332.

_____ 'Fethullah Gülen: A Sufi in His Own Way' In: Yavuz, M. H Yavuz and John L. Esposito, *Turkish Islam and the Secular State: The Gülen Movement.* New York: Syracuse University Press, 2003.

_____ and Griffith, Sidney, 'Fethullah Gülen and 'the People of the Book': A Voice from Turkey for Interfaith Dialogue,' *The Muslim World*, 95, (2005), pp. 329–340.

_____ 'An Islamic Approach to Peace and Nonviolence: A Turkish Experience,' *The Muslim World*, 95, (2005).

_____ and Ünal, Ali, 'An Interview with Fethullah Gülen,' *The Muslim World*, 95 (2005), pp. 447–467.

Schimmel, Annemaria, *Mystical Dimensions of Islam*, Chapel Hill: University of North Carolina Press, 1975.

Sevinç, Bayram, *Diyalog ve Korku: Postmodern Bir Dilamma*, İstanbul: İz, 2012.

Sevindi, N., *Fethullah Gülen ile New York Sohbeti.* İstanbul: Sabah, 1997.

Sezen, Yümni, *Dinlerarası Diyalog İhaneti: Dini, Psikolojik, Sosyolojik Tahlil*, İstanbul: Kelam, 2011.

Shabbir M.H. Alibhai and Michael Gordon, 'A Comparative Analysis of Islamic and Jewish End-of-Life Ethics: A Case-Baed Approach,' *Muslim Medical Ethics: From Theory to Practice*, (eds) Jonathan E. Brockopp and Thomas Eich, Columbia: The University of South Carolina, 2008.

Shogar, Ibrahim, 'Ethical Discourse in the Qur'an: An Analytical Study of the Term *huda* in Izutsu's Conceptualization,' in *Japanese Contribution to Islamic*

Studies: The Legacy of Toshihiko Izutsu Interpreted, (ed) Anis Malik Thoha, Malaysia: IIUM Press, 2010.

Siddiqui, Ataullah, *Christian-Muslim Dialogue in the Twentieth Century*, London: Macmillan Press, 1997.

Staerklé, C., J. Sidanius, E.G.T. Green and L. Molina, 'Ethnic Minority-Majority Asymmetry and Attitudes Towards Immigrants Across 11 Nations, *Psicologia Politica*, 30 (2005), pp. 7–26.

Steele, David, 'Contributions of Interfaith Dialogue to Peacebuilding in the Former Yugoslavia' in *Interfaith Dialogue and Peacebuilding*, Ed. David R. Smock, Washington DC: United States Institute of Peace Press, 2002.

Steger, M., *Globalisation: A Very Short History.* Oxford: Oxford University Press, 2003.

Steinbock, Bonnie, John D. Arras and Alex J. London, *Ethical Issues in Modern Medicine,* New York: McGraw-Hill, 2009.

Suyuti, *al-Itqan fi Ulum al-Qur'an*, Beirut: Dar Ibn Kathir, 1993.

Swanson, Mark N., 'On the Teaching of Islam at Luther Seminary,' in *Teaching Theology & Religion*, Volume 8/3, (2005), pp. 172–175.

Swyngedouw, E., 'Globalisation or glocalisation,' *Cambridge Review International Affairs*, 17/1, (2004).

Şeker, Mehmet, *Müsbet Hareket*, İstanbul: Işık, 2006.

Şimşek, Said, *Günümüz Tefsir Problemleri*, Konya: Kitap Dünyası, n.d.

al-Tabari, Ibn Jarir, *Jami al-Bayan an Ta'wil Ay al-Qur'an*, Egypt, 1954.

Tahawi, *Sharh al-Ma'ani al-Athar*, Beirut: Dar Kutub al-Ilmiyya, 1996.

Takim, Liyakatali, 'From Conversion to Conversation: Interfaith Dialogue in Post 9–11 America,' *The Muslim World*. Hartford: Jul 2004, Vol. 94, Iss. 3.

Tirmidhi, Muhammad b. Isa, *al-Jami al-Sahih*, Beirut, n.d.

Tavernise, Sabrina, 'Turkish Schools Offer Pakistan a Gentler Vision of Islam,' *New York Times*, May 4, 2008.

Uygur, Selçuk, 'Islamic Puritanism as a Source of Economic Development: Contributions of the Hizmet Movement,' in Conference Proceedings, London, Leeds: Leeds Metropolitan University Press, October 2007, pp. 176–197.

Ünal, S., *Hoşgörü ve Diyalog İklimi.* İzmir: Merkür, 1998.

Ünal, Ali and Alphonse Williams, *Fethullah Gülen: Advocate of Dialogue*, Fairfax: The Fountain, 2000.

_____ *The Qur'an with Annotated Interpretation in Modern English*, New Jersey: Tughra Books, 2008.

Vahide, Şükran, *Beduizzaman Said Nursi,* Malaysia: Islamic Book Trust, 2011.

Voll, J., 'Fethullah Gülen: Transcending Modernity in the New Islamic Discourse,' M. Hakan Yavuz and John L. Esposito (eds). *Turkish Islam and the Secular State: The Hizmet Movement.* New York: Syracuse University Press, 2003.

Waardenburg, Jacques, 'Between Baghdat and Birmingham: minorities-Christian and Muslim,' *Islam and Christian-Muslim Relations*, 14/1 (2003), pp. 3–22.

Waqidi, Muhammad b. Umar b., *Kitab al-Maghazi*, Oxford, 1966.

Watt, David Harrington, *Muslims, Fundamentalists, and the Fear of the Dangerous Other in American Culture*, V. 12 (2010), pp. 1–13.

Webb, L. E., *'Fethullah Gülen: Is There More to Him Than Meets the Eye?,'* İzmir. Mercury, 2000.

Wieseltier, Leon, 'The Jewish Face of Fundamentalism' in *The Fundamentalist Phenomenon: A View from Within, a Response from Without*, Edited by Norman J. Cohen, Grand Rapids: Eerdmans, 1990, pp. 192–196.

Yavuz, M. Hakan and John L. Esposito, 'Introduction,' M. Hakan Yavuz and John L. Esposito (eds). *Turkish Islam and the Secular State: The Gülen Movement*, New York, Syracuse University Press, 2003.

_____ 'Islam in the Public Sphere: The Case of the Nur Movement,' M. Hakan Yavuz and John L. Esposito (eds). *Turkish Islam and the Secular State: The Hizmet Movement.* New York: Syracuse University Press, 2003.

_____ 'The Hizmet Movement: The Turkish Puritans,' Hakan Yavuz and John L. Esposito (eds). *Turkish Islam and the Secular State: The Hizmet Movement.* New York: Syracuse University Press, 2004.

Yıldırım, Suat, 'Vefatından Elli Yıl Sonra Bediüzzaman İle Helallaşma (Fifty years after Said Nursi's death), *Yeni Ümit*, 88, (2010).

Yılmaz, İhsan, 'State, Law, Civil Society, and Islam in Contemporary Society,' *The Muslim World*, Volume 95/3, (2005), pp. 385–412.

_____ 'Ijtihad and Tajdid by Conduct: The Gülen Movement,' in *Turkish Islam and the Secular State: The Gülen Movement*, (eds.) M. Hakan Yavuz and John L. Esposito, New York: Syracuse University Press, 2003, pp. 208–237.

_____ 'Changing Turkish-Muslim Discourses on Modernity, West, and Dialogue' presented at Congress of the International Association of Middle East Studies, Freie Universitat, 5–7 October, Berlin, 2000, pp. 1–14.

Yücel, Salih, 'Muslim-Christian Dialogue: Nostra Aetate and Fethullah Gülen's Philosophy of Dialogue,' *Australian eJournal of Theology*, 20/3, (2013), pp. 197–206.

_____ 'Fethullah Gülen: A Spiritual Leader in a Global Islamic Context,' *Journal of Religion and Society*, 12, (2010).

_____ 'Spiritual Role Models in Gülen's Educational Philosophy,' *Tawarikh, International Journal for Historical Studies,* 3(1), 2011, pp. 65–76.

Zarkashi, *al-Burhan fi Ulum al-Qur'an*, Beirut: Dar al-Ma'rifah, 1990.

Unnamed Articles:

'A Farm Boy on the World Stage,' *The Economist* (March 6, 2008). Available online at www.fethullahGülen.org/press-room/news/2851–a-farm-boy-onthe-world-stage.html. retrived 2.3.2010.

'Top 100 Intellectuals in the World,' *Foreign Policy*, May/June 2008.

'Gülen Inspires Muslims Worldwide,' *Forbes*, Jan 21, 2008

Translation of Qur'anic verses: www.usc.edu/schools/college/crcc/engagement/resources/texts/muslim/quran

Internet references:

Abu Dawud, *Sunan*, www.al-islam.com.

Ahmad b. Hanbal, *Musnad*, www.al-islam.com.

Aksoy, S., 'Prenatal Diagnosis: Watching Unborn Babies,' (1998), www.fountain-magazine.com/article.php?ARTICLEID=608.

_____'Abortion: Mercy or Murder,' (1997), www.fountainmagazine.com/article.php?ARTICLEID=250.

Aydüz, Davut, 'Fethullah Gülen ve Kur'an'ı İdrake Açtığı Ufuk,' www.yeniumit.com.tr/konular.php?sayi_id=959&yumit=bolum2.

Beşer, Faruk, 'Kürtaj ve Ceninin Yaratılış Safhaları,' *farukbeser.com/yazi/kurtaj-ve-ceninin-yaradilis-safhalari-9.htm.*

Bukhari, *Sahih*, www.al-islam.com.

Ebaugh, Helen R. and Doğan Koç, 'Funding Gülen-Inspired Good Works: Demonstrating and Generating Commitment to the Movement' in *Muslim World in Transition: Contributions of the Hizmet Movement.* International Conference Proceedings, October 25–27, 2007, pp. 539–551 London: Leeds Metropolitan University Press. Available online at Gülenconference.org.uk/userfiles/file/Proceedings.pdf (retrieved on January 6, 2011).

Ergene, Enes, 'The Hizmet Movement, Dialogue, and Tolerance,' 5 August 2008, www.fethullahgulen.org/about-fethullah-gulen/an-analysis-of-the-gulen-movement/3022–the-gulen-movement-dialogue-and-tolerance.html.

Gannusi, Rashid, 'İslam diyalog dini, radikalizm ise fitne ve kaos çıkarma projesidir,' *Zaman*, www.zaman.com.tr/gundem_islam-diyalog-dini-radikalizm-ise-fitne-cikarma-projesidir_2082413.html retrieved 25.4.2013.

Ghazali, *Ihya Ulum al-Din*, www.alwarraq.com.

Hermann, Rainer, 'Fethullah Gülen Offers Antidote For Terror,' *Fethullah Gülen Web Site.*

Ibn Hisham, al-Sirat al-nabawiyya, cited in www.herkul.org/kiriktesti/index.php?article_id=7075 'Üslupta istikamet,' by Fethullah Gülen. retrieved 10.8.2012.

Ibn Kathir, *Tafsir al Qur'an al-Karim* www.altafsir.com/Tafasir.asp?tMadhNo=1 &tTafsirNo=7&tSoraNo=19&tAyahNo=47&tDisplay=yes&UserProfile=0& LanguageId=1 retrieved 2.27.2010.

Ibn Seyyid al-Nass, *Uyun al-Athar*, www.risaleforum.net/islamiyet-72/resu-lullah-aleyhisselatu-vesselam-90/117592–allahim-sen-kavmimi-bagisla. html and cited in www.herkul.org/kiriktesti/index.php?article_id=3471 retrieved 2.4.2011.

Kalyoncu, Mehmet, 'Civilian Response to Ethno-Religious Terrorism,' *Muslim World in Transition: Contributions of the Hizmet Movement* at SOAS University of London, House of Lords and London School of Economics on 25–27 October, 2007, en.fgulen.com/conference-papers/contributions-of-the-gulen-movement.

Köksal, Asım, *İslam Tarihi,* www.darulkitap.com/oku/tarih/islamtarihi/islamtarihiasim/indexana.htm (retrieved on December 24, 2010).

Kurucan, Ahmet, *Gülen's response to legal questions in 1970s,* (unpublished work).

Michel, Thomas, 'Two Frontrunners for Peace: John Paul II and Fethullah Gülen' (en.fgulen.com/content/view/1944/13/).

_____ 'Toward a Dialogue of Liberation with Muslims,' www.sjweb.info/dialogo/index.cfm.

Muslim, *Sahih,* www.al-islam.com.

En-Nedvi, Ebu'l-Hasan, *İslam Önderleri Tarihi-1,* İstanbul: Kayıhan Yayınları, 1995, p. 453, www.darulkitap.com/oku/tarih/islamonderleri/indexaan. htm (retrieved on January 8, 2011).

Newby, Gordon D., 'House Health Care Bill Discriminates Against Religious Freedom,' *www.religiondispatches.org/archive/2034/house_health_care_bill_discriminates_against_religious_freedom* (December 14, 2011).

Özgüç, Orhan, 'Islamic Himmah and Christian Charity: An Attempt at Inter-Faith Dialogue,' in proceedings of the conference, *Islam in the Age of Global Challenges: Alternative Perspectives of the Hizmet Movement, Georgetown University,* November 14–15, 2008, pp. 561–582, available at en.fgulen. com/conference-papers/gulen-conference-in-washington-dc/3102–islamic-himmah-and-christian-charity-an-attempt-at-inter-faith-dialogue (retrieved on January 2,2011).

Polat, Çemen, 'On the function of Gülen-inspired educational initiatives as business enterprises in the philanthropic fashion,' *The significance of education for the future: The Gülen model of education International Conference Proceedings,* October 19–22, 2010 at The State Islamic University, Jakarta, Available online www.fethullahgulenchair.com/index.php?option=com_content&view=article&id=666:dr-cemen-polat&catid=75:conference-papers&Itemid=255.

al-Qurtubi, *Al Jami li-Ahkam al-Qur'an,* www.altafsir.com/Tafasir.asp?tMadhNo=
    1&tTafsirNo=5&tSoraNo=20&tAyahNo=44&tDisplay=yes&UserProfile=0
    &LanguageId=1 rerieved 8.10.2011.

al-Qushayri, Abd al-Karim ibn Hawazin, *Lata'if al-Isharat bi Tafsir al-Qur'an,* www.
    altafsir.com/Tafasir.asp?tMadhNo=3&tTafsirNo=31&tSoraNo=20&tAyahN
    o=44&tDisplay=yes&UserProfile=0&LanguageId=1 retrieved 8.10.2011.

al-Razi, Fakhr al- Din, *Tafsir al-Kabir* www.altafsir.com/Tafasir.asp?tMadhNo=1
    &tTafsirNo=4&tSoraNo=19&tAyahNo=47&tDisplay=yes&UserProfile=0&
    LanguageId=1 retrieved 1.2.2013.

Spencer, Robert, 'A Vatican Apology for the Crusades?' www.frontpagemaga-
    zine.com, March 22, 2005.

al-Tabari, Muhammad ibn Jarir, *Jami al-Bayan an Ta'wil Ay al-Qur'an* www.
    altafsir.com/Tafasir.asp?tMadhNo=0&tTafsirNo=1&tSoraNo=7&tAyahNo
    =23&tDisplay=yes&UserProfile=0&LanguageId=1, retrieved 2.8.2013.

Tabatabai, Muhammad Husayn, *Tafsir al Mizan,* www.altafsir.com/Tafasir.asp?t
    MadhNo=4&tTafsirNo=56&tSoraNo=6&tAyahNo=108&tDisplay=yes&Pa
    ge=3&Size=1&LanguageId=1 retrieved 11.9.2012.

Tirmidhi, *Sunan,* www.al-islam.com.

Tuncer, Faruk, 'Fethullah Gülen's Methodology of Interpreting the Qur'an,'
    www.fethullahgulen.org/conference-papers/the-fethullah-gulen-move-
    ment-ii/2240–fethullah-gulens-methodology-of-interpreting-Qur'an.html.

Ondřej Valenta, 'Relationship Between Minority and Majority Population Groups:
    Examining Factors of Spatial Concentration of Ethnic Minorities,' http://
    www.postemoderne.net/ondre/centrum/skola_soubory/Prirodoveda/
    rocnikovka.htm, accessed in 05.05.2014.

Yazır, Elmalılı Muhammed Hamdi, *Kur'an-ı Kerim Tefsiri,* www.kuranikerim.
    com/telmalili/nuh.htm retrieved 5.10.2012.

Yücel, Salih, 'Fethullah Gülen: A Spiritual Leader in a Global Islamic Context,' in
    Journal of Religion and Society, 12, (2010), moses.creighton.edu/
    JRS/2010/2010–4.html, (retrieved on January 11, 2011).

al-Zamakhshari, Mahmud ibn Umar, *Al-Kashaaf,* www.altafsir.com/Tafasir.asp?t
    MadhNo=1&tTafsirNo=2&tSoraNo=2&tAyahNo=21&tDisplay=yes&User
    Profile=0&LanguageId=1.

Fethullah Gülen's Works

Gülen, Fethullah, 'Kur'an,' *Yeni Ümit,* 2/6 (1989).

_____ 'Kur'an-ı Kerim ve İlmi Hakikatler–I,' *Yeni Ümit,* 5/16 (1992).

_____ 'Kur'an-ı Kerim ve İlmi Hakikatler–II,' *Yeni Ümit,* 5/17 (1992).

_____ 'Kur'an-ı Kerim ve Meali Üzerine,' *Yeni Ümit,* 17/68 (2005).

_____ 'Dar Bir Zaviyeden Düşünce Sistemimiz,' *Yeni Ümit,* 13/49 (2000).

_____ (1992).'Tekye,' *Sızıntı*, 14 (163).

_____ (1998). 'Varlığın Mana Buudu,' *Sızıntı*, 230.

_____ *İnancın Gölgesinde-1-2*, İzmir: Nil, 1996.

_____ *Fatiha Üzerine Mülahazalar [FÜM]*, İzmir: Nil, 1997.

_____ *İrşad Ekseni*, İzmir: Nil, 1998.

_____*Hoşgörü ve Diyalog İklimi,* eds. Selçuk Camcı and Kudret Ünal, İzmir: Merkür, 1998.

_____ *Zamanın Altın Dilimi*, İzmir: Nil, 1998.

_____ *Kuran'dan İdrake Yansıyanlar [KİY]*, İstanbul: Feza Gazetecilik, 2000.

_____ *Asrın Getirdiği Tereddütler-3,* İzmir: Nil, 2001.

_____ *Yaratılış Gerçeği ve Evrim,* İzmir: Nil, 2003.

_____*İnsanın Özündeki Sevgi*, (prepared for publication by Faruk Tuncer) İstanbul: DA, 2003.

_____ *Sohbet-i Canan*, İstanbul: Gazeteci ve Yazarlar Vakfı, 2004.

_____ *Kalbin Zümrüt Tepeleri-1-2-3-4,* İzmir-İstanbul: Nil, 2005–2008.

_____ *Fasıldan Fasıla-1-2-3-4-5,* İzmir: Nil, 1995 and 2008.

_____ *Prizma-1-3-6,* İzmir: Nil, 2002 and 2011.

English Works

Gülen, Fethullah, *Prophet Muhammad: The Infinite Light*, London: Truestar, 1995.

_____*Criteria or the Lights of the Way*, London: Truestar, 1996.

_____'Science and Religion,' *Knowledge and Responsibility: Islamic Perspectives on Science,* İzmir: Kaynak, 1998.

_____*Essays, Perspectives, Opinions.* New Jersey: Light, 2002.

_____*Toward Global Civilization of Love and Tolerance*, New Jersey: Light, 2004.

_____'In True Islam Terror Does Not Exist,' *An Islamic Perspective: Terror and Suicide Attacks*, New Jersey: Light, 2004.

_____*Key Concepts in the Practice of Sufism*, New Jersey: Light, 2004.

_____*Muhammad: The Messenger of God*, Trans. by Ali Ünal, New Jersey: Tughra Books, 2011.

Short Newspaper Articles

Gülen, Fethullah, *Financial Times*, 20.9.2012

_____ *Gurbet Ufukları*, 221–3; Zaman Gazetesi, (01.09.2006)

_____an interview with the Italian Journalist Michele Zanzucchi

_____ *Violence is not in the tradition of the Prophet*, Financial Times, 20.09.2012.

Internet

Gülen, Fethullah, 'The Necessity of Interfaith Dialogue,' www.fethullahGülen. org/about-fethullah-Gülen/messages/972–the-necessity-of-interfaith-dialogue-a-muslim-approach.html, accessed January 6, 2009.

_____ www.herkul.org/kiriktesti/index.php?article_id=8785 retrieved 23.4.2013.

_____ 'Teknit Adabı ve hakka hürmet,' www.herkul.org/bamteli/index. php?article_id=5244 Retrieved 10.3.2013.

_____ www.herkul.org/kiriktesti/index.php?article_id=7905 retrived 10.10.2010.

_____'Fazilet Ehlinin Dört Şiarı,' www.herkul.org/index.php/bamteli/bamteli-arsiv/9176–fazilet-ehlinin-doert-siar reterived 25.03.2013.

_____'Üslup ve Hikmet,' www.herkul.org/index.php/krk-testi/kirik-testi-arsiv/7905–%C3%9Csl%C3%BBp%20ve%20Hikmet retrieved 20.4.2013.

_____'Toplumun İleri Gelenleri ve Gönüllerin Fethi,' herkul.org/index.php/krk-testi/kirik-testi-arsiv/8785–Toplumun%20%C4%B0leri%20Gelenleri%20ve%20G%C3%B6n%C3%BCllerin%20Fethi, retrieved 25.4.2013.

_____'Tatlı Dil ve Firavunlar,' www.herkul.org/index.php/krk-testi/kirik-testi-arsiv/2647–Tatl%C4%B1%20Dil%20ve%20Firavunlar retrieved 1.27.2013.

_____'Fitne Zamanı ve Çekirdek Toplum,' herkul.org/index.php/bamteli/bamteli, retrieved on May 22, 2013.

_____'Değirmenin Suyu,' www.herkul.org/bamteli/index.php?article_id=1646.

en.fgulen.com/press-room/news/2412–fethullah-gulen-on-abc-radio-nationals-encounter retrieved 25.04.2013.

en.fgulen.com/content/category/148/160/10/.

www.herkul.org.

Index

A

Abd al-Qadir Jilani, 132
abortion, xi, 147, 152, 156, 157, 158, 159, 160, 162, 163, 164, 165, 175
Abraham, 25, 40, 41, 74, 75, 194, 196
Abu al-Suud, 183
Abu Hanifa, 104, 164
Abu Jahl, 48, 139
Abu Talib, 46
activism, 6, 109, 117
Adam, 39, 40, 94, 169, 196, 197, 200
Ahmad Yasawi, 104
Akbar Shah, 49
akhfa, 184
alienation, 12, 60
Alusi, 48, 183
Alvarlı, 110
Aristotle, 111
asceticism, 11, 113, 117
Askari, 28
assimilation, 8, 12, 59, 60, 61, 66
atheism, 11
Australia, 7, 21, 26, 35, 59, 109, 125, 131, 132, 142, 216, 217, 220
Ayoub, 27, 28, 216

B

Barton, 6, 8, 30, 125, 142, 216
Battle of Yarmuk, 139
Baydawi, 183
Bistami, 116
Bosnia, 16, 31, 36, 67

Bradley, 132, 221
Büyükçelebi, 111, 119, 142
Byzantines, 97

C

Catholic Church, 22
Chowdhury, 131, 132, 217
Christianity, 21, 24, 65, 68, 76, 77, 78, 85, 86, 87, 157, 217, 219
Christians, 21, 22, 23, 28, 30, 31, 32, 36, 46, 54, 59, 64, 71, 73, 76, 77, 78, 80, 81, 85, 86, 87, 89, 98, 103, 124, 174, 191
clash of civilization, 17, 67
coexistence, 15, 153
common good, vii, 12, 70, 84, 154
common ground, 17, 27, 33, 79
cooperation of civilizations, 27, 123
creation, 9, 10, 19, 103, 105, 124, 149, 151, 162, 178, 182, 209, 210

D

da'wah, 33, 72, 131, 132, 133, 134, 135, 138, 140, 144, 145
death, xii, 9, 40, 49, 56, 97, 115, 116, 125, 129, 134, 147, 150, 151, 157, 158, 159, 160, 168, 170, 171, 172, 173, 174, 175, 204, 212, 224
democracy, 4, 37, 120
Descartes, 111
Dhu al-Qarnayn, 192
dialogue, vii, viii, ix, x, 3, 7, 14, 15, 16, 17, 18, 19, 21, 22, 23, 24, 25, 26, 27,

28, 29, 30, 31, 32, 33, 47, 57, 58, 61, 62, 63, 64, 65, 66, 67, 68, 69, 70, 71, 72, 73, 75, 76, 77, 79, 80, 81, 82, 83, 84, 85, 86, 87, 88, 89, 91, 102, 103, 104, 105, 109, 120, 122, 123, 124, 125, 126, 141, 152, 188, 192, 213, 215, 225, 226, 229

diversity, viii, 3, 15, 16, 59, 61, 62, 64, 67, 69

E

Ecevit, 128
education, 7, 9, 10, 11, 12, 13, 14, 15, 16, 17, 18, 19, 26, 30, 60, 67, 68, 87, 88, 89, 101, 102, 110, 111, 113, 118, 121, 126, 143, 166, 219, 226
ensoulment, 158, 159, 160, 161, 162, 163, 164, 165
eternity, 151, 182
ethics, xi, 12, 44, 74, 92, 128, 147, 152, 154, 162, 181, 206
Europe, 21, 26, 37, 61, 62, 63, 114, 140, 215, 217, 220
European Union, 120
euthanasia, xi, 147, 156, 165, 169, 172, 173, 175
Eve, 39, 40

F

faith, ix, x, 6, 9, 11, 12, 19, 26, 27, 28, 31, 35, 38, 40, 51, 54, 56, 58, 63, 64, 65, 70, 74, 76, 77, 84, 85, 88, 98, 100, 105, 109, 110, 113, 117, 121, 122, 135, 138, 141, 149, 183, 185, 193, 197, 205, 209, 226
fanaticism, 11
Faruqi, 28, 29, 218
Fazıl, 110
freedom, 4, 9, 65, 157, 174, 226
French Revolution, 37
fundamentalism, 36

G

Ghazali, 56, 104, 114, 115, 118, 129, 132, 159, 160, 162, 202, 216, 225
globalization, vii, 3, 4, 5, 6, 8, 10, 13, 15, 18, 19, 65, 122, 126
Gog and Magog, 192
golden generation, 9
Göle, 122
Gündem, 114, 127, 218

H

Hamidullah, 28
happiness, 11, 13, 16, 64, 66, 69, 92, 94, 98, 103, 138, 144
hermeneutics, xii, 177
himmet, 119, 141, 142
hizmet, viii, 3, 12, 83, 109, 111, 113, 114
Hujwiri, 116
human existence, 9
humanity, viii, 3, 8, 9, 12, 14, 17, 18, 27, 33, 45, 77, 92, 94, 99, 100, 104, 105, 111, 114, 118, 121, 144, 149, 151, 154, 156, 168, 197, 204, 212

I

Ibn Kathir, 41, 42, 43, 44, 45, 50, 134, 183, 223, 226
Ibn Khaldun, 129
Ibrahim Haqqi, 117, 203
ideology, 4, 30, 35, 38, 101, 126, 144
ignorance, 17, 22, 44, 45, 66, 69, 111, 151
Imam Rabbani, 49, 104, 203, 218
information, iv
injustice, 35, 39, 40, 41, 44, 46, 53, 56, 88, 94, 101
intercultural, vii, x, 7, 14, 15, 16, 18, 19, 25, 57, 61, 64, 67, 70, 72, 88, 120, 125, 141
interfaith, viii, x, 14, 15, 16, 23, 24, 25, 26, 27, 28, 29, 31, 32, 33, 64, 66, 69,

71, 75, 76, 77, 79, 82, 87, 91, 120, 123, 124, 141, 152, 213, 229

Islam, viii, ix, x, xi, 5, 6, 8, 9, 10, 14, 15, 17, 18, 19, 22, 23, 24, 25, 26, 29, 30, 31, 32, 35, 36, 37, 38, 39, 40, 43, 44, 46, 47, 49, 50, 51, 52, 53, 54, 55, 56, 59, 62, 63, 65, 66, 67, 68, 70, 71, 72, 73, 74, 75, 76, 77, 78, 79, 80, 82, 83, 84, 85, 86, 89, 91, 92, 93, 94, 95, 96, 97, 98, 99, 100, 101, 102, 103, 104, 105, 109, 110, 112, 113, 115, 116, 117, 118, 119, 121, 122, 123, 124, 125, 127, 129, 131, 132, 133, 134, 138, 141, 144, 148, 149, 150, 151, 152, 153, 154, 155, 156, 157, 160, 166, 168, 169, 170, 171, 174, 175, 180, 189, 190, 199, 201, 215, 216, 217, 218, 219, 220, 221, 222, 223, 224, 225, 226, 228

Islamism, 6, 36

Istanbul, viii, 25, 26, 30, 98, 143, 219, 220, 226

J

Jacob, 48, 194

Jerusalem, 23, 25, 26, 64, 190

Jews, 30, 31, 46, 54, 71, 76, 78, 89, 103, 124, 167, 191

jihad, x, 35, 48, 91, 94, 95, 96, 104

John Paul II, viii, 7, 23, 24, 25, 31, 63, 64, 65, 120, 123, 226

Jonah, 39, 42, 43, 193, 203

Joseph, 47, 178, 195

Judaism, 22, 65, 68

justice, 6, 21, 27, 33, 39, 48, 95, 99, 185

K

Kamalpashazadah, 183

Kant, 111

Kestane Pazarı, 111

khafi, 184, 199

knowledge, 10, 11, 13, 40, 73, 96, 110, 113, 115, 116, 117, 144, 152, 178, 193, 196, 198, 207, 209

L

law, 11, 62, 63, 72, 94, 95, 96, 97, 98, 99, 115, 119, 127, 128, 152, 153, 154, 156, 158, 163, 168, 169, 181, 182, 195, 196, 197, 201, 206

love, 9, 19, 25, 27, 39, 49, 56, 77, 78, 82, 103, 104, 105, 113, 115, 117, 122, 123, 127, 138, 166, 197

Luqman, 46

Lütfi, 110

M

madrasa, 7

Magna Carta, 22

Marowich, 25, 30

Marx, 54

materialism, 11, 122

Mawdudi, 28, 37, 38, 220

Medina Charter, 31

Mehmet Akif, 110

Mehmet Vehbi, 183

modernity, 5, 8, 11, 117, 121, 122, 129

Moses, 39, 41, 42, 46, 194, 197, 205

Muhammad, 11, 28, 31, 38, 39, 40, 43, 44, 45, 46, 47, 48, 49, 52, 55, 73, 77, 78, 79, 93, 94, 96, 97, 103, 112, 113, 115, 117, 119, 121, 131, 134, 136, 138, 139, 164, 180, 183, 190, 193, 197, 201, 202, 215, 217, 223, 224, 227, 228

Muslims, viii, ix, xii, 5, 8, 12, 14, 17, 19, 21, 22, 23, 24, 25, 27, 28, 29, 31, 32, 33, 35, 36, 37, 38, 39, 40, 43, 44, 45, 46, 47, 48, 49, 50, 51, 52, 53, 55, 56, 58, 59, 60, 61, 62, 63, 64, 65, 70, 72, 73, 74, 75, 76, 77, 78, 79, 80, 81, 82, 84, 86, 87, 88, 92,

93, 94, 95, 96, 97, 98, 100, 101,
102, 103, 105, 110, 118, 120, 121,
122, 123, 124, 125, 134, 140, 144,
145, 152, 153, 154, 157, 159, 160,
165, 168, 169, 171, 172, 174, 175,
177, 178, 179, 186, 187, 188, 190,
191, 192, 197, 198, 199, 207, 208,
216, 218, 224, 225, 226
mysticism, 11

N

naturalism, 21
Noah, 48, 134, 196
Nostra Aetate, viii, 21, 22, 23, 24, 27, 28,
32, 64, 218, 224
Nurculuk, 110
Nursi, xi, 7, 10, 11, 21, 22, 24, 26, 29, 38,
44, 46, 49, 51, 53, 56, 65, 66, 72,
99, 102, 103, 110, 111, 112, 114,
116, 125, 131, 135, 136, 137, 138,
139, 140, 144, 148, 149, 150, 151,
181, 196, 203, 220, 222, 223, 224
Nurullah, 133, 215

O

Omar ibn al-Khattab, 136
Osman Ghazi, 132
Ottoman Empire, 21, 37

P

paradise, 9, 19, 76, 138, 170
peace, x, 14, 16, 17, 18, 23, 24, 28, 29,
31, 32, 33, 38, 45, 53, 65, 74, 80,
89, 91, 92, 93, 94, 95, 96, 98, 101,
102, 104, 105, 110, 112, 113, 115,
117, 120, 122, 144, 180, 190, 197,
201, 202
Pettifer, 132, 221
pluralism, 14, 61, 78, 153
Pope Benedict XVI, 22, 23, 88
poverty, 17, 22, 57, 101, 136, 138, 160

Q

Qur'an, ix, xii, 6, 7, 15, 23, 28, 36, 38, 39,
40, 41, 42, 43, 44, 45, 46, 48, 49,
50, 51, 65, 68, 71, 72, 73, 74, 78,
93, 94, 95, 97, 98, 99, 100, 110,
112, 114, 115, 116, 117, 124, 133,
134, 135, 138, 139, 144, 145, 148,
149, 150, 151, 154, 155, 156, 159,
160, 161, 162, 163, 168, 169, 177,
178, 179, 180, 181, 182, 183, 184,
185, 186, 187, 188, 189, 190, 191,
195, 196, 197, 198, 199, 200, 201,
203, 204, 206, 207, 208, 209, 210,
211, 212, 213, 215, 218, 220, 222,
223, 224, 226, 227
Qushayri, 41, 44, 45, 116, 134, 227

R

radicalism, 37, 38, 118
rationalism, 11, 122
Razi, 40, 42, 43, 44, 45, 48, 134, 183, 227
reconciliation, 24, 80
religion, viii, 8, 11, 12, 14, 29, 35, 43, 45,
46, 51, 55, 62, 74, 75, 76, 81, 85,
89, 92, 93, 95, 98, 99, 100, 101,
102, 103, 104, 105, 111, 113, 117,
121, 122, 123, 124, 125, 128, 131,
156, 170, 171, 175
representation, viii, 13, 19, 31, 32, 80, 82,
131, 138, 151
responsibility, 17, 50, 63, 65, 142, 164, 193
resurrection, 150, 151
Risale-i Nur, 7, 65, 110, 111, 148, 222
Rome, 23, 26, 31, 63, 86
Rumi, 30, 54, 55, 104, 114, 116, 129, 132,
203

S

salafis, 117
Salah al-Din Ayyubi, 49, 55, 132

Samarqandi, 183

Sarıtoprak, 24, 25, 27, 32, 38, 46, 115, 116, 129, 199, 222

schism, 17

science, viii, 7, 9, 11, 110, 111, 117, 121, 186, 195, 205, 206, 207, 208, 210, 212

service, viii, 3, 7, 8, 12, 31, 66, 83, 109, 114, 135, 174, 202

Shuayb, 134

sirr, 184

social change, 10

spiritualism, 11

Sufi, 30, 71, 110, 114, 115, 116, 117, 124, 125, 129, 220, 222

Sufism, 18, 30, 69, 103, 113, 114, 115, 116, 117, 122, 124, 129, 201, 228

Suleyman the Magnificent, 132

T

Tabari, 40, 41, 42, 43, 45, 47, 48, 50, 93, 134, 138, 139, 183, 223, 227

tabligh, 134

Ta'if, 46, 47

taqwa, 11, 14, 15, 113

Tariq ibn Ziyad, 132

tawhid, 39, 73, 77, 78, 93, 202

temsil, viii, 13, 131

terror, ix, x, 17, 91, 92, 93, 94, 95, 100, 102, 103, 104, 119

terrorism, vii, x, 5, 17, 91, 92, 93, 94, 95, 98, 101, 102, 119

tolerance, x, 7, 14, 15, 16, 17, 18, 19, 24, 29, 51, 52, 55, 56, 62, 66, 67, 69, 75, 88, 91, 103, 104, 116, 123, 126, 225

Turam, 120, 121, 217

Turkey, vii, viii, ix, x, 6, 7, 8, 12, 15, 25, 27, 29, 30, 37, 46, 54, 57, 58, 63, 64, 65, 67, 68, 69, 70, 71, 80, 81, 83, 84, 86, 87, 89, 91, 102, 109, 114, 118, 119, 120, 121, 122, 123, 124, 125, 126, 127, 128, 140, 141, 144, 157, 218, 219, 221, 222

U

Uhud, 48, 51

V

violence, 4, 17, 18, 32, 35, 47, 56, 66, 92, 94, 95, 101, 103, 119

virtue, 11, 16, 94, 144

Voll, 6, 122, 223

W

war, vii, x, 4, 5, 16, 17, 57, 67, 88, 91, 94, 95, 96, 97, 98, 99, 101, 104, 132, 139, 164

Western civilization, 4

Western cultures, 5

Western powers, 8, 64

worship, 12, 44, 45, 56, 66, 72, 79, 96, 97, 111, 113, 114, 131, 190, 202

Y

Yazır, 48, 110, 183, 227

Yıldırım, 49, 68, 69, 111, 224

Yusuf Ali, 133

Z

Zamakhshari, 43, 134, 183, 227